MY
LIFE
IS
ART

War Child

MY LIFE IS ART

11 Pillars for a **Positive** and **Purposeful** Life

Emmanuel Jal

COUNTERPOINT
BERKELEY, CALIFORNIA

My Life Is Art

First Counterpoint edition: 2023

Library of Congress Cataloging-in-Publication Data
Names: Jal, Emmanuel, author.
Title: My life is art : 11 pillars for a positive and purposeful life / Emmanuel Jal.
Description: First Counterpoint edition. | Berkeley, California : Counterpoint, 2023.
Identifiers: LCCN 2023034735 | ISBN 9781646220380 (hardcover) | ISBN 9781646220397 (ebook)
Subjects: LCSH: Jal, Emmanuel. | Self-actualization (Psychology) | Resilience (Personality trait) | Meaning (Psychology)
Classification: LCC BF637.S4 J339 2023 | DDC 158.1—dc23/eng/20230801
LC record available at https://lccn.loc.gov/2023034735

Jacket design by Farjana Yasmin
Jacket photograph by Emmanuel Jambo
Book design by Laura Berry

COUNTERPOINT
2560 Ninth Street, Suite 318
Berkeley, CA 94710
www.counterpointpress.com

Printed in the United States of America

10 9 8 7 6 5 4 3 2 1

I dedicate this book to the souls and spirits of those who are trapped in their horrific past experiences. To those who are locked in any type of mental prison ruled by anxiety and fear, and those who are robbed of their present experiences by negative events from the past and negative ones imagined in their future. My hope is that the pillars outlined here can give them a stepping stone to reengineer their lives and create a desired future, guided by their purpose.

On a more personal note, I dedicate this book to my children and to a positive world in which I hope they will thrive: Nyakang, Athiey, and Shang Jal.

CONTENTS

INTRODUCTION

MY NAME IS EMMANUEL JAL. I AM A FORMER CHILD SOL-
dier. I am a musician. I am a writer. But more than anything I am a
human. Sometimes we spend so much time defining what makes us
different that we forget what actually makes us the same. Whoever we
are, whatever our background, wherever we are from, we have com-
monality. Trauma affects a child ensnared in civil war the same as it
does a young person chasing a dream or someone trapped by a pandemic in an apartment block. So do a thousand other emotions. How
do I know? Because all those people are myself. And to survive, all of
them have needed to access an education, a bible of survival, formed in
the starkest of circumstances.

At the time, I was never aware that a seemingly endless parade of
life-threatening challenges were instilling in me a knowledge denied
the majority of those on this planet. Even had I realized, it would have
provided little comfort. Hunger, isolation, and the specter of death allow little room for consolation. And yet pillars of support were building
beneath me. Together they would form a structure of such solidity that
even the all-consuming grip of the worst sinking sands would never
be able to topple either it or me. I have come to see the structure as
invincible—not because doing so makes me feel safe, but because that
has absolutely proved itself to be the case.

Over time, I came to give each pillar a name. Whatever issue might
come my way, I knew I could lean on one or more of them not just to
deliver me through to the other side but to imbue me with a positivity
I could never previously have imagined.

These pillars should not exist merely for me. They were made for all, and that is why I take such intense pleasure in sharing them here. I call them My Life Is Art. Why? Because we are all self-portraits unfolding before our eyes. Sometimes that image has clarity; at other times it is blurred, be it through tears, misfortune, or unexpected circumstance—in other words, daily life.

I want you to enjoy this book not as a life lesson, but as a way of uncovering the limitless possibilities within yourself. I want the strength contained in these eleven pillars to be passed on to you, to inhabit your cells just as they do mine.

I want you to reach the end of *My Life Is Art* with a single overriding thought—"My Life Is Art, too."

Enjoy the journey,

Jal

MY
LIFE
IS
ART

1

THE PILLARS OF MY LIFE IS ART

WHO OWNS YOUR MIND?

I WANT TO ASK YOU A QUESTION. WHO OWNS YOUR MIND? Is it worry, anxiety, poverty, or death? Is it perhaps your partner, your friends, your boss, a favorite brand, maybe even sugar? Or is it fear: of what lies outside the front door, of the future? Perhaps it's the most basic fear of all—of losing loved ones.

Who owns your mind? It is a question we must all face up to if we are ever going to paint an honest self-portrait of our inner selves. The mind is where all our battles take place, in graphic, life-altering detail. The heart will also play its part. If the mind is the battleground, the heart is where victory is felt most emotionally and keenly.

Who owns your mind? I have asked that simple question again and again in schools, colleges, conferences, and universities around the world. The answer I always receive is "I own my mind." Only two people have ever said otherwise. One was a seven-year-old girl who believed sugar owned her mind. Sugar is big when you're seven. The other was a man who felt that a Somali woman owned his. But are the majority correct? According to the Nuer people of South Sudan, from whom I originate, all humans are made equal by the creator, or shah. The greatest gift the creator has given you is your mind. With your mind you, too, can create. That relationship is divine. You do indeed own your mind, but there will always be those seeking to steal or influence it.

Take note: whoever or whatever owns your mind owns you and everything you create. Lose to the conflicts in your head and you become a slave to whatever it is you have allowed to take away your inner self. It is important then that you fight always to own the mind the creator has given to you. Owning your mind allows you to possess your gifts and talents and use them to create the life you want. Owning your mind allows you the mental space to think, plan, strategize, organize, create, and have peace of mind. Owning your mind allows you to connect with your purpose, which in turn unites your heart and mind. The human body is a kingdom, and any kingdom that is not united shall be destroyed. If your heart and mind are not united, you as a person shall be destroyed.

For many years, what owned my mind was fear, anxiety, poverty, and the prospect of loved ones dying around me. What owned my mind was fear of being deemed insignificant. But what dominated my mind more than anything else was trauma.

WHERE DID MY TRAUMA COME FROM?

"The world will end someday," my mother used to say. She was describing the coming of Jesus, judgment day, when bad people would be cast into the abyss and burn for eternity while the good would head heavenward.

I was four years old when the clouds first closed in. There was no hint of what was to come. It was a beautiful sunny morning, just one of so many others. Everything seemed so normal, except that our dogs seemed restless. I looked upward and noted the songbirds' absence from the sky.

I was playing with a bicycle by our *tukul*, the thatched round hut in which we lived, when hell unleashed its fury. Such was its ferocity, I thought the world had ended. The ground was lifting, falling, shaking, and as it did so I was bombarded with terrifying, other-worldly noises. I heard the thunder of a thousand storms, the hissing of a million snakes. I fell to the ground and screamed. The songbirds had indeed flown, replaced by mechanical vultures, blades whirring in the sky. Bombs were dropping from their confines. Between eardrum-shattering explosions, I could hear people yelling, crying, terrified as they ran for their lives. I knew I had to run, too, which was when I realized the bicycle had fallen on top of me. It was old and heavy. My left leg was trapped in a fire upon which a pot had been boiling merrily. The pain consumed me as the flames ate me up. I was screeching with the horror, the agony. I looked around. Hell was everywhere but Jesus was nowhere to be seen. His absence planted a seed deep inside of me. "If Jesus has not come," I thought, "then we must be the bad people." That thought would only grow and grow. It took me a long time to remove it.

Only when my aunt, in her own panic to escape, tripped over the bicycle was I dragged away. The smell of my burning flesh was nauseating, overwhelming. The pain was excruciating, and there was no one to fix it. No doctors, no painkillers. The only "drug" to keep my pain in check was sugar—and lullabies. My foot was heavily scarred. Even now it delivers pin-sharp reminders of that morning, delivering red-hot poker shots of pain and becoming infected easily. It is a physical part of me, capable of bringing back so many sad, tragic memories.

I should probably mention that when I talk about my age, I am using only guesswork. I do not know my birthday. All I know is that I was born in the early 1980s in southern Sudan at a time when my country was at war with itself. Sharia Law had recently been introduced. With it came a belief that the land was given to Arabs and Muslims by Allah along with everything in it. This belief was used as a justification to enslave Black Africans. People who became Muslims were treated better than those didn't, so many converted. A resistance was formed, which led to rebellions across the country. At the age most children are becoming acquainted with fairy tales, I was already intimately acquainted with death. The first person I saw shot was my mother's bodyguard. He took the bullet in his stomach. His intestines rushed out—accompanied, my infant mind noted, by a steam like a light cloud of smoke. Blood followed. It was too late for my mum to cover my eyes. Not that it mattered. Horror was becoming a constant backdrop to my everyday life. The worst excesses of human violence were interspersed with devastating flashes of hell.

Perhaps I ate too much sugar during my recovery from my burns—my first trip out of the village after the attack was with my aunt Sarah to buy more. I was so excited as we turned toward home, hoping I would get a taste of our cargo when we got back. And then a government soldier appeared before us. He wouldn't let my aunt pass. The only access he would grant was to the blank metal door of the *tukul* ahead. He dragged my aunt inside. "Leave her alone!" I shouted, but I knew my protests were useless. I could only watch through the mesh of the window as he forced her to the floor and inflicted on her what I would later come to understand was rape. That image, her silent acquiescence, knowing resistance would result in her death—and possibly mine—has never, and will never, leave me. A real-life childhood nightmare transplanted with every vile detail into the adult, becoming a seemingly impenetrable stronghold of my trauma, and one that causes me flashbacks even now.

My early years were spent running from village to village, attack after attack. Again and again, places of childhood freedom were reduced to giant graveyards. Instead of playing, children buried their dead, as we, too, buried our own. Rivers of blood ran across parched soil. Dead soldiers became waxworks in the sun, their broken limbs sticking out at odd angles, or lying detached, spread randomly nearby, like driftwood on a beach.

War meant my idyll, the place of safety that every child should have, had been snatched away in the most graphic and awful of ways. It really did feel like I had been transported to the deepest bowels of hell, to the extent that the smell of smoke and fire forever filled the air. My food tasted like gunpowder.

Eventually, the attack that changed my life forever came. A surprise attack doused our village in gunfire. We ran, but my mother turned back for the medical box that could save us if we were injured.

"Run for the river." Those were the last words I ever heard her speak. She disappeared into a maelstrom of grenades, bombs, and gunfire. Did she survive? For months I had no idea. Eventually, I discovered death had claimed her, as it had all her sisters. My family was large and sprawling. I had many uncles. They loved to talk, but only two would survive to tell this tale.

My father, meanwhile, lived a largely separate life. He had joined the Sudan People's Liberation Army and was away forming battle plans against the enemy. He arranged for me to be sent to a school in Ethiopia, but the school didn't exist. Instead, after a long desert march on which many of my fellow children died of exhaustion, I found myself in a refugee camp, a place where children with swollen bellies and empty fly-specked eyes stared, with all hope lost, into a morass of others like themselves. I survived by my wits and yearned for life as a child soldier, a "future" that offered both escape and revenge. To carry a gun and fire it into the hearts of my people's tormentors was all I wanted. I found my way, via ritual violent abuse and the structural reassembling of my soul, into the same murderous mindset carried by those who had inflicted such misery on our own people, into those ranks. I was Emmanuel Jal—with an AK-47. This was my time to wreak hell, to find mental satisfaction. But war can never be a counselor. My life as a child soldier delivered only more despair. The lowest point was being forced to march for weeks, with neither food nor water, across a vast barren wasteland to a different encampment. I watched as children, weakened, emaciated, hopeless, died before my eyes. I saw others eat their fallen comrades. I didn't judge. I was tempted to do the same. I survived only by drinking my own urine.

The flashbacks from that journey haunt me more than any others. It was the final truly dreadful experience of my childhood. My battle-field experiences—the grotesque disdain for human life—haunt me, too, but it seems they prefer to reappear in nightmares.

WHAT IS TRAUMA?

Make no mistake, trauma is immense. I define it as mental genocide, a soul murder, an invasion of demons. Flashbacks in the day; nightmares at night. Trauma glues you to the past. Without help, trauma becomes a negative energy. It feeds off your life. Like a parasite, it grows stronger as you weaken. Some don't know they have trauma. Some are in denial they have it. Some know they have it and seek help. Others know they have it but have no idea how to get help.

Everyone's definition of trauma will be different. As small children, my younger sister Nyaruach and I were separated by the raging violence and unforgiving brutality of the Sudanese Civil War. Nyaruach endured truly terrible violations of her mind, body, and soul. At age ten, she was raped by enemy soldiers. It would happen time and again during a childhood lost beneath a deluge of cruelty. Forget concerts, cinema, theater—Nyaruach had a front-row seat on genocide. At a time when most young people are discovering independence and freedom, she was chained to slavery, starvation, savage attacks, and forced marriage.

I ask Nyaruach for her definition of trauma. "Hell inside my body," she tells me. "I am on fire twenty-four hours a day."

Take your eyes from the page for a moment and internalize that image. Imagine those flames burning your insides. Imagine your stomach as a furnace, never satisfied, fueled by hate.

"At any moment," Nyaruach continues, "my brain could explode. I am constantly alert, always looking for danger."

Nyaruach's experience of people as a relentlessly malevolent force means that if she perceives somebody as threatening or harmful, her desire is to cut that person to pieces and share with them the fire that rages within her. Let them live her horror. Let them see how evil consumes its victims.

She prefers talking to listening. That way other people's words cannot hurt her. She longs for peace but is drawn to dramatic situations. In a way that only the deeply traumatized will understand, dramatic situations offer comfort because they are all she has known. Real peace of mind comes only through music, an escape into an alternate world where she can breathe safe and easy.

I recognize only too well Nyaruach's description of trauma. I recognize the constant agitation, the flame flickering on the inside, the debilitating fatigue that snares you in the mindset so you are unable to jump the wire to the green fields on the other side. Trapped in your head, you create fantasies to hurt those who delivered your wounds. There is a delight—fake, unworthy—in inflicting pain on those individuals. Normally, you would flinch from such thoughts. But at those points you have no control. Afterward, it makes you sad to think that your negativity was unseen by yourself. You wish it hadn't happened, but you know also your mind forced you to tread that twisting path of darkness.

My own inner longing for peace ran parallel to my sister's. Whenever that peace came, I failed to recognize it. Dramatic situations offered the security of familiarity. They felt safer than peaceful ones. My education, when it came, was a case in point. In the classroom, I was labeled stubborn and problematic. I was involved in fights and expelled from several schools. One principal decided to test my IQ. The result was low. IQ tests don't take into account intelligence learned from adversity rather than from encyclopedias. I was told that school was not the place for me. I should concentrate instead on carpentry, manual labor, something using my hands. We cannot judge the individual on tests that treat us all the same. We are all different. Experience shapes us all. We do not all emerge from the same mold. For some of us, there was no mold. It lay shattered in a million pieces before we were even born.

At primary school, a teacher would enter the room. A pen would be stuck in my hand, a lesson would be taught, and I wouldn't remember a thing. I'm not sure what the other pupils were thinking, but my mind was under attack from flashbacks of broken limbs, bodies with bones sticking out at right angles, rotten corpses, burning villages, the cacophony of heavy fire, the chest-thudding impact of dropping bombs. In that classroom, I wasn't experiencing the smell of pen and paper. In my nostrils was the odor of blood. My nervous system raced with fear. There were no walls, just a clearing containing a single terrified child. How I wished the teacher would stop for a second, look my way, and ask a simple question: "Young man, what's on your mind?"

But nobody ever asked me anything.

My traumatic experiences caused multiple setbacks at all levels of education. I ended up repeating Year 12 four times, which I found deeply humiliating. Only when I gained a scholarship at Brookhouse School in Nairobi, with its forward-thinking and open attitudes to education, creating a welcome environment for all students, did I finally begin to feel comfortable in the classroom. It was a long, long time coming.

Trauma acts like a virus. The vaccine—peace—that can stop it entering the human body is in the ownership of mankind, but we have yet to release it. The virus is single-minded. It searches every vein, muscle, and artery until it has hidden, or preferably deleted, the good programs installed to make a person function positively. Others watch helplessly as that normal person they knew—gentle, loving, joyful, generous, peaceful, intelligent—is wasted by an invisible force. A new character takes over. Childlike, it is stripped of focus. The person's ability to think for themselves, their courage, their confidence, their dignity, all are snatched away, as if monsters have entered their being and claimed them. The murder of a soul, replaced by bitterness, a hedonistic lack of self-respect. Their will to stay alive, their drive to do something constructive, to better their life, is snatched away, incinerated alongside self-motivation and self-worth. Everything they know about life has lost its meaning. Everything has become hard. The person is locked in a different world, a slave to a force invisible to our eyes. We see only the way they act, and pass judgment on them in those terms. Meet a person you knew before they were struck by trauma and you will not recognize them, let alone know how to communicate with them. The lock has been installed. The sign has gone up. Their mind is out of order.

In my own traumatic times, every conversation became a debate, every discussion an argument, both inevitably yielding negative results. I didn't want any dispute to stop, even if I was on the losing side. My mind would insist I was right and ignite the debate again. The blurred lens through which I viewed life meant a clash of perspectives was inevitable. If someone paid me a compliment, I was offended. I lacked the self-confidence and trust in others to see it as sincere. The lies I told myself instantly became the truth. When people were nice to me it made me suspicious; I would think they were up to something. I picked apart every word of every conversation, every tone of every voice, and applied my negative filter without logic or reason. I could only trust stories, jokes, music, art, dance, movies, nature, wilderness, rivers, which inspired me and helped me move forward. I was guided by stories that flowed from a source of openness and honesty. I loved them. I don't live that life now, but, like many others who have been through traumatic experiences, I still suffer flashbacks.

THE FLASHBACK THAT MADE ME ATTEMPT SUICIDE

It was in a refugee camp in Ethiopia, a place of death and starvation, that I met Dr. Koang Tut. A man of great care and consideration, he prescribed me extra nutrients. In a world that seemed so heartless, to come across someone who exuded rays of sunshine from his very core meant a lot to me. I struck up a friendship with my savior, occasionally visiting him by surprise at his compound. Even though it was protected by guards, I always found a place in the fence to sneak through when they weren't looking. I had done just that one day when I came across a woman's red leather shoe on the ground. It was the first time I had seen anything so wondrous. I was admiring its beauty when an Ethiopian woman saw me, picked up a big stone, and stormed toward me screaming "*Leba! Leba!*" ("Thief! Thief!") I tried to run but it was too late. She threw the stone at my head, and I was knocked to the ground. Bleeding from my nose, mouth, and head, I was like a wounded animal as I tried forlornly to scramble up and escape. My assailant picked the rock up to finish me off completely. In such places, punishment doesn't come via a courtroom. It was then, as I thought I had met my end, that Dr. Koang came to my rescue. He heard the commotion—her shouts, my screams—and ran over, stopping the woman in her tracks as she held her weapon high, ready to deliver the fatal blow. The doctor looked at the blood gushing from my head and shouted to his aides for me to be rushed to the hospital. The nurses stitched me up the best they could, but I have the scar on my skull to this day. In my younger life I saw many, many sights no child, no adult, no animal should ever see, but the incident with the woman and the shoe remains ingrained in me, a moment of such innocent wonder reduced to one of such brutality.

Anything can trigger a flashback. It could be a sound, the smell of a certain food, the sight of officialdom, a soldier, even a word. When that flashback comes it can last between two to ten seconds and is so visually clear it might as well be in high definition. The flashback itself is far from a pleasant experience, but what follows is deadlier and more disturbing. If the flashback is like a kick in the guts, then the aftermath is ten times worse. Physical pain is one thing, emotional pain entirely another. In my highly sensitized state, my confidence disappears, my immune system is crushed. I am defeated. My entire body hurts, muscles become inflamed, I feel tense, my chest tightens, and my appetite vanishes. I have no peace of mind as a muddle of negative thoughts crashes around my head. I just want to isolate myself. Suicidal thoughts kick in, as do flashbacks of other traumatic events.

For a long time, I didn't have a term to describe the feeling that comes after a flashback, but I now call it semi-depression. Why semi? Because my heart has a backup power. When I am lying on my bed, feeling so terrible and defeated, there remains a spark. As I say little prayers, my attention focused on my breathing, I visualize that tiny spark as both hope and light. I ask it to flow through me, and as I do so it charges my entire body. Eventually I will slip into sleep. By the next morning I have the energy to get up and source other means to help me out.

When there is no tiny spark in my heart, I become possessed by demons. I become bitter. I hate people and want to kill either them or myself. I have attempted to end my life several times, all because the spark was no longer there. One such occasion lives with me still. When I was in Ethiopia, I saw a man shot in the head, his brain spilling out. Instantly I was taken back mentally to the woman who threw the stone at my head, which itself proved the catalyst for numerous vivid recollections of other desperate incidents from my childhood. At that point, the spark of joy in my heart was snuffed out as surely as if an invisible hand had pinched it between thumb and forefinger. I was barren inside and had no idea how to reach out for help. How could I reason with myself when my head was occupied by so many different negative voices talking to me? I found the strength to go to Dr. Koang and describe the pain inside of me. He prescribed some medication, but as I was heading home to my *tukul*, I heard some women talking. "If someone takes all the tablets the doctor gives them," one stated, "it will be all over. They will die the next day."

Their conversation planted a seed in my head. That night I swallowed all the tablets. It was the worst pain I have ever gone through. My head felt like a lead weight atop a body that was being punctured by a thousand knives. I wanted to throw up but couldn't. Speech, too, was impossible. My tongue couldn't communicate; my mouth couldn't say a word. Throughout the night, my head was in endless agony. Its working parts had been removed, replaced by snakes. I genuinely believed my skull was about to spill its contents out through my ears. My heart was beating fast and my eyes were aching terribly. A woman called Nyahon DK gathered women to sing songs and pray over me throughout the night. No one around me had any idea what I was going through. This was my own private hell. I believe their prayers were answered. By the second night I was at least beginning to feel a glimmer of recovery. The pain in my head reduced to a more tolerable ache and I was hungry. Another twenty-four hours on and I had recovered, but that flashback to the woman and the red shoe almost ended my life.

Thankfully, over time I have learned the art of keeping that spark glowing in my heart twenty-four hours a day. It helps me navigate my life and keeps me standing in all situations. It is my internal and eternal flame.

Trauma and Hurting Those Who Love You

Emma McCune, a British aid worker who rescued me and smuggled me to Kenya, would shed tears every week. I was the cause of a lot of them. Why? Because I could not understand the love she was providing me. My learned distrust was such that I thought she was playing a game, fattening me for the kill, for the day when she would reveal her true self and sell me. I had no idea she was an angel sent to save me.

That distrust led me to bad acts to test her commitment. They varied from the inane—leaving the toilet unflushed, slamming doors, throwing bones on the carpet, chasing the dogs outside the house— to the more serious—stealing or taking other kids' toys by force. The change in circumstances was just too much. In South Sudan my mind had been in constant survival state. I had orders and routines and sets of rules to follow. If I broke any of them, punishment was swift. In

Nairobi, however, there were no rules. I couldn't understand the level of freedom; I was not familiar with it. I was disturbed by Emma's attempts to give me the childhood I'd never had. She was so patient and kind, but when that affection came, I would respond only with something unkind. My behavior in Nairobi was my mind creating familiar wars for me.

One of my worst acts was aimed at Emma's brother, Johnny. He came to Nairobi to see her and meet me. I found him the loveliest of men—and that was what threw me. I couldn't understand why this man was so happy. At that point, I asked myself a question. *How can I give him a bit of my pain?* When he left me with his car in a parking lot at Emma's funeral, I spotted my chance. I saw some street boys hanging around and sold them one of his tires. He found us unbolting the back wheel and was so mad. I pretended I was sorry but inside it made me happy. I actually found it funny.

Trauma often involves the manipulation of others. A person can become self-centered and try to create a world that revolves around them. It is important to note that they may not even be aware they are doing this. A traumatized person can do mean things to their loved ones and not even remember; a traumatized person can be ungrateful and not recognize the kindness of others; a traumatized person can find it a challenge to have hope; a traumatized person can act like the most selfish person in the world—because they think that the world is against them. When trauma comes, the usual narrative of life is replaced by the legends of demons. They enter and occupy your mind. Your loved ones may be around you, but you are absent to them. They can't help. They don't know what is going on inside you because they can't see it. They only see the character you have adopted, your physical appearance. Similarly, you don't see them. Neither do you see the opportunities that may come your way. You don't view life the way everyone else does. Everyone and everything seems to act against you. You become childlike again, asking endless questions about the world and your place in it. When somebody offers a good explanation, you don't understand.

My behavior brought Emma to tears. My heart was hard, and my mind was manipulative and incapable of trust. The only people I felt I could trust were soldiers because, as someone who first wielded an AK-47 at the age of eight, we had something in common. I still viewed myself as one of them. Normal people were mere civilians.

But Emma, incredibly, no matter what I did, however I let her down, never moved me on.

THE UNIVERSALITY OF TRAUMA

Every human in this world is going to experience trauma someday. The trauma will vary, but it will happen. Extreme trauma can come from an endless number of sources: violence, abuse, heartbreak, a lost job, or bad news related to health. At the other end of the scale are lesser incidents related to work, school, and a million other daily activities. But all trauma can lead to stress, worries, and depression.

Extreme trauma can often come out of the blue. Rarely does it announce its imminent arrival. For example, if you had never before experienced violence and were enjoying a peaceful environment, only to witness someone being stabbed, or several people murdered, that would qualify 100 percent as extreme trauma. That image is now installed in your head just as surely it would be on a laptop or phone. It just keeps playing, playing, playing, playing. It is there forever, ready to reappear as a flashback and ruin your life.

Take a person who has been raped. What happens in their mind? Everything stops, their head goes blank, and the damage begins. On top of the grotesque physical trauma, they have been robbed of the most valuable asset in their life—their mind. Their character changes. They become dead and alive. Dead walking. Dead talking. Dead living.

Trauma can reprogram you. If not treated, those new personality traits and behaviors can be passed down to the next generation. But the good thing is that as human beings, even if the positive survival software has been corrupted or deleted, we can reprogram ourselves. That is what you will learn about as you continue to read this book.

Every person on this planet has immense talents they can use to contribute to the betterment of themselves and of humanity. In their DNA, they have the information needed to survive. DNA is powerful. It features the genes from both our parents that are best suited to our survival and contains hidden ways to deal with previous happenings, current events, and future needs. Few realize that DNA mutates every seven years, both allowing and encouraging us to introduce new skills into our lives. Used properly, the information encoded in our DNA can help us to enjoy our lives holistically. It can allow us to escape trauma by defining ourselves not by a single event but as a whole person. Positive stimulation of our DNA is as vital as the positive stimulation of our emotions.

The blockage of progress happens in both the psychological and physical state, but by recognizing how it happens, it can be healed. Trauma occupies our mind, body, and cells. It takes up a huge space and affects our conscience, intuition, subconscious, memory, and imagination. The human brain weighs just 2 percent of the entire body but consumes 20 percent of the energy. If that energy is negative, then trauma has its fuel. It blocks our connection to reality, so we become a slave to an invisible force that those around us can neither see nor understand. Inevitably, because we mean so much to our loved ones, their lives become infected by our condition. If they don't know how to handle us or where to find help, it can mess them up big time. Physical scars fade, but psychological scars can take a lifetime to heal. Those scars are all too easily transferred to loved ones. Internal scars may be invisible, but they hurt and create chronic pain. Understanding our trauma's effect on others is as vital as understanding its effect on ourselves.

THE MIRACLE OF SURVIVING TRAUMA

Every person who has been traumatized yet manages to live a normal life is a miracle. That person is born again. They are living a new life. They have reprogrammed themselves, tapped into their DNA to find the information not just to survive but to thrive. They are creating new and positive habits to help them make good choices and live a life with meaning. They begin to remember the way they used to function. They install new software for their survival and use it to contribute to a higher calling for humanity.

It is the only way I can explain my own survival. I have endured nightmares, terror, and flashbacks. I have also battled with the devil inside me, who tried to prevent me from moving forward and, ultimately, told me to commit suicide. Those things are not easy to deal with in any environment, but especially so when you come from a culture where men are not allowed to cry or show vulnerability. I always kept my innermost emotions to myself. Such cultures are dangerous and damaging.

I know I am lucky today to be here, to be able to live like a normal person. I have encountered the very worst of people, those who feed on evil, controlling humans through fear, poverty, starvation, torture, and death. They use one hand to give and the other to kill. They use violence, they rape, they chop people's hands off, they loot property, burn villages down.

They kill children.

All the time they are installing software into the minds of thousands, millions, so they can control them for the rest of their lives. Meanwhile, those close to their victims are too infected by hate, anger, and pain. If they get an opportunity, they will hurt those who violated their families in even more violent and awful ways. In such an environment, war quickly thrives, communities are torn apart. Fear dominates the minds of all, whatever their loyalties, whatever their background.

Fear infected me like an illness. My past was ugly; my past was a living hell, running away from death and cursing the day of my birth. My present, meanwhile, is disturbing. I constantly fight elements of my history that try to suck the calm out of me and replace it with crippling stress. But what is great is that my future is a beautiful, peaceful place, just as I have imagined since my childhood. Every day I wake up I walk to this place in my mind. It gives me peace, keeps my hope alive because I can see it. In the physical world I have yet to get there, but I can see it, and that's what matters.

What has allowed me to get this far? I saw so much suffering that I had to stay alive and be part of the solution. I had to unshackle myself from trauma and find new sources of purpose. Gratitude, for instance, is one of my key principles. It gives me a joy that doubles as my painkiller of choice. Forgiveness, meanwhile, keeps my hope alive. My forgiving heart has become my secret weapon to blow away negative energy fields hiding inside me.

Reprogramming is the burning desire to install new and positive habits into my life. I have other go-to elements to keep me afloat. A positive mindset allows me to achieve my goals. It is the shield that deflects my worries. Courage is the force that helps me overcome fear. Calm allows me to control my emotions so that I can see clearly. Love is the light inside me that allows me to see and makes my work easier. Loving is giving without expecting anything in return. Care is how I maintain my body so I can be healthy and perform my work, while faith is how my heart and mind unite to achieve what I desire. Feeding my soul is how I constantly provide myself with supplies to continue in these struggles.

There are so many things a traumatized person needs to go through if they are to experience psychological improvement and recovery, if they, too, are to become a miracle. It is incumbent on us all to make sure they do not have to undertake that journey alone. Each and every person in the universe knows somebody who has been traumatized. There is no challenge in finding someone who has been through hell. The challenge is in helping them, and the best way to help a traumatized person is to create an environment where they feel they are loved. That is the aspiration of any loving parent. Dealing with a person who is traumatized is no different. They have effectively become a child again. It is time for everyone around that individual to recalibrate. They need to ask the same questions they would of someone who has yet to step out on life's path. If you want to reprogram a traumatized person, discover what they really want to do in life. Find out what they care about, what dreams they have. And then think what opportunities you can provide. Can you, for example, direct them to an environment where they will be surrounded by a lot of positive people? Those are, after all, the environments with the power to reprogram our DNA, our subconscious view of the world. In new and vibrant surroundings, it is easier to reprogram ourselves by installing new programs that can help us function. This is exactly what happened to me. I had to install new programs into my life so I could operate like a normal person. This would have been impossible had I never had a dream, a purpose, and if my environment had not changed.

Every human being who has moved on from a traumatic situation is miraculous. Imagine someone who has experienced sexual violence, or a war child, still talking about peace and love. Think of a person who has had their legs blown off in combat, waking every day to the physical reminder of their loss, and then spending the rest of that day helping others. That to me is truly extraordinary. Yet everybody has that ability inside of them. Every human being, when floored by trauma, has the capacity to stand and walk again, to control flashbacks, to find a way to use memories to serve the greater calling of humanity, to share their experience with others for personal, social, and emotional learning. Through recovery they learn incredible truths about themselves, the world, and humanity.

It is possible to forgive.
It is possible to regain courage.

It is possible to regain joy, purpose, gratitude, and peace of mind.

It is possible to regain faith and positivity.

It is possible to find a new calm.

It is possible to feed a soul with positivity again.

It is possible to reprogram.

It is possible to add value to the lives of others again.

It is possible to regain self-worth, confidence, and productivity.

It is possible to regain a hundred times over what was stolen from you.

HOW DID I ESCAPE TRAUMA?

I escaped trauma through a process called My Life Is Art. And that same process can work for you.

There are eleven principles to My Life Is Art. In the early years, I didn't have a name for these principles—I may not even have recognized them as such—yet I practiced them intuitively and diligently to the point they became a lifestyle. I have now applied a structure to those principles that allows you to make them a lifestyle too.

My Life Is Art will allow you to put your life in order. Like everyone, there are times when my heart loses courage. Times when my mind is full of clutter. Times when my ability to achieve goals and think clearly and strategically is drained by past defeats, or challenges both current and future. When those times come, My Life Is Art provides me with the tools to think clearly, gain strength, increase my mental power, be calm—joyful even—and positive. It allows me to move forward with purpose and engage my mind to achieve my goals.

My Life Is Art is a 360-degree approach to life, a commitment to self-development through daily practices that increase our ability to think, plan, organize, strategize, be compassionate, love, and exhibit wisdom, knowledge, and understanding. My Life Is Art delivers purpose and vision to our goals and creates an alignment to produce positive outcomes.

My Life Is Art recognizes our life as a work of art, one that is ever changing as we seek conscious awakening, a full spiritual understanding of who we are—the journey we take to own our minds. Only by embarking upon that journey can we truly access our spiritual and physical wealth. My Life Is Art delivers a beautiful portrait, one that reflects the new us, the person who has undergone change, the person who has found their true inner self awakened.

When I think about my own ongoing journey, I become excited. My Life Is Art has given me the power to influence my future by revealing what I want and generating the necessary emotions, habits, and beliefs to get me there. It has turned me into a master artist, collaborating with my environment to create a vision of myself I both like and recognize. That picture was within me all the time. My Life Is Art drew it out. It challenged me to search for the ingredients—the colors, the textures, the perspectives—I needed to create that work. In so doing, it made me reassess my challenges as blessings, because without addressing them, I couldn't genuinely apply brush to canvas.

It all comes back to evolution. Millions of sperm raced to fertilize the egg in my mother's womb. All of them died except one. That one informed the million and one ever-changing elements that make up me. The beauty of life is that we are always evolving. Often I am still surprised to discover a new facet of myself. And that is the point—I will only be complete as a piece of art when I transform to the next life. We are not the complete work until we reach that point.

There is a saying in Africa that the child is raised by the village. It recognizes that the many people we encounter as youngsters have an influence on us. But what it fails to recognize is that the adult needs support and influence too. Yet the adult's ongoing story is too often forgotten or overlooked. It is important to respect other people's art and remember that we never see the complete picture while they are alive. Only those left in this world after me will be able to say if I was a beautiful piece of art, a heroic piece of art, or someone from which most people would rather avert their gaze.

I know also that my mother's art was influencing me before I was even born. When I was in her womb, I could hear what was going on around me. I was so excited by the prospect of entering the world, yet sometimes it scared me. At such moments, my mother would whisper, "Don't be afraid, son. It's a beautiful world." With typical joyousness, she would add, "Everyone out here is waiting to throw a party for you."

Other times, it was the creator's voice I heard. "The world is waiting for you," he reassured me. "You will leave your mark. You will be great."

Heaven and hell could exist in Mama's womb—the road to birth is never easy for either mother or baby—but I felt certain that the world was the place to be. If anyone had told me what actually awaited outside my mother's womb, I don't think I would have made it out. When finally I did emerge, before I could breathe the oxygen, smell the environment, open my eyes, the devil pinched me and told me, "Welcome to planet Earth." I screamed with so much pain. He told me not to tell anyone.

Had I been born in hell? Sometimes it seemed that way. But a village elder once told me, "Son, it is your choices which will define your destiny. You have the power to shape your destiny."

He was right. I had been born in a world where dodging lies was as important as finding truth. But once I found that truth, it was incumbent on me to protect it from the lies and use it to shape my direction.

My Life Is Art became my road map to a fulfilled life. I want to share that map with all those who want to take those same turns and directions to a better life and better world.

Each of the letters of My Life Is Art represents a fundamental principle of how I live every day. The eleven steps of My Life Is Art brought me this far, and I am sure they will take me further. I work every day to further immerse myself in them. We can master all the principles of My Life Is Art, but I promise you that if you master just one, your life will be transformed.

THE PILLARS AND PRINCIPLES OF
MY LIFE IS ART

M   Meditation

Y   Yearning

L   Leading

I   Ideas

F   Focus

E   Endurance

I   Intuition

S   Sagaciousness

A   Action

R   Reading

T   Training

2

MY LIFE IS ART

PRINCIPLE 1:

Meditation

M FOR MEDITATION

MEDITATION IS AT THE CORE OF MY LIFE IS ART. UNDER-standing its deep-seated roots, meaning, and incredible life-changing benefits is vital to grasping the ethos. Over the following twelve chapters, I will unveil the key pillars of meditation. Invest in these learnings and you will have a clear path on the journey that follows—the journey that is My Life Is Art.

What Is Meditation?

- Meditation is a lifetime commitment to internal self-development.
- Meditation is about finding yourself and the best you.
- Meditation is the journey you take to unite your mind and heart.
- Meditation is the journey you take to unite your spirit, soul, and body.
- Meditation is a commitment to the designing and redesigning of the self.
- Meditation is about owning your mind and using it to gain spiritual wealth.

■ Meditation is about adding order and structure to your life.

■ Meditation is about maintaining peace, love, harmony, and productivity.

How Meditation Came to Me

When I was a youngster, my dad was often away fighting with the Sudan People's Liberation Army. Life lessons from him were rare, so it was down to my mum to fill in the missing parts. Mum was like a god to us growing up. She had great courage, and her courage became our courage. Her fears became our fears. Her tears became our tears. She was the absolute center of our existence, as much a part of us as our lungs, our livers, our arms, our legs.

As the war devoured both young and the old, Mum held us together. She shielded us from everything and was there with us all the time, teaching us, comforting us, giving us security, and nurturing us. She made sure we ate even when it seemed there was no food.

The challenges of life were not so difficult to overcome when Mum was with us. She made us laugh. She loved to tell stories as we lay on the ground with our bellies facing the clear night sky. Looking at the stars, my eyes could see as far as they ever could.

Mum told us those stars were cattle. The tiny ones were calves, medium ones cows, and big ones bulls. When there were many stars in the sky, she would say the fox was on duty. If there were few, it meant the hyena was in charge. The moral of the story was that the fox knew how to take good care of the cattle and the hyena did not. The hyena was greedy and would eat those left in his charge. My mum wanted us to be like the fox, canny and smart. She taught us through stealth, through tales that contained deep values, all told in a soothing and relaxing voice. We didn't need pictures; we had our imaginations. Our wonder would take us to the end of the universe and back.

Mum was ahead of her time. Nowadays her technique would be

called "guided meditation." Before she could finish a story, I would be so relaxed that I would have fallen into a deep sleep.

Mum meant everything to me. Yet when I lost her during the civil war, it took a while before the pain could burn me. I was in denial and couldn't comprehend the fact of her death.

"Mum will return one day," I kept promising myself. But the wait never ended. My mind played tricks on me many times. When refugees came by our village, I would head over to them, hoping to see my mum among their weary faces. Sometimes my mind fooled me into actually seeing her in their midst. I could hear her voice. Recognize her dress. She was back. Everything was going to be okay again.

Then she would disappear. It was as confusing as it was torturous. I didn't know how to deal with it. How could any child know how to deal with it?

I craved stability. Normality. But I was living in a war zone. Childhood security is the first casualty of any conflict. Instead of my much-yearned-for mum, I was placed under the care of cousins, aunties, step-mums, grandmothers, relatives I barely even knew existed. Other times my caregiver was simply "the village," whichever that happened to be at any given time. Nothing, no one, could ever be as grounding as mum. Every time I began to settle, the earth would vanish from beneath me and I'd plunge into yet another cavernous unknown. Down there in the darkness, bedtime stories were the stuff of distant dreams. Real life became all-consuming and overbearing. Some of my "caregivers" put me to work. If I made a mistake, there was a beating.

As neighboring children grew fat, flesh and muscle was stripped away from me until I was as skinny as a flamingo's legs. Every day we ate *wal wal*, a porridge made of fermented sorghum flour. It was all I had to look forward to, indicative of just how bereft of tenderness, sensitivity, love, and care my life had become. Lost in hunger and misery, I could only reflect that having no mum was having no home.

A physical escape from this mental maelstrom seemed impossible. But an incident led me to discover that escape can be found in a place that, to others, has no visible existence.

One sunny afternoon I went hunting with the big boys. It was a beautiful experience, clear sky, mile upon mile of flat green savanna grassland, a few scattered trees, fresh wind blowing in our faces. I felt more grown up than ever before as I walked with them, clutching a spear. A sudden rushing sound spread through the group like a buzz, signaling imminent action. In the distance, a herd of gazelle kicked up a cloud of dust as they stormed toward us.

I was six years old. My first reaction was utter panic. But then I remembered the instructions one of the boys had given me: "Throw your spear at the weakest animal." I quickly found a position that would allow me the best chance of hitting my target, but I was so busy watching the oncoming pack that I didn't notice the hole beneath me, fashioned by an elephant's foot. I screamed as my leg slid in at a horrible angle. I managed to pull myself free, but I was convinced that the leg was broken. An overwhelming desire to rest and inspect the damage was overridden by the thundering herd nearly upon me. These wild and unpredictable animals could easily trample me.

I bless the heavens that I quickly identified a huge but clearly weak bull. I was shaking with fear, but that same fear gave me focus and allowed me to channel my strength. I drew back my arm and the spear flew at the gazelle's neck.

"Black bull!" I shouted. "Black bull! That's my spear!"

I didn't manage the kill, and some of the boys laughed at my attempt. But the bigger boys were proud of me. I had injured the gazelle enough to slow it down, allowing them to move in and finish it off. My prize was a leg and the intestines. Now all I had to do was get my share home before sunset—that was when the real big beasts came out, the lions, the hyenas, all no doubt attracted to me by my bloodied gains. My goal was to eat, not to be eaten. But a gazelle leg is heavier than you might think. It was touch and go whether I would get it back in time.

Many times weariness overtook me, and I considered giving up. It would have been much easier to leave my quarry and travel the rest of the way unencumbered. But I pressed on, powered only by sheer determination.

When I finally got home, starving and exhausted, the relatives I was staying with were excited to see me—or at least the food I was carrying. As ever, these people weren't close. I was stranded with them, as my brothers and sisters were in different villages. The war and its accompanying lack of food meant it would be burdensome for one person to look after four kids.

"This child is going to do great things," someone shouted as, incredulous at such rich pickings, they settled down to prepare the feast. The smell was unbelievable as the leg cooked on the fire. It was a banquet compared to what we were normally faced with.

I was given none of it.

I slept hungry that night. I had never missed my mum more. I boiled with rage. The anger, the disappointment, and the feeling of being forgotten mixed together to make a vile stew in my stomach. The pain felt like being kicked by a cow. My chest was tightening, suffocated by my own despair. All I could do was wait for the dawn to come. I had one plan—to go and be alone in the forest.

As soon as morning came, I rushed out. I didn't tell anyone where I was going. It would only have got me in trouble. Beneath the trees, sparse sunlight dappled the forest floor. I asked for death to come and take me to my mum. I wanted to die. I cried and cried until I ran out of tears. Anger, humiliation, and frustration forced me down into the earth until I was lying flat on my back, facing the sky. It was the exact same position I used to be in when Mum told us her stories. In that moment I began talking to her. "Mum, where are you? Can you see the suffering I am going through now?" I said prayers to God, wondering why he, too, had abandoned me. Eventually, the words ran dry. My head contained nothing. All I could hear was the flow of my breath, the sounds of the birds, the cows and their calves, the frogs, the wind moving in the branches. The rhythms I felt between myself and nature were new to me. A sense of absolute beauty cocooned me as I slipped into a deep sleep, waking six hours later with so much energy and an inner assurance that I was not, in fact, alone. Others were with me mentally and spiritually. I felt light and creative as I ate the wild fruits, okra, and health-giving plants that festooned the forest floor. The despair of the previous night was forgotten. I made my way home with a joy and happiness far removed from my mood the night before.

At the time, I lacked the words to name the place where I found myself that day. Now I refer to it simply as heaven. I now know that the experience that took me there was meditation. I could not, would not, trade that experience for anything.

That journey into the true power of the mind laid a foundation upon which I would build. Saying prayers, being positive about myself, using my imagination to picture the future, and then just lying down and breathing made a huge difference. Had I understood the true power of meditation then, I would have done it every day. Even so, whenever I felt overwhelmed by life, I would recall that moment of being so in sync with my surroundings and mentally transport myself there. The experience gave me the mental space to seek answers to any predicament. It gave me peace of mind and peace of heart.

Now that I have grown up, meditation has become my medication. I also call it the Pyramid. Why? Because its strength comes from layers, blocks, each supporting the others. The Pyramid is a solid, impenetrable structure, capable of withstanding the storms and attacks of millennia. Look down on that pyramid and see how it broadens, gaining its power. When we meditate, that's exactly what we are doing too. We are opening our minds, widening our perspective, raising our awareness. Meditation gives us the mental space to create and think clearly.

THE 10 PILLARS OF THE PYRAMID

- ◘ Gratitude
- ◘ A forgiving heart
- ◘ Faith
- ◘ A positive mindset
- ◘ Programming or reprogramming of self
- ◘ Purpose
- ◘ Calm
- ◘ Courage
- ◘ Feeding of the soul
- ◘ Love of yourself and your neighbor

How the Pyramid Is Built

When we are born, the world revolves around us. Those who occupy our world must listen to us, nurture us. Without knowing it, we are at the center of everything. As we carry on into our early life, we do so with an underdeveloped consciousness. If we are not exposed to the right environments, we may end up growing into an adult with a self-centered lifestyle, marked by poor moral habits and distorted beliefs. Such a lifestyle takes and rarely gives. It is destructive both to the self and to others.

Self-centered people are empty, sad, and angry. They spend their joyless lives looking for happiness in material items. In contrast, those who cultivate a wider level of consciousness find strength and purpose in their community. They realize they have family: brothers, sisters, grandparents, aunts, uncles, and cousins. They share their love, knowledge, and wealth with these people and in return receive happiness and joy. Others extend their giving beyond their family, looking out for their community, their friends, their country, and perhaps even addressing global issues by contributing to restore balance to the planet. These people have joy in abundance. They have explored all areas of the Pyramid.

MEDITATION AND YOU

Life has taught you that challenging situations will always come your way. In order to counter them, you must raise your mental power; your social, physical, emotional, and spiritual status.

Meditation means allocating time to reprogram yourself, find self-peace, pray, dance, and cultivate any of a million and one things that can bring you happiness. Meditation delivers self-empowerment, self-motivation, and purpose. It is the process a person takes to own their mind and engage with it to find what they truly want. It is the time a person needs to build themselves and seek courage to face their fears.

Through meditation, a person can acquire self-healing and spiritual wellness. Just as you can heal your body by eating healthy, so you can heal the soul by feeding it with positive messages, whether by listening to motivational speakers, reading religious books, or conducting spiritual rituals.

Meditation is a holistic approach to your well-being. It is an integration of your soul, spirit, mind, and body and an examination of purpose. Are you living your life the way you want to? Doing what you really want to do? Through this process of self-investment and analysis, a person comes to know themselves better and believe in themselves. But you must make time in your life to do it. For instance, I create time for myself first thing in the morning. Even if it is just two minutes, I make sure to seize my day before it even starts. In this way, I create a defense mechanism so that if and when I encounter negative forces, my body can resist them without my giving in and engaging negativity.

Other times, I read something inspiring, write lyrics, listen to a powerful speech or positive music. I might read a verse from my favorite book, the Bible, or the words of other beliefs, keeping my eyes and ears open for any positivity that might come my way. The Bible says not to conform to the pattern and standard of this world. Better to be transformed by the renewal of your mind.

I recite positive things about my life. I practice them in my head and write them down to see how I can refine them. Sometimes I reinforce the words by using an external voice to talk me through why they are relevant to my circumstances.

Mental uplift can come from yoga or singing. It can come from spiritual reflection or from isolating yourself from your surroundings and empowering yourself. It can also come from searching for your purpose, acquiring healing for your body, or self-motivation.

Through meditation, you can see the future, identify your vision, and set your goals before heading out into the big wide world. Meditation brings order where there is chaos. It brings courage where there is fear. Meditation means you, like me, get to review yourself and your values and challenge yourself to live by them.

How Meditation Came to Rescue Me in My Teens

As a teenager living in Kenya, I was a troubled young man with many issues. It was a point in my life when I actually had some stability. I had found relief in education and an understanding that maybe I could find my place in what previously seemed such an unforgiving world. Yet, as the experience of real war retreated, a cold war started in my mind. I would hear people screaming, gunshots, and bombs that were not there. Nighttime was the worst. Unable to sleep, my head became a torture cell. I refused to share my secrets with anyone because I was afraid to be seen as having a weak mind or labeled as different.

The nightmares were more tormenting than the battlefields. Sometimes, in the darkness, I would lie there feeling sorry for myself and wishing I had never been born. The suffering of my people, not knowing where my family was, created a fire that burned fiercely within my stomach. My ribs constricted and crushed me. I suffered terrible migraines. Any mental freedom I achieved was quickly buried beneath worries about my future and poisoned by the bitterness in my heart. Forces of evil attacked my mind. I became suicidal as the images got worse and worse—the burning of my village, the dead bodies left to rot, vultures fighting over dead soldiers and children. I didn't want to eat, think, breathe, nothing. I began fighting with God.

"You love the tears of poor people," I told him. "The longer they stay in that situation, the more they will keep singing your praise and worshipping you."

One day I locked myself in a closet. I talked to myself. I told myself good things. "I am wise. I am smart. I am a giver. I am a thinker. I solve problems. Things will get better, Jal, don't give up."

Just as I had in the forest as a six-year-old, I had turned to meditation without knowing it.

I talked about the future, asking questions and waiting and listening. Nothing happened on the first day, but each day I repeated the process I felt better. I began to mix the questions with songs, prayers, and writing my thoughts down. My mind stirred from its torpor and became engaged. I started reading scriptures from the Bible and the Quran, listening to stories about Mahatma Gandhi, Nelson Mandela, and Martin Luther King Jr.

Through meditation, I was able to process the positive words of great leaders and further my healing and willingness to forgive. Through meditation, I created self-motivation and an autonomous lifestyle, and I began to use music as a therapy to soothe the pain. Through meditation, I was able to build faith in myself.

One day I remembered my mother's words to me as a small child: "If someone says bad things to you, use your inner voice to say good things to yourself. Tell yourself 'I am good, I am going to do big things.'" Her wisdom resonated with me. If another child or an adult told me I was stupid, I would start an internal conversation with myself: "I am a good child. I am smart." I would divert their words from me by dancing, praying, singing, writing, listening to music—any method available. I still do it. Words allow me to reflect, to keep the Pyramid strong.

> *Cold War makes my whole body sore, flashback of my childhood experience roar.*
> *Walking on the street, a strong stench punches through my nose.*
> *I am aroused. I look around and I pause.*
> *My whole body shakes. Migraines, my skull is boiling open.*
> *My throat tightens, my cells and tissues frighten.*
> *My lungs shrink.*
> *My internal organs, stomach and intestines, want to come out through my mouth.*
> *No "ambulance" as I lose my balance.*
> *A moment of a silence, of internal violence.*
> *Soul murder, internal genocide. An invasion of demons, nowhere to hide.*
> *I stay calm and pray, my body breathes peace.*
> *Breathe, breathe, breathe, peace.*
> *You are safe, forgive, so you can be free.*
> *Relax, you are experiencing the past.*
> *Your experience was your preparation for greatness.*
> *You are safe, breathe in, breathe out.*
> *A word of gratitude to the pain—"Thank you for reminding me of the past."*
> *And thank you, creator, for trusting me with these experiences.*
> *I will use them to learn—social, emotional.*
> *You believe I have the power to overcome.*
> *To show others that storms only last for a while.*
> *And then come blessings.*

These lyrics, inspired by my relationship with meditation, give me an amazing uplifting energy. The ten pillars of the Pyramid do the same.

My goal is to take my life to the next level. Thanks to meditation, the process is simpler than it has ever been. Its central guidelines have become my lifestyle.

Look at the pillars. Believe in them. Follow them. They will allow you to carry out internal engineering, to design and redesign your life.

3

—

GRATITUDE

MEDITATION PILLAR 1

I HAVE COME TO UNDERSTAND SOMETHING VERY IMPOR-
tant in life. What takes away my joy are the things I want. What brings
me joy are the things I give. It may seem counterintuitive, but this truth
becomes clear when understood from the perspective of gratitude.

Gratitude is a positive attitude toward life that sparks a positive reaction in the soul, body, spirit, and mind. It takes us from a
state of complaining to a state of appreciation. It helps us to identify
opportunities.

Gratitude is walking in complete awareness. It is noticing the gifts
that Mother Earth and the universe have made available to us. It is the
appreciation of experience. When we appreciate something from the
bottom of our heart, we cultivate joy. Appreciate something without
expectation and it gives us so much. It connects us to our universe and
makes us operate on a higher frequency.

When I pray to God for help with a challenge and yet I am defeated, I am struck hard by disappointment. My energy levels are al-
tered in a negative way. When I set up a goal and don't achieve it, I feel
upset. When a friend, colleague, or family member lets me down, my

joy, my lifeblood, is snatched away. When feeling ill means I miss out on life, I get frustrated; my day becomes worse, and I become worried and anxious. When I am disrespected or offended, my joy vanishes as fast as the hurt arrives. When I fail to meet people's expectations, my heart shrinks a little inside.

At times in my life I've been a taker, putting my needs and wants before those of others. That attitude made me full of myself. It made me believe my pain and vision was bigger than everyone else's. I was inspired to change this attitude by the great and inspiring African leaders whom I learned about during my childhood in Kenya. They gave more than they received. They worked harder than others. They did their best to live by their word. They were purpose-driven individuals who surrendered their pain to the cause.

The question I had to ask myself was how I could reprogram my heart and mind to ensure joy could be with me 24/7. What I loved as a kid was to see people smile, dance, feel happy, and be joyful. That never changed. I always wanted to be part of the solution, never the problem, and create experiences that delivered those great emotions.

As ever, I could draw on strengths forged in adversity. I was once slung in prison in Ethiopia with a group of Sudan People's Liberation Army commanders and officers waiting to be sentenced. The fate that awaited us was death. The cell we shared was dug into the ground. On top was placed a metal sheet. When it was sunny, the heat in the pit was stifling. When it rained, water would seep through and we would slowly be drenched, shivering as temperatures plummeted at night and the cold crept into our bones from the damp earth that was our bedding. Our sustenance during this misery was one meal a day, made up of sorghum grain and bland beans. It was, to put it mildly, an uncomfortable place to be.

In that squalid hell, I asked myself a question. "What can I do to make these men smile, or at least lift themselves by sharing stories among each other? What can I do to build togetherness between us, so we work together positively as human beings?"

I was eleven. I was not a psychologist, a teacher, or a leader of men. I was a boy. So I started by cracking jokes. No one laughed. I told stories. The only response came from one of the officers telling me to shut up.

"You talk too much," he barked at me.

But an older officer intervened. He said he liked my chatter: "Keep talking, my son."

For two more days, I shared funny stories, again to no reaction. But then, on the third day, it was as if the group had been injected with a life serum. They, too, began sharing jokes and stories. From then on, we somehow found fun amid these deathly circumstances. Even though my own contributions didn't make all the soldiers smile, I was glad to have sparked a modicum of joy in that literal hellhole.

Sometimes, while we may not ultimately be the one to drive a message home, we can still be the one to put the fuel in the engine. All those soldiers were awaiting execution. My own fate was less clear, but I had a clear conversation with myself. If I was to be taken to the firing squad, I wanted to die with joy in my heart.

All too often, as soon as joy appeared, something would come along to take it away. The ultimate challenge was to make joy long-lasting. I was in my mid-twenties when the power of gratitude finally began to dawn on me. I was embarked on a process of internal engineering, examining my inner self and assessing what needed updating or changing. Something clicked in my mind. If I accepted everything that came to me with gratitude, I would have joy for eternity.

I took that revelation seriously. It shifted my perspective. I began to accept my past difficulties as great lessons. Future challenges were repositioned as incoming blessings or missions. It was a moment of such eye-opening clarity that I felt I had been trusted by the universe with infinite intelligence. Instead of my background as a child soldier being a source of dark, disjointed nightmares, I realized that my shapeless, malformed existence had given me rules to follow. There was a structure, and it gave my life both purpose and meaning. When a mission came my way, as with any soldier, I got on with it no matter how difficult it was. I drew on that experience and applied it to my current world. If my mission was to feel joy and help those around me feel it, too, then I would accept it with gratitude.

I grew up as a Christian, so gratitude has always been in my life. Giving thanks for whatever comes to us drives the Christian culture. Across my early years, I was also exposed to many different cultures that further influenced my perspective on gratitude. But the shift I made following my revelation was to apply gratitude in a deeper way across every possible area open to me—positive experiences, negative experiences, the living and the nonliving. I would be as grateful for my family and friends as I would be for strangers, for the sun, moon, stars, oceans, rivers, mountains, birds, animals, fish, plants, insects, fire, wind, nature, silence, violence, and peace. Everything that is and everything that isn't. Everything that had helped me overcome my obstacles. The revelation of the power of total gratitude made me so excited that it took a while to sit properly within me.

The beauty of gratitude is that it takes us from a state of complaint to a state of appreciation; to one where we can, with crystal-clear vision, unblemished by negativity, identify opportunities. People who are not grateful face many challenges that overwhelm them, whereas those who carry gratitude with them as surely as they carry their heart recognize defeats as learning experiences that will make them stronger, smarter, and wiser. Victories, of course, are also recognized. Big or small, they are never insignificant.

Gratitude is an attribute whether we are in situations of abundance or of poverty. It gives us the ability to create happiness for ourselves even out of nothing. Gratitude is made for difficult situations. A person who practices gratitude will never be a victim. They can't be because they have chosen to live a life where such a status doesn't exist. They have created a force that affects their environment so much that they are experiencing heaven on Earth.

If you believe yourself to be in a place where everything is running smoothly and there are no problems, I propose you run for your life because a bomb is about to explode. Problems are a way of life. They have no end, so best to prepare for them.

Bear in mind also that it's the problems we solve that make us who we are. The more problems we solve, the more valuable we become as people. Look at your life that way and then every challenge becomes a gift, a blessing, or an opportunity. We become born again, we become new, and our experience in life will be different. The universe is our ultimate life trainer. It will always throw up lots of problems. The more you handle the problems, the better person you become.

These days when I face a difficult situation, I count my blessings and say thank you to the creator of all things. "Thank you for trusting me with this challenge that I am facing today. Thank you for trusting that I am smart, a reservoir of wealth, a well of infinite wisdom."

One of the biggest challenges I have faced over the years is that my throat is twisted to the right, making it difficult for me to sing, rap, and talk. Not great when what you want to do most in life is sing, rap, and talk!

My right shoulder is always tense, and pain afflicts the muscles on the right side of my face as well as my neck, eyes, throat, jaw, and chest. On a bad day, the pain is a nine out of ten. It can take up to a week for it to reduce to a three. At its worst, I will lie in bed and refuse to talk to people. I will have a headache that feels like my skull is cracking. The pain can be so bad that it almost drives me into unconsciousness, making it difficult to wake up again. Could I really be grateful for this? I had to figure out a way for that to be the case, to live through that pain via gratitude. So every morning I put one hand on my chest, the other on my throat, and give thanks to the creator for my life. I breathe in and out slowly, use chanting, and sometimes speak out loud to thank the pain. When I go through that process, the discomfort drops to a one or a two. If I go too long without expressing gratitude, the severe pain comes back again. At that point, I become annoyed, and my mood can be affected. The same happens when I reflect on my childhood. If I don't practice gratitude for my early years, then haunting visions return. The situation becomes overwhelming.

Gratitude gets me up in the morning. It activates my higher purpose, which in turn gives me joy. Forget pharmacies, forget drugs. Gratitude has become my painkiller. It is what I use in every challenging situation because it has never failed me. Gratitude is a safe place for my soul. It stops me from throwing gasoline on negative thoughts.

Gratitude is a reservoir of infinite potential. Don't just take my word for it. Scientific research has shown that regularly expressing gratitude changes the molecular structure of the brain, making us healthier and happier. It can, among other things, affect our immune systems and cardiovascular health.

HIGHER PURPOSE GRATITUDE

Sometimes, I express what I call a higher purpose gratitude. I thank my lungs and heart, my intestines, stomach, throat, skin, kidneys, liver, appendix, blood, and skeleton. And then I invite my organs, tissues, muscles, nails, hair, every cell and living tissue inside me to thank their creator, because the creator deserves to be given thanks and praise without the caveat that we want something back. When I do this my whole body feels incredibly light, infused with so much energy. Sometimes it feels like I am floating or flying—an amazing experience.

Other times, I use my imagination to place myself high in the clouds. From there I dive into the ocean, swimming with sea life of all shapes and sizes—shrimps, crabs, sharks, whales, turtles. Sometimes I imagine swimming in the Nile with the hippos and crocodiles. I fly to Africa and feel intense gratitude for the giraffes and elephants, the forests, the birds, or any other of the thousands of other majestic animals that grace that great continent.

I am also grateful for the landscapes that I will make into a cinema-scape in my mind. I love that I can transport myself into the body of a being unlimited by gravity, looking down at the Earth and then soaring up away into the galaxies to enjoy the beautiful view offered by the stars, at all times giving gratitude for these beautiful creations. The peace I receive from this kind of gratitude has no explanation. It makes me feel drunk with joy.

I look at humanity in exactly the same way. When I meet a human being who has done something extraordinary, I offer appreciation for their work; when I meet someone and am amazed by their beauty, I tell them how beautiful they are. Whether the origin of the beauty that surrounds me is an ultimate creator, the Big Bang, or whatever, I am simply grateful for the chance to see what surrounds me. I am grateful because I, too, am part of creation. I am related, as we all are, to the living and the nonliving.

Open yourself up to gratitude and you open yourself up to a seventh sense. I will discuss this further later, but for now all you need to know is that the seventh sense is the highest form of conscious awakening. It is a life-giving, renewing, and invigorating experience we should all experience some day, and preferably every day.

YOUR JOYS AND YOUR CHALLENGES

Before we go any further, I need you to ask yourself two questions:

1. **What are the top ten things you are grateful for?**
2. **What are the top ten things robbing your peace of mind?**

Make a list for each. Hold one in each hand. Sit for a short while and analyze them. You will notice that one list feels light, the other feels heavy. Now I want you to consider a technique I have found to invite gratitude into my life.

First, I lie on my back, my hands open, and my palms facing the sky. Into my right hand, I invite my challenges, the scenarios making my life difficult, be they financial issues, pain, worries, or fears. I open that palm to stress, family issues, work, politics, business, every challenge of every kind. I acknowledge and accept those challenges. I become excited about the learning experiences those challenges will bring. I prepare my entire self to observe, study, listen, and fall in love with them, to accept them as the route to positive rewards. I visualize every challenge and transform it into something beautiful. The joy and peace that comes from that process is incredible, so overwhelming it is almost impossible to express.

Yet the process is only half complete. Into my left hand I invite my rewards, those both living and departed who continue to give me happiness and joy. In those moments, I give my gratitude to those who have sacrificed their time, money, and life for me. I remember my family and my childhood friends, the lessons my mother gave me, the love of my grandmother. I think deeply of my friends, my colleagues, and the mother of my children. My hand will draw in the air, oxygen, water, fire, wind, and land. As I offer this invitation to the world around me, its people, its beauty, its elemental grandeur, I smile and allow every cell in my body to experience the moment. I am joy. Joy is me.

As I bring the session to a close, I rise slowly and bring my hands to the prayer position without quite allowing them to touch. I let the energy between them exchange, visualizing a sky-blue light, and then bring both hands together, producing an incredible supernova where I imagine my entire body lighting up.

As with the electricity that illuminates a light bulb, the power of gratitude can only come from a combination of negative and positive forces. I envision my challenges as electrons (the negative force) and my rewards as protons (the positive force). Neither can be created nor destroyed, but both can be transformed from one to the other.

The Gratitude Bowl

The gratitude bowl is great for training the brain to find a meaning in each stage of suffering. It is worth trying for anyone in a difficult situation who needs to build themselves back up. The idea is to do the gratitude bowl every day for thirty days, and then pare it back to once a week or once a month.

- Fill a large bowl with water and place it between two smaller bowls. The bowl on the right represents negativity—plans or goals unreached, trauma, financial worries, relationship difficulties, health problems, or any other challenge. The bowl on the left represents everything that gives you joy and happiness.
- Take two deep breaths and slowly exhale.
- Measure your negativity by taking teaspoonfuls of water from the center bowl and putting them in the right-hand bowl. Each teaspoonful represents an element of negativity.
- Mark something good in your life by taking teaspoonfuls from the center bowl and putting them in the left-hand bowl.
- By the end of the exercise, the bowl in the center should be empty. Now compare left and right to see which one has more.
- Drink the water in the left-hand bowl and imagine it giving your body energy.
- Look at the right-hand bowl, full of negativity. Pick one of your current challenges. Meditate to find a meaning in its existence. Be grateful for the challenge it has given you.
- Take a teaspoonful of water from the right-hand bowl, transfer it to the left, and drink it. In so doing, you are converting the challenge into a positive.
- End with a gratitude meditation.

Life Waves

I hated birthdays. They hit me hard, triggering my traumatic childhood memories. I would pretend I was enjoying them—I would laugh and dance—but behind the façade I was hurting. I was reminded of being alone without a real family. That torture went on for years until I found a way to overcome it with a technique I call the life wave.

I drew a waveform across a graph. Surfing the tops of the wave were people, events, and activities that made me feel better by lifting me up. In the wave troughs were those people and things that sought to destroy me.

As I completed the activity, I was reminded of a friend who told me how he didn't have to worry about money at major times in his life because of the support of his mother and father. The COVID-19 pandemic had recently ravaged my industry, and I had exhausted all my reserves. The recollection threatened to wreck me. Unlike my friend, I lacked the protection of family. The only resource I had was my joy and peace of mind, which I protected with gratitude.

But then I remembered the woman who triggered so many beautiful events in my life by leading me to the life wave graph: Heather Dennison. Out of the blue, Heather called my manager. She said that the Lord Jesus had sent her to check on my well-being and provide financial support. While greatly touched by my friend's gesture, I instructed my manager to donate the funds to my Gua Africa charity so it would help children in need. Heather insisted, however, that the money should come directly to me as Jesus instructed. COVID-19 had decimated the music industry, causing financial hardship, and she wanted me to be able to continue my work because many people, herself included, benefited greatly from it. I could not accept Heather's generosity as a simple handout, but I accepted it on the basis that we use the funding as a grant to provide free online activities and youth coaching.

I should have known that Heather would appear. Whenever I face a tough challenge, a woman always turns up to pull me back up to the top of the wave (as we shall see throughout the rest of this book). Heather made me see that I have family all over the world, and that the universe has a way of taking care of its own. Family doesn't just mean those who are blood connected. Family is the individuals who walk with us, help us face our fears, and use their skills and resources to help us overcome our perils. I drew a new life wave that day—one with a safety net.

On January 1, 2021, I celebrated my fortieth birthday. It became the first birthday I ever celebrated with the right intention and purpose; the first where I experienced joy in abundance, knowing I could move forward armed with a new belief brought about by an individual who had entered my wave. I look forward to celebrating birthdays properly from now on, working on training my mind further to enjoy them. December and January, which have tormented me for so long, are now going to be joyful months.

MEDITATION AND GRATITUDE

Remember the ten pillars of the Pyramid? Remember the power of meditation, of taking a step back and evaluating your life? Here we will apply those principles to gratitude.

First, a breathing exercise:

1. Take a deep breath.
2. Exhale.
3. Take another deep breath. This time, slowly fill up your lungs. Imagine your belly as a balloon that you are filling with air.
4. Exhale slowly.
5. Regain your normal flow of breathing.
6. Take a minute to simply enjoy that flow.

Now, out loud or in your head, say the following words:

Gratitude is having a positive attitude toward life.

It takes us from a state of complaining to a state of appreciation.

It allows us to identify opportunities.

I am grateful for all the good and the challenges I have in my life.

Thank you for life, for peace, for joy, and for the wealth I have in abundance.

Thank you also my heart and my mind.

Thank you my bones, my brain, my hands, my legs, my eyes.

Thank you my ears, my mouth, my tongue.

Thank you my skin, my muscles, my cells.

Thank you my soul, my body, my spirit.

Thank you every living organism within me.

Note: Whoever or whatever it was that created you—please thank that higher power.

Now:

Pause. Enjoy a moment of silence. Then take a short time to give personal gratitude for all the blessings in your life. In your mind, pick a place—perhaps the ocean, the sky, the openness of space, the forest—connect with it, and appreciate the creative force for the sight that you behold in your mind.

Out loud or in your head, say the following words:

I understand the law of thermodynamics. That energy can be neither created nor destroyed, but only transferred from one form to another.

I invite all my challenges into my right hand. (**Be specific as to the nature of those challenges—feel them, acknowledge them, allow the joy within yourself to soothe the pain.**)

I am grateful to the creator for these challenges. I am grateful for the lessons I am learning. I view these challenges as an infinite source of potential energy which I will use as a foundation to walk with purpose and create many beautiful things.

I thank you, creator, for giving me the calmness and humility to endure and accept the things I cannot change.

I thank you for giving me the courage to face my challenges.

I am grateful for the wisdom, knowledge, and understanding that you have given me to be able to create beautiful things and to tell the difference between what I can manage and what I cannot.

On my left hand, I smile with joy as I notice my breathing, feeling my blessings and everything beautiful around me. I invite everything that gives me joy and happiness into my left hand. **(Feel free to be specific about what you are grateful for. Allow the joy to engulf your entire body.)**

I thank you, creator, for all my blessings.

I thank you for family, friends, and colleagues. I thank you for my community, the country, the sun, the stars, the fish in the ocean.

All the beautiful things you created have a purpose. Everything in this world has a purpose.

Now:

As your eyes close, bring your hands slowly toward the prayer position until you feel them repelling or attracting.

Imagine your entire body as a light bulb. Your challenges and problems represent electrons; your rewards/blessings represent protons.

Imagine your right hand as a cathode and your left hand as an anode. Bring your hands together and allow the energy to flow through you. Let your entire body light up. As you do so, make a connection with everything that is precious to you—those from the past, those from the future, loved ones, friends, forests, beaches, vast open spaces, the four walls that enclose your love and security.

Enjoy the feeling for however long you like. You can repeat this process at any time.

Close the session with the following words:

I am gratitude. I have gratitude.
Thank you, creator, for giving me gratitude.
I am gratitude. I have gratitude.

Remember, gratitude is a principle you must practice every day. Do so and you will find a joy you never knew yourself capable of possessing.

4
—

FORGIVING HEART

MEDITATION PILLAR 2

HOW DO WE OBTAIN A FORGIVING HEART? IT IS A QUES-
tion that eats away at so many of us. How can we ever forgive those who
have so terribly wronged us? Yet the answer is right there in front of us
if we open our eyes to the truth, hard as that may seem. A forgiving
heart comes from a single core action: forgiving those who have caused
us harm without expecting them to ask for forgiveness. We back that up
by forgiving ourselves for the harm we have caused others and ourselves.
If we make both of those mindset adaptations, we create an impenetrable
defense to keep us healthy and productive. We gain a forgiving heart.

I would like to take you to the genesis of the bitter experiences that
form the foundation of my invisible internal war. In doing so, you will see
the immense value forgiveness has brought into my life. You will see that
forgiveness allowed me to live. The alternative was to shrivel away and die.

THE FOUNDATIONS OF MY BITTERNESS

We were in the back of a truck, one of many in a convoy snaking
through this war-torn land, heading to what we hoped was the safety

of my grandmother's house in South Sudan. My mother, uncle, brothers and sisters, and I sat close, as nervous of our fellow Arab passengers as we were of being ambushed by the Sudan People's Liberation Army. It was rumored the SPLA stole children and ate those left behind. The Arabs were the enemy of the SPLA, but their conversation, overtly aggressive demeanor, and guns made them just as frightening. Gesturing at those we passed on the roads and in the fields, one of them snarled, "These Blacks are slaves. Their land and everything in it has been given to us by Allah. We own these Black people, plus their cows, chickens, and goats. We are the ones to decide the fate of their souls." I was confused by such words. We had Muslim neighbors and none of them had ever said anything like that.

Food, as ever, was everything. We had ours, *tahnia*, a sugary paste made of sesame, in a box. At least I thought we did. I looked up and saw one of the Arab men eating it. My uncle tried to get it back but was set upon. Mama tried to help. Fists pummeled into her mouth and stomach. I felt sick as I watched this woman, so benevolent, so forgiving of others, being thrown around like a rag doll. I couldn't just sit there. Jumping up, I seized the foot of one of her assailants and sank my teeth into his flesh. But I was a small boy. I could never match his strength. He grabbed my neck and tightened his hands around my throat. The world shrank away, as if I were entering a tunnel, until I blacked out.

When I came to, my uncle's face was swollen with bruises. He had two puffy black eyes and blood streamed from his nose—as it did mine. My mum's injuries were largely internal. It took her weeks to recover from the punches and the kicks she suffered. A strange feeling occupied my heart in that moment. It possessed so much power and crackled with an intense energy. Any thoughts or flashbacks of terror I experienced became fuel to carry on in the struggle. But it came with a price. My imagination turned to hate and pushed me to seek to destroy those who brought hell to my home and raped the soul of my homeland. I didn't know what to call it then, but I would soon recognize it as bitterness.

The catastrophic events I witnessed in the Sudanese Civil War, when the Sudanese government sought to terminate our existence—death, famine, rape, disease—confirmed the seriousness of that Arab's words. My mother used to tell me that the world would end one day, and as a kid I would imagine how it would happen. My mind would throw up images of a great flood, or all-consuming fires coming from the sky and beneath the earth. I would see devils on horseback cutting people to ribbons with swords. In South Sudan, I experienced precisely what I had imagined. The sky did rain fire. The ground did shake. People ran in every direction, everywhere and nowhere—there was no escape. It was devastating to watch my mother, so strong, so driven, cry helplessly.

As we trudged from village to village, we passed rotting bodies, fresh bodies, lost souls, and frozen spirits. Death was omnipresent, to the extent that mothers no longer covered the eyes of their children. There was no rest. Everywhere we went was on fire, matching the relentless pain I felt inside. Refugees in our homeland, the tangled roots of bitterness spread from my heart and into every cell of my body. The more pain I experienced, the thicker the walls of bitterness became, and the narrower my perspective.

Bitterness Gave Me Strength

Ultimately, my anger would drive me to become a child soldier for the SPLA. The training nearly killed me. It did kill others. On one occasion, we were made to crawl for five hundred meters until our elbows were bruised and bleeding. One small boy couldn't take it anymore. He raised his face, and the trainer kicked him hard on the back of the head. The boy began vomiting blood. Soon after, he died. The trainer had used the boy's life to drive his pitiless message into our hearts.

I wanted to escape the training camp, but every time I got near to doing so, I would be haunted by flashbacks—the tears of my mother, the rape of my aunt, the burning of my village, the humiliation of the truck convoy, and the loss of everything we owned. Those images made me say words that charged my body to the core—"I want to kill as many Muslims and Arabs as possible." Saying these words empowered me. They sent an electric charge through my body. It was as if I had been plugged into the power grid.

"I will finish the training for my mother, my brothers, sisters, and my village," I told myself. Bitterness got me through to the end.

By the time I was required to turn that training into action, to wreak vengeance, I was a child deeply disturbed by the insanely cruel world I had become part of. But bitterness soon overruled empathy. I didn't feel sorry for myself. Instead, I'd found a sense of purpose out in the killing fields. I was consumed with looking for the man who had beaten my mother in the truck, the Arabs who had burned my village down, the man who had raped my aunt. Those who had killed our animals, poisoned our water, and starved us to death.

One day, we managed to capture an Arab officer alive. I was elated. We all wanted him to die in pain. Each of us agreed to take turns beating him with a machete, a bayonet, or the butt of our AK-47. The guilt of taking a man's life was tempered by turning it into a shared action. We felt justified. Flashbacks from my childhood provided my fuel. At thirteen years old, if I'd had a nuclear bomb I'd have known exactly where to drop it. My hate for Arab Muslims was real and knew no bounds, yet if I had met you then, you would have never known. My bitterness was invisible to the naked eye. It was internal. I was good at hiding it.

I knew something else at that time: killing the officer was scary and exciting, but the joy we felt was hollow and meaningless.

MY TRANSFORMATION FROM BITTERNESS

Initially, what I loved about church in Kenya were the free cookies, juice, and music. As soon as the pastor got up to preach, I would leave. Then one day I decided to stay and listen. The sermon he delivered was about how Jesus expects us to forgive. His words made me angry.

I walked out of that church in a rage. On my way home, I told Jesus my life didn't relate to his. He didn't lose his mother, his brothers and sisters, his aunties, his uncles. His father was God. Had either of them forgiven Satan?

I distanced myself from the church and went back to embracing meditation and prayer, but one day, a voice came out of the dark.

"Do you want to experience joy and complete peace of mind?" it asked.

There was only one reply. "Yes."

"To do so," the voice told me, "you will have to forgive. You must forgive yourself and those who have hurt you." The voice made me angry. It reminded me of my childhood experiences, the screaming of people in burning houses, the desperate running for cover, the shooting, the bombing, the loss of my loved ones. It reminded me of the day I was taken away from my family and made into a child soldier. It reminded me of the terrible things I did to others just as they had done to me.

The message bore no relation to my suffering. How could I forgive the loss of so much in such a violent, hideous, viciously inhumane, and wholly unnecessary way? I clung to my pain and felt justified in doing so. I felt my meditation had let me down by bringing such a voice into the sanctuary of my darkness, so I carried on with my daily life, holding on to my childhood traumas and the bitterness inside my heart. With my shuttered mind, closed heart, and rigid attitude, I saw forgiveness as an ambush. Everywhere I went it seemed to jump out at me. Every signpost seemed to point one way. When the universe, God, or any other infinite intelligence wants to deliver a message, it will not allow you the excuse that you didn't hear or see it. At school, the movies, football games, everywhere, the message of forgiveness was waiting for me.

I was at a secondhand market in Nairobi. I'd been there many times before, but this time was different. I heard two men talking.

"Brother, if you don't forgive," one told his friend, "then you are the one who has swallowed the poison. It won't kill your enemy."

His words stopped me in my tracks. The fog cleared and I could suddenly see clearly. If I did not forgive, I would always be a slave to the person who caused me harm. I remembered also how warriors from the Nuer tribe are not allowed to fight if they are bitter. Such emotion makes them reckless; it puts them in the control of the enemy. Before they fight, the Nuer ceremonially cleanse themselves of evil spirits.

The men's conversation reminded me of why villages are burned down, why men and women are raped, why genocides are committed. As a general once told me, it is to the crush the spirit of the enemy, to control them for their lifetime, and then pass the curse on to the next generation. That conversation was one of thousands taking place that day in that market in Nairobi, yet it was the only one I heard. It awakened a great spirit within me and sent me on a path of no return.

That evening, I returned home with my mind opened and my heart ready. "I am going to forgive," I told myself. I didn't know how to do it, but at least I now understood what forgiveness meant.

In Naath (which is the Nuer's name for themselves), they have a phrase, "*palah kah*," which means to let go without expectation. In my meditation space, I made sure there was no one around to interfere. Then I began.

I took a deep breath, exhaled, and started speaking.

"My heart lets go," I said. "My mind lets go. My body lets go. My organs let go."

Why my organs? It is important to respect that our entire body can hold trauma, so while our hearts may forgive, other facets of our being may not do so quite so easily. It is vital that we allow our entire bodies—our cells, muscles, skeletons, and vital organs—to understand that we are starting anew without bitterness and that they, too, must be part of the forgiveness process.

I thanked the creator. In my silent surrender to an invisible force, a gentle spark of joy came first into my heart before distributing around my body. As I was enjoying this peace, a soft voice told me to forgive myself too.

It was so simple, if a little strange, to trust this voice in my head—the voice, according to whichever doctrine you believe, of the holy spirit, guiding spirits, or the wisdom of ancestors. But trust it I did. It was the first time in my life that I tasted freedom in full. I became more creative and active in the community, leading to my founding Gua Africa, an organization that works with families, individuals, and communities to overcome the effects of war and poverty.

Forgiveness also led me to work with the Sudanese Muslim musician Abdel Gadir Salim, a collaboration that gave me an international platform to drive home the messages of peace and self-improvement I feel so passionately about. Forgiveness has given me the energy that still charges me today. Forgiveness has made doors open.

Letting go of hate became the foundation of healing. My heart and mind finally united, allowing a positive new perspective into my life. The joy in my heart and the peace in my mind made me feel alive. I was, at last, a human being.

To forgive is to relieve oneself of the psychological, emotional, and physical torments that bitterness brings. Bitterness has an energy field that attracts negative energy. It creates setbacks and insecurity and makes it impossible to forge long-term relationships. A bitter heart burns bridges. It creates self-destruction.

But do not ever think that forgiveness is easy. You have to persuade your subconscious to understand its importance to you. You must work to make forgiveness an inseparable part of your life. Only then can your mind and body truly let go of bitterness and rage. Forgiving is keeping hope alive. Forgiving is saying that tomorrow will come. Forgiving is freedom.

Letting Go of Genetic Bitterness

My grandmother believed that more than anything else, the suffering that brings us down is caused by bitterness and fear. It destroys us internally and affects our communities and loved ones. She also believed in curses and that hate and bitterness were the key ingredient in activating them, inviting negative spirits to possess us.

As a child, I would hear her talking to other women about such curses, passed down from previous generations. "Just as we inherit blessings," they would say, "so we inherit curses." The only way to break a curse, my grandmother claimed, was through forgiveness. A cursed person would have to purify themselves before undergoing a ceremony to break the curse.

Such conversations were a little deep for me to understand at the time. But I do believe that when we are bitter, we become an altar for evil and can be used to do its work. A bitter heart is a dangerous thing.

Based on these traditional beliefs and what I have learned from Indian American spiritual guru Deepak Chopra, I firmly believe that our ancestors' trauma and bitterness can be passed down into our lives, just the same as our own pain and bitterness can affect those around us. That is why, when we ask for forgiveness for ourselves, we must also seek the same for our ancestors. Our work to banish bitterness is about far more than just us.

SOUL-TO-SOUL FORGIVENESS

Everyone has a soul. Every soul has a purpose, is forgiving, and is omnipotent. Few realize, however, that souls can communicate. I can talk to the souls of those I have caused harm, apologize, and seek their forgiveness, just as they can to me. I have taken huge mental relief from that. Communicating with the souls of others has allowed me to clear my conscience and clean my heart on several occasions. Soul-to-soul forgiveness can also be extended to people who have passed away, but it is not an easy way out. It requires a deep mental connection and above all must come from a place of truth, with deep sincerity, for it to work. One's own actions, one's own soul, must be thoroughly examined and cleansed.

As with so much in my life, the root of my soul-to-soul forgiveness lies in my childhood. My mother raised us always to tell the truth, to walk in the light, but sadly, it takes courage to tell the truth all the time. I lied to her many times. Lies fed other lies, so scared was I of the repercussions if I told her the truth. But my conscience never made it easy. I so wanted to look into my mother's eyes without guilt, yet I could not do so without telling her the truth. Facing this quandary one day, a wise counsel entered my head.

"Find a quiet place in your heart to apologize to your mum," it advised. "Tell her that you are sorry and will do your best not to lie to her again."

It was more than words. Mum would not be able to sense I had done something wrong after I had cleansed myself. My posture would be different, my mind retuned. I was renewed.

I performed soul-to-soul forgiveness not just with my mum but with all the other adults who had been on the end of my many untruths. Immediately, my psychological state improved. It became a secret practice, apologizing to people privately and doing my best to not knowingly repeat the deceit. When I could find the courage, I would tell the truth to their faces, but I knew also I could apologize later alone in my quiet place where no one was able to hear me.

Soul-to-soul forgiveness should never be seen as a coward's way out. It takes strength to achieve psychological liberation. The mental pressure of guilt is incredible. Soul-to-soul forgiveness delivers a solution when the alternative is too painful, too unrealistic, too dangerous to consider.

I am not alone in this approach. Look at the Catholic church's tradition of confession. As an altar boy in Kenya, I found it an amazing way to relieve personal darkness as I mixed my mother tongue with English and confessed my sins to a priest who would make the sign of the cross and tell me I was forgiven. The act of confession made me feel clean and free from guilt. I would go home with happy dancing feet. Soul-to-soul forgiveness lightens the load we all carry.

FORGIVENESS IS A PROCESS

Forgiveness must be continually practiced if it is to succeed. I thought I had a forgiving heart, and that bitterness would never catch me again after I forgave myself and those who stole my childhood in the Sudanese Civil War. I thought the anger and pain were gone. But on December 15, 2013, as I stood in my home in Canada talking on the phone with my sister in South Sudan, something took over my whole body. I heard her and her children screaming. Gunshots could clearly be heard in the background. The government of South Sudan had begun the genocide of its own citizens.

My sister's phone cut off, immediately followed by a call from my brother Marnath, in shock. He, too, had heard the atrocity unfolding while on the phone to our brother Kueth. A death squad instructed Kueth to call his loved ones and say his final prayers. He was shot dead before he could even finish, while Marnath listened on the other end of the line. A South Sudanese soldier then picked the phone up and told Marnath they were looking for him and he would be next.

My home village was wiped out a few months later. Young girls were raped, boys were castrated, and families were burned in their homes. Of the village elders, there was no trace.

Sixty members of my family were murdered. I felt helpless and was filled with incredible anger and frustration. I knew also that for my own well-being, I needed to get the rage out of myself as soon as possible. I prayed, read the Bible, chanted, wrote a song even, but it was impossible. What I didn't realize until a few months later was that bitterness had once again found a way into my heart.

I needed that old familiar voice to enter my head again, to tell me what to do next. As ever, for by now I trusted it as my friend, it arrived. It told me to mourn for those I had lost, an emotion that was swept away in the flood of anger. It also told me I must perform a ritual for them. I should cover myself with white paint, hair included, and dance naked in the park. I know—crazy. But I trusted it. I remembered a similar healing ritual from our village where young and old would dance together, covered in white ashes from burnt cow dung.

I called my manager and lawyer and told them what I wanted to do. It didn't go down well. They pointed out that dancing naked in a park in Canada could put me straight into a psychiatric ward. My heart wanted to do the ritual, but my head agreed with their advice. However, my friend, the photographer and writer Cari Flammia, told me I would not be the first artist to dance without clothes in public. It had happened in the United States on numerous occasions. That was all the encouragement I needed. I painted my entire body and made my way to a nearby park. Dancing, though, was difficult. My body felt heavy; when I tried to dance, I fell down. On my fourth attempt, I pushed to remain upright and, as I did, I began to feel something come alive in me. I felt light and knew I had regained my inner joy. I was back: not just to how I had been, but with added mental clarity.

Forgiveness is a living organism—it requires different techniques to manage it. I danced naked to grieve for those who were lost, but also to heal myself. My mental freedom was important to me if I was to continue walking the long path of struggle, doing the work I wanted to do. I wanted to be like the warriors from my village who know they will succeed only if they do not have bitterness in their hearts.

Where I was raised, trauma and bitterness are removed from the body through music, stories, and rituals. In the west, they remove trauma and bitterness through therapy. I believe all forms of forgiveness are valuable. We should look for what works for us. Even if that means dancing naked in our local park.

THE NATURE OF UNFORGIVING

I have experienced situations where one day I have forgiven and then the next woken up with nothing but the opposite on my mind. When this happens, we must go through the process of letting go again. We must tell ourselves that we forgave once and can repeat it. We must keep speaking to our hearts and minds, reminding them we have let go; we must say thank you to our entire self for forgiving ourselves and others. We should also bear in mind that forgiving does not mean forgetting. It's a good thing to remember what can hurt us. But we must do so with context. I have been stung by a scorpion four times. On each occasion, it took me three to seven days to recover. But I have never woken up hating scorpions. I am aware of them, nothing more, nothing less. It's the same with fire. Flames may burn us, but we still work with fire to make our food. When a human hurts us, however, we pass judgment; we want justice; we want them to feel our ire. A forgiving heart is a heart that lets go. Remember, letting go is the genesis of all healing. It allows our body to restore itself to its natural state. It delivers a positive mindset, which helps us gain confidence, calmness, and stable mental health. Letting go keeps hope alive. It gives us a 360-degree view of life. Stress and anxiety, on the other hand, release adrenaline and cortisol into our bodies, toxic when released without purpose and potentially leading to high blood pressure, heart attacks, mental illness, and a weakened immune system.

I will continue to embrace a forgiving heart. I will stay open, spread compassion, and aspire to be like those I so admire, such as Gandhi and Nelson Mandela, who spread their own message of forgiveness.

We forgive to be free, to set others free, to break the generational chain of trauma. We forgive so our bodies can create a defense mechanism to keep us healthy and productive. We forgive to liberate our souls from captivity and have joy in abundance.

BEGINNING YOUR FORGIVENESS JOURNEY

Who would you like to forgive?

Write a letter to that person. State exactly what they have done to you. If you want to use strong language, do so. Don't leave anything out. At the end of the letter, write two words—"I forgive."

You do not need to send the letter—remember soul-to-soul forgiveness? Imagine it as a cancellation of debt owed. Imagine forgiveness as a gift you are giving them without expecting anything in return.

You can repeat the process, only this time seeking forgiveness from someone you feel you have wronged. If you feel the person doesn't want to forgive, don't let that hold you back. The most important thing is that you have done it. Imagine instead that they have heard you and let go.

Similarly, you could write a letter to yourself. Write in detail what harm you have caused yourself.

Place one hand on the paper and one on your heart, take a deep breath, and let it all go.

Allow the cells in your body to feel the pain disappearing. Expel the toxins.

You may also want to program your heart to forgive by reading other stories of forgiveness. Instill the rhythm of forgiveness into your heartbeat by chanting, "I am a forgiving heart. Thank you, creator, for giving me a forgiving heart." Repeat this chant many times across thirty days.

FORGIVENESS MEDITATION EXERCISE

- Take a moment of silence.
- Inhale for twelve seconds, exhale for fifteen seconds.
- Let your breath return to normal, with focus on breathing in and out through the nose. Find your flow of inhale and exhale.
- Allow your thoughts to fade away. Every time your mind drifts, bring it back to your breathing.
- Allow your brain to scan your life for those you need to forgive.
- Allow your thoughts to fade away, bringing yourself to a state of forgiveness.

Say these words out loud or in your head:

I am grateful my heart has learned the art of forgiving, by developing defense mechanisms to keep me healthy and productive, and by forgiving those who have hurt me without expecting them to ask for forgiveness. I am grateful my heart has mastered the art of forgiving myself for the harm I have caused myself and others, and I ask for soul-to-soul forgiveness for causing harm to others.

I forgive those who have caused me harm.

I forgive myself for the harm I have caused myself and others, and I ask for soul-to-soul forgiveness for causing harm to others both knowingly and unknowingly.

My cells forgive me for the harm I have caused them.

My cells forgive those who have caused harm to my parents, my grandparents, my ancestors, and my cells. My cells ask for forgiveness from the souls of those my parents, grandparents, and ancestors have caused harm to.

I am forgiving; I have a forgiving heart.

Thank you, creator, for giving me a forgiving heart.

I am forgiving; I have a forgiving heart.

5

FAITH

MEDITATION PILLAR 3

FAITH IS HOPE IN ACTION. FAITH IS WHEN OUR HEARTS AND minds unite in a desire to succeed. Faith is acquiring spirituality. It is believing in something bigger than us.

One thing is obvious: without belief there can be no hope. Faith builds a structure in the mind to help it function. Faith is the catalyst, the scientist, the magician, the chemist that makes nothing become something. It is the hidden guru, the willpower, the persistence, and the endurance—the invisible force that makes the impossible happen. Faith is the core strength of the soul, but it will vanish if we do not nurture it. We must believe in ourselves and show courage and self-confidence.

LOSING AND GAINING FAITH

I always wanted to live in the United Kingdom. It was a country that appeared strong, secure. As a child soldier, I used to listen to the generals. "If you want to be great, you must learn from the great," they said. To my mind, the U.K. possessed greatness—history told me so.

Thus, aged ten, I prayed to be allowed to go to this land of conquerors. Thirteen years later, my prayers were answered.

Immediately, I was amazed by its beautiful architecture, its values, its institutions, and its free medical care. For someone such as myself who has struggled so hard to attain an education, I marveled at the U.K.'s system of free schooling. Equally, I was impressed by its hard-working spirit, freedom of speech, and democracy. This was a place where people used their brains to find solutions, without resorting to violence. I was tempted to cast off my past and stay there, especially when I was admitted to the University of Westminster to study electronic engineering. My plan was to acquire knowledge and use it to help my people back home, but to do so I first needed to marshal resources in this new country. I began networking, seeking out those who could facilitate my stay, sponsor my education, and provide the mental and financial support I needed. I had faith that those people existed and indeed they did. I felt more settled than I had ever been. I put a lot of effort into my learning, staying up late and waking early to study. My grades were high. My life was finally in order, and I was settling down mentally. I was certain that I was going to be an electrical engineer.

But without warning, a barrier was lowered, and a lid was placed on my ambition. I was told my visa was wrong; I would have to leave the country and reapply for the correct student visa. Advice was split. Some said once I left, I would be denied the visa—much better to stay and seek asylum. My heart told me to go home; my mind said stay. I decided to go with my heart. I departed the United Kingdom for Kenya. Five times I applied for the visa. Five times, heartbreakingly, I was denied. On every occasion, I would pray for an intervention, but the visa was always refused.

I felt certain I qualified for the visa, so I couldn't understand the problem. Negative thoughts invaded my mind, and I became bitter and angry.

In my negative state, I devised an evil plan. I waited outside the

British Embassy, looking for those I believed had denied me my visa. I was convinced they were deliberately destroying my life and blocking my opportunities. I would find out where they lived and kidnap two of them. My plan was to murder one and keep the other alive to tell the story. I could make that happen. I had access to guns. I didn't really care what would happen to me afterward. Hate consumed me. In private, I spat bile. "F***ing British c***s, I am going to put a gun in your asshole and fire."

At this point I was staying with my adoptive mother, Mrs. Mumo, a very important person in my life. Mrs. Mumo was measured and immensely knowledgeable. She urged me to pray. She also told me things would only start working out when my sister came to Kenya.

The morning I was to execute my plan, Mrs. Mumo called me for prayers in the living room. As she said the final "Amen," she looked straight through my eyes into the window of my soul. She knew I was going to do something terrible.

"Forget your plans," she told me. "The Lord has other plans for you. Do not let your thoughts control you. Forgive the British. They don't know the real you."

She reminded me that the same forces that protected me in Sudan remained at my side.

"Trust in them," she whispered, "and the door to the U.K. will open at the right time. You will travel the world. You will meet with kings, queens, presidents, and address nations. I know because the Lord has told me so."

Mrs. Mumo was a prophet. Her words rejuvenated me. I threw off my negative thoughts and cloaked myself instead in forgiveness. In doing so, I found peace in my heart and mind. My faith that I would return to the U.K. became strong. I didn't know how it was going to happen, but I knew ultimately it would, and so I thanked the creator in advance for the opportunity he was to send me.

My beloved sister Nyaruach had indeed come to Kenya. She was battling her own demons, having been raped several times during the

Sudanese Civil War. As I waited for my opportunity to return to the U.K., I focused on my music and on making an album with Nyaruach.

Expressing ourselves through music brought both of us not only joy but a feeling of worthiness. One song in particular, "Gua," epitomized our renewed positivity. The title means "good" in Nuer and "power" in Sudanese Arabic. It became a hit across Kenya. Our story attracted the interest of news outlets across the globe. *USA Today* featured us, as did the BBC in the U.K. One journalist, Peter Moszynski, a friend of my first savior, Emma McCune, played a key role in making the magic happen by finding me a record deal, and in 2005, I was invited to perform at Live 8, a charity concert highlighting global poverty and featuring a host of African talent at the Eden Project in Cornwall, southwest England. The lineup was brought together by Peter Gabriel, the internationally renowned singer, composer, and activist. Peter would pay me the ultimate compliment by describing me as having the "potential of a young Bob Marley." Live 8 was the bridge to my becoming a recognized and respected artist. I was being interviewed left and right and getting booked all over the place. I never in my wildest dreams thought that music could pay my bills, leaving extra to send back to family and friends. Yet it did.

I saw firsthand the power of faith, of believing, of hoping tomorrow will come. I have traveled to the U.K. many times now and every time the memory of this story inspires me. When we believe something should happen, we need to control our frustration and carry on trying, believing. It may seem impossible, but that does not mean it won't happen. It will happen, and it will do so at the perfect time.

Faith can be both gained and lost. The denying of my U.K. visa crashed my faith. I lost hope and became bitter. If Mrs. Mumo hadn't intervened to restore my faith, my life today would have been a different story. Maybe I would have no life. I refound faith through another's positivity. Having a community of believers, elders, and mentors around us can strengthen our faith. Belief needs to be nurtured, and sometimes we require others to provide us with the means to do so. When our faith matures, we are unstoppable. We have it within us to become like the great names that have transformed our planet's history in the most positive of ways. We are all great names in our own right.

REBELLIONS ARE BUILT ON HOPE

As a child soldier, I played dominos with William Nyuon Bany, one of the founding fathers and third in command of the SPLA. While doing so, I learned my greatest lesson. Nyuon liked talking to young people because they were honest and would ask him questions that made him think deeply. My question was simple and to the point: When will this war end?

"Soon," he promised.

I spoke for my people. "We are suffering. The enemy is better equipped; we are outnumbered, and too often on the losing side."

He looked at me intensely. In his eyes were power, hope, strength, passion, and courage. He told me something I will never forgot.

"To tell you the truth, young man," he said, "I don't know when the war will end. But I am committed to this struggle and will fight to the end of times. I know our freedom will come, but the government forces are stronger and have greater firepower. They have tanks, jets, helicopters, and heavy artillery. They have food, medicine, transportation, and more skilled fighters than us. But what keeps us going is the hope that one day we will be free to enjoy the fruits of our land. There will be no more enslavement of our kind or possession of our wealth by these oppressors.

"No one is born brave," he continued. "We learn from one another to be brave. And when we are afraid our shared purpose gives us courage. If we believe we can beat them, our hearts and minds are united. Never think that we cannot beat them. Freedom is coming, young man. The devil is afraid of human beings with united hearts and minds."

I understood what he was telling me: that the less you have, the stronger you are. The strength that comes from having nothing to lose.

"Our lack of methods and the resources we desire to beat the enemy," he stated, "will only make us smarter, tougher, and stronger."

It is our faith that will create the world we want for ourselves. The consequences of losing faith or letting hope go are enormous, leading to depression, bitterness, hopelessness, and unworthiness. Losing faith strips us of discipline, persistence, focus, patience, and endurance. Faith pulls together all the ingredients we need to create the success we want.

Faith is a positive state of mind driven by a plan and a purpose. It is the master key that allows heaven to open the floodgates and pour its blessing on us.

Faith is hope in action. If we unite our hearts and minds with purpose, belief, wisdom, knowledge, understanding, and a plan, faith will create a positive outcome. Faith that comes without those elements is blind faith.

Wisdom, knowledge, and understanding can draw from a variety of wells. We can drink deeply from the positivity of our surroundings, our families, communities, books, podcasts, and speaking to mentors and elders. Even though my family wasn't there to support me in my teens in Kenya or my adulthood on tour globally, faith brought along others to help with my journey. My faith was not built by myself. I did not arrive here alone. Angels carried me on their backs. Faith comes from different directions. If someone gave me milk, they told me I had worth. If someone gave me clothes, the same. Look closely and we will see the examples of faith that are around us every day. No challenge comes to us without the grace to help us overcome it. Faith is our secret weapon. With it we can move huge obstacles, shape our lives, and manage our fate.

Remember, though, that while our faith may grow as we learn, it needs to be nurtured to maturity, like a child, to deliver its potential.

Sadly, many people have more faith in failure than in success, so we must work hard to remove doubt and worry. When I have tried as hard as I can with a situation, when my faith and imagination have been stretched to the fullest yet the future looks bleak, empty, and impossible, I will apply gratitude. Why? Because I know I have learned from the experience. I have worked my hardest, and therefore I have strengthened my faith rather than weakened it. It is better to seek a solution than to give in from the start. If you give in, you will never find your way out of the maze.

I take peace of mind from knowing there is a creator out there who wants the best for me. Such knowledge means that when I am doing something, I know I am not alone. I have that force behind me, supporting me. I know also that not everybody leans on a creator for support. If that is the case, I suggest instead you believe in yourself. Draw also from a wider energy. Faith is derived from love for the self and others. It comes from understanding that you are never alone. Make that spiritual connection and you will find your faith is either bolstered or restored. It is why we should respect the beliefs of others—because they, too, are building faith. Their internal message is the same. We all need someone or something to look to for direction and safety. We function better when we have that center of gravity. We are all just big kids looking for comfort and love when things go wrong. We must create daily practices that provide the right atmosphere for our faith to grow.

FAITH MEDITATION

- Take a deep breath and exhale.
- Take another deep breath. Imagine your belly as a balloon filling with air.
- Exhale slowly.

Find your normal flow of breathing and revel in it for a minute.

Now focus your thoughts on faith.

Out loud or in your head, state:

Faith is the positive outcome of needs and wants hoped for and the proof of the unseen.

Faith is when my heart and mind unite to achieve what I desire. With a plan, action, purpose, and belief, I will get it.

Action

Pause for a moment of silence, then answer the following questions. Either write your answers down or keep them in your mind.

- What are you hoping for?
- What is your motive or purpose?
- What plan do you have in place to make it happen?
- What action have you taken to make it happen?
- Who are your mentors?
- Do you have a positive community and environment to nurture your faith?
- What are you doing to nurture your faith?

To Close

Either out loud or in your head, say:
I have faith that what I hope for will come to pass.
I am faith. I have faith.
Thank you, creator, for giving me faith.
I am faith. I have faith.

6

POSITIVE MINDSET

MEDITATION PILLAR 4

A POSITIVE MINDSET IS THE ABILITY TO ENGAGE YOUR MIND to do what you want. You speak it. You imagine. You think it, plan, strategize, visualize, and act with a burning desire to achieve. Thinking, organizing, visualizing, and achieving all become much easier with a positive mindset. Imagine it, and you can create it.

A person who has slipped into a negative mindset, perhaps through trauma, or through feeling marginalized, loses the ability to deal with the everyday requirements of life. I know this from personal experience. Instead of seeing the bigger picture, the person with a negative mindset becomes lost, ineffective, and irrational. To find a better way to resolve the situation takes a lot of mental power.

A WORLD OF EMPTINESS

My savior Emma McCune died young. She was just twenty-nine when she was killed in a car crash. She gave me the key to a new life in Kenya with possibilities and opportunities. But I still found living hard. The war, and its bleak, violent imagery, still haunted me. I was drowning in my fears and thoughts. My soul was suffering.

After Emma died, my mental state worsened. I would run out of the house imagining it was under attack, ducking into the trees or behind objects for cover. I could see no way forward. I felt useless, and my world was empty.

I knew if I was to survive, I had to find a way back, so I came up with a plan. When a negative thought dragged me down, I would immediately fight back. When an internal voice told me "You're useless," I would punch back with "I am useful." If the voice told me "You're a failure," I would state exactly the opposite. If it told me I knew nothing, I would tell it how I had seen more in my short life than most people see in a lifetime; that I didn't need to pass exams to be part of a solution to the world's problems.

I could argue logically that I wasn't a failure, and if logic didn't work, I would think back to massaging the elders' feet in Kenya. The smell was terrible, but the stories were great. As well as giving free advice and prophecies, they always made me laugh. With the elders' words in mind, I would make another appointment with my negative thoughts and confront them with confidence and purpose.

Other times, I would create images in my head, visualizing myself helping others or performing with great positivity in front of a crowd. I would listen to Christian radio, read the Bible or the Quran, or listen to the teachings of others, all to gain the positivity with which to fight the demons in my mind. Words, dance, music, and simple daily tasks paved a way for me to keep my head above water. I never wanted a day to pass without experiencing something positive. Nowadays, I call it feeding the soul.

Switching from a negative to a positive mindset always pays dividends. At school in Nairobi, my heart was willing, but my mind was elsewhere, as if a passing fly had taken it. I would think about recent setbacks or, worse, have a blinding flashback of a disturbing childhood incident. The effect was physical as much as mental. As soon as the lesson began, my body would start itching, my head would hurt, and I would want to go to the toilet. The bell for the end of the session would ring and again, I had missed an opportunity to learn.

I would set targets to study at home, but my mind would veer off into a distant cloud. My heart pushed me to study; my mind refused to engage. Other times, I would rise at 4:00 a.m. to study. I desperately wanted to challenge my brain, but it had no interest in taking part. Instead, I would spend the day playing football and hanging out with friends. Those pursuits are not bad in themselves—they provide valuable mental space—but they overwhelmed other vitally important areas of my life. I was not doing the things I needed to do. It reminded me of being a child soldier and how I would be punished for failing to do my duty. On one occasion, I was appointed to grind sorghum. Instead I played football. The group had to eat harsh boiled grain that evening. My indiscipline earned me twenty lashes, and I was sent to collect firewood in the forest, a job I hated because of lurking snakes and scorpions. My fear made me nervous, so the firewood I picked from the edges of the undergrowth was much lower quality than that selected by braver children much younger than myself. Most of the time it was unusable and again I would be punished.

I wanted to find a way of breaking this pattern of behavior. My desire to understand my tendency to self-sabotage gave birth to a positive mindset. I came to realize that before I could encounter more technical thought processes, my brain needed to travel a path of healing from my earlier trauma. The brain needs balance to help a person achieve. Anyone who has been through trauma, poverty, or difficulty must understand that the right mindset is vital to achieve personal goals.

I understood that sometimes to beat problems I needed to raise my conscious state. I began to see myself as an electronic device. I needed to charge myself with positivity to make myself work properly.

I realized that we have to fight and win some battles from the inside. A positive mindset, I concluded, is the key to overcoming.

THE POWER OF THE MIND

So much of what we see before us now existed in the mind before it existed in the physical. Cars, planes, guns, radios, war, mobile phones, sport, films, slavery, the pyramids—none of it just appeared out of the blue. The first picture of any of these things was in the mind. They existed in the spiritual realm way before they made it into the physical.

We need to remember that elements such as worry, fear, and anxiety also exist in the mind. As with physical objects, we have a role in deciding whether we allow them to progress into reality.

Protecting our minds from unwelcome intruders is vital. A positive mindset means keeping our inner selves free from negative occupations. If you feel negative in your mind, you may well experience negativity in everyday life.

I know from my own experience how a single negative thought has the magnetic capacity to attract others. Between them they suck up my energy, make me agitated. In no time, I lose patience, focus, and attention to detail. I say and do the wrong things. My day becomes a mess of negative emotions. I react by eating unhealthily to comfort myself, which further impacts my energy, and therefore my positivity levels.

We live in a world of troubled souls. Who among us does not grapple with issues that affect mind, body, and soul? Many of us feel the stress of circumstances, fears, and past defeats. Remember, the brain forms just 2 percent of our weight yet uses 20 percent of our energy. Little wonder that negative emotions can manifest themselves in such a physical manner.

Think about how worry and fear make us feel, how so easily they dominate our minds, make us miserable, and prevent progress. A mind full of worry and fear is a mind in survival mode. It cannot think long-term as it is traumatized, trapped in endless daily battles.

To rise beyond our challenges and achieve success, we need to recognize that positivity works in the same way. It is from positive thoughts in our spiritual realm that we produce positive outcomes in the physical one. How do we do that? By seeking to be positive in our everyday lives: sharing, being kind to others, and working hard to deliver our objectives. When my mind becomes filled with negative thoughts and the ugliness of my past, I stand back and imagine the beautiful future I have a chance to make.

Keeping the mind positive is a lifestyle anyone can master. Engaging our minds to serve us and be productive is a daily undertaking fostered through mental dialogue. "How am I feeling? How can I engage with today to make myself feel better? Who can I help? Where can I be of benefit to others?"

Only through positivity can our hearts and minds unite. It is then that the life we think about can manifest as the one we lead.

VISUALIZATION

Visualization engages the mind in a positive direction. It can be useful, for instance, to visualize how we see ourselves in the future. However, before we can employ visualization, we need to recognize our inner filter. The brain's reticular activating system sieves our environment, leaving only what needs to reach the brain. Its selections are based on how we were programmed in early childhood. Its scope is therefore limited. Occasionally, it can even be damaging. The good news is that through visualization we can reprogram it. Over time, the system will learn to filter out the negative. It will automatically increase our ability to manage our environments and make the right decisions.

Programming Your Mind for Visualization

- Look at an object and study it in detail until you can see it with your eyes closed.
- Use your hands to explore an unknown object and then allow your mind to create an image in your head (this could be a fun activity with friends).
- Imagine a positive future and visualize it.
- Visualize a landscape you have visited and imagine yourself in it.
- Create pictures in your mind as you tell or listen to stories.
- Visualize objectives, goals, plans, and strategies. Only react to positive thoughts aligned to them. Don't be distracted by other thoughts.

The next step is to break down thoughts into goals.

Take a Moment to Consider

- What would you like to engage yourself with today?
- What is your purpose?
- What is your vision?
- What is your mission?
- What is your goal for the year? The month? The week?
- What are the goals, objectives, and tasks for the day?

On weekdays, visualize your daily goals. At weekends, visualize goals for the coming weeks, months, and year. Now the question is, how are you going to achieve them?

Developing a Positive Mindset

- In a quiet place, take three deep breaths, then breathe normally with your eyes closed.
- Speak your goals. Do so from the heart and let the words flow.
- Enjoy the feeling. Appreciate the impact of your words on yourself.

◘ Ask yourself how you can achieve your goals. Understand the obstacles and embrace the opportunities. Capture positive thoughts. Use them as a blueprint for success.

◘ Connect the dots by conditioning your mind to find the route of least resistance with the greatest rewards.

◘ Stay in this visualization zone for as long as you can, up to a maximum of an hour. Your body should be charged with a burning desire to achieve.

You should by now be feeling the strength of positivity. Further the visualization techniques that deliver positivity through meditation.

Blue Background and Bright Triangle Meditation

This exercise is all about training your mind to focus on targets and creating what you desire through imagination. It will help you become disciplined. If you can create images in your mind, you can also plan, imagine, and see your future in the physical realm.

◘ In a quiet place, take a deep breath, then breathe normally with your eyes closed.

◘ Imagine you are walking on a beach.

◘ As you enjoy the view, create a blue background from the ocean and sky. The blue delivers peace of mind and calmness. That blue is you.

◘ Create a super bright triangle connecting sea and sky. The bright triangle is the best you can be—your purpose, your vision. It is peace, joy, love, courage, kindness, and prosperity. It is the force of creation.

◘ Stay in the visualization for as long as you can. When different images appear, acknowledge them, but reclaim the original picture by using your inner voice to say, "I want a blue background and bright triangle." These distractions mirror those that crop up when you try to achieve your real-life goals.

◘ If you get too distracted or can't maintain the triangle, no problem. Just try again next time.

ENGAGING YOUR POSITIVE MIND TO SOLVE PROBLEMS

Now it is time to use your visualization technique alongside your positive mindset to solve problems and shape your life the way you want it. Take the following steps and you will reach your destination more quickly.

Step 1: When a problem arises, acknowledge it. Thank the creator for trusting you with it, and believe you have infinite intelligence to overcome it. Remember, solving problems adds value to your life and those of others around you.

Step 2: Forgive. That way your mind can travel light and is better placed to be creative. Apply soul-to-soul forgiveness to those who have caused you harm and those whom you have caused harm.

Step 3: Employ rigorous thinking.* Think like a general. Put away emotion, opinion, and perspective, and use only the conscious, targeted mind to do your thinking. Rigorous thinking is popular in the military. As a child, I would listen to generals planning an ambush. At no point was there room for assumption. The only thing that mattered was logic, reason, and accumulation of fact. Rigorous thinking can help us avoid obstacles and make the right decision.

---

* *There are two ways to approach rigorous thinking: positive reasoning and negative reasoning.*

Positive reasoning is when all the facts believed to be true are carefully analyzed and sifted in order of importance to draw a conclusion. Positive reasoning is the most important part of thinking. It shuns emotion in favor of hard facts that can add value to your life.

Negative reasoning is a conclusion based on facts assumed to be true. It should be avoided at all costs because it can lead to disaster.

Step 4: Think of a problem in your life. Write down the solutions. Condition your subconscious by allowing your chosen solutions to occupy your mind for the whole day. Virtually unnoticed, your mind will soon start to work with you to make the answers happen. It will put you in auto mode.

Step 5: Visualize your desired outcome. Plan and strategize a route to your chosen goal—better health, independence, success, or whatever it might be. By doing so you are training your mind to attract only things that will push you forward and achieve what you desire.

Step 6: Do two or more things every day to confront your situation. Have faith and persistence to solve your problem. Allow yourself to be excited about the process of engaging your mind. Don't let the sun go down before you achieve your tasks. Don't let the sun go down before doing something that sets you up for success—an activity to support a goal.

Step 7: Expand your imagination. Be curious, ask questions; seek knowledge, wisdom, and understanding. Fuel your mind with the content it needs to do its job well.

Step 8: Analyze your day without judgment. Afterward, take at least ten minutes to listen to yourself breathing normally, allowing the thoughts to complete the stories without reaction. Then think of something positive, just a few words you would like to say to yourself. Make it your positive mantra. It will clean your mind, connect your emotions to the positivity process, and unite the cells in your body to fight with you.

Step 9: If negative thoughts do occur, use positivity and purpose to outsmart them. Think of negative thoughts as not being real. It is your real (positive) thoughts that contain truth and purpose.

Step 10: Train your mind to banish worry and keep only your dreams alive. Worry occupies too much space where creativity should lie.

Step 11: Dance until you sweat! Then, using the methods you learned earlier, meditate to clear your mind. In so doing, you will create the mental space to handle all your problems—past, present, and future—with positivity.

You are now equipped with a tool more valuable than any sold in any shop. One that can, quite literally, achieve anything: a positive mindset.

7

REPROGRAMMING

MEDITATION PILLAR 5

THE SUBCONSCIOUS IS A HUGE PART OF WHO WE ARE. IT manages our thoughts and prompts us to believe certain things about ourselves and others. It influences our habits, beliefs, and ability to solve problems. Its role in our goals and visions is huge. The question is, how can we hack into the subconscious and influence it?

A good starting point is to analyze our belief system. It can quite easily be split into two. Positive belief gives us courage to stand up and be ourselves. Negative belief steals our power and makes us unable to resist. We need then to apply that belief system to the following three areas:

1. What we believe about ourselves
2. What we believe about others
3. What we believe others think of us

What Did I Believe About Myself?

Growing up, I lost a lot of people close to me. Family, friends, young, old—it seemed every time I got close to someone, something terrible happened to them.

When I was just five years old, a soldier befriended me. He would show me wild birds, play with me, and tell me stories and jokes. Then one day he never appeared. My mum told me he died. It wouldn't be long until she was dead too.

As a refugee making my way with thousands of others in a horribly overloaded boat to Ethiopia, I became good friends with a great kid. He was bigger and stronger than me. The boat capsized. Of the 250 children on board, only sixty survived. He wasn't among them. The rest of us were placed in a convoy and ordered to walk the remainder of the journey. Again, I made friends, but they, too, fell by the wayside, from exhaustion and starvation.

In Ethiopia, as a child soldier, I watched as friends I made in the ranks were killed in action.

I was ultimately rescued from this life thanks to Emma, who took me to a new life in Kenya. But she, too, was killed, in the car accident I mentioned earlier.

By that point, I'd come to believe that I was bad luck to anyone who got too close, but Emma's death was different. Previously, I never cried when somebody died, not even my mother. But with Emma, tears hung in my eyes. A voice in my head kept repeating, "You killed her!" It was all I could hear, so firmly did I believe anyone close to me was doomed.

Almost immediately that belief was further reinforced. Following Emma's death, Mrs. Mumo, whom I came to consider a second mother, took me in. I became close with her family, only for her husband to be killed in a car accident. Mrs. Mumo was badly injured but survived.

I began pulling away whenever anyone tried to get close. It was safer that way for everybody. My attempts to protect others created serious commitment issues with girlfriends. How could I commit to someone when I believed doing so was akin to handing them a death sentence?

My ability to bring death and destruction raining down on those close to me was, of course, not real. It existed only in my mind. It was one of many damaging beliefs I clung to. Some of these I was aware of. Others were clearly seen by those around me while remaining invisible to me. To progress, I would need to radically reprogram my brain.

What Did I Believe About Others?

I used to believe that our neighboring tribe, the Dinka, were cannibals. I had a Dinka friend as a kid and was afraid of sleeping next to him. I thought he would grow a tail, his face would become that of the devil, and he would eat me. I would monitor his movements at night, sleeping with one eye and one ear open, but it didn't stop me having nightmares that I was being eaten.

This belief was deep-seated. It stayed with me until I was twenty-five years old, passed down to me, just as it had been to those who told me. The story was used to justify raids on Dinka villages, to steal their cows. I am equally sure the Dinka had their own stories to justify their raids on us.

Those stories created a psychological barrier that prevented me from ever fully enjoying my childhood. They also meant I felt nothing when a Dinka person died. Even though I had a Dinka friend, I never lost the belief that he might eat me at any time. Only when I was exposed to new cultures in Kenya did I come to see my fear as irrational.

What Did I Believe Others Thought of Me?

The Arabs I grew up with believed Black people were only good for labor, that we were ugly and should just be slaves. In Kenya, kids, teenagers, and adults alike made fun of my dark skin. One girl even refused to date me because of it. If I was just "slightly brown," she told me, we could date. It broke my heart, and I swallowed my tears.

Every incident added to my belief that Black people were cursed and my dark skin was ugly. Only a trip to New York finally disabused me of the lie. I was stopped on the street by a beautiful young lady with blue eyes and blonde hair. She reminded me of blue-eyed fish I caught in my village when I was six years old. She looked like an angel.

"I love your skin," she told me. "Can I touch it?"

"Yes," I replied. She touched my arm. "It is so smooth and beautiful," she said. Her words warmed my heart.

Later, in Harlem, an African American woman screamed at me that I was a Nubian king. I had no idea what she meant, but I've loved New York ever since. The city planted a seed in my heart and mind to make me believe Black is beautiful.

THE POWER OF THE SUBCONSCIOUS

Things to consider when programming ourselves:

- The conscious mind learns through curiosity and the subconscious learns through repetition.
- The summation of emotions we generate every day makes our decisions, and the summation of decisions we make every day creates our lives.
- The subconscious makes 95 percent of our decisions.

The subconscious is led by our history. It makes decisions based on our accumulated habits and beliefs. It also draws on our DNA. The positive skills and talents of previous generations exist within us, but so, too, do trauma and fear. Inevitable then that our subconscious has the power to dictate our lives in a negative way if we don't create habits and beliefs that allow us to make the right choices.

To access the positivity in our subconscious, we must have a conscious awakening and renew our minds. In order to program your mind, you must know your purpose and vision and change your environment. Only by reprogramming can we truly transform ourselves.

We must create a vision of our future selves or propagate a change of environment. Think about it: If you are born poor, chances are you will be poor for the rest of your life—unless you have a vision, a purpose, a change of environment. Equally, if you are born into wealth, the likelihood is you'll be wealthy for the rest of your life—unless you have no vision, no purpose, and alter your environment terribly.

Therefore, the three fundamental areas we need to address to reprogram ourselves are:

◘ Vision
◘ Purpose
◘ Environment

Vision gives us a burning desire to seek wisdom, knowledge, and understanding. Along the way, we acquire skills and polish our talents. Vision also provides strong emotion to help us create new habits. It gives us the courage and the confidence to move forward, to knock on doors, to ask for help, and to keep up the fight. It delivers the humility to listen to those from whom we can learn and the power to choose whom we spend time with.

Purpose grounds us and keep us in balance. It makes us rise beyond what we could not possibly imagine. Only purpose can give our lives meaning in every stage of suffering. If we don't find a meaning in our suffering we will exist to suffer.

Environment is responsible for how we look, what we eat, and what we become. It is responsible for our culture, nature, character, perception, and beliefs. There are two types of environments relevant to our well-being: the external environment and the internal environment. Both work hand in hand. Change one and we change the other.

The **external environment** is our surroundings. It refers to what and who we are exposed to. For our vision to be realized, we must charge our surroundings with positive people whose presence will influence our minds on a subconscious level. We can then begin to encode ourselves with the desired skills.

There is a saying: *hang around wise men and you will be wise; hang around thugs and you will be a thug.* But there is more to the equation than that. To hang around with positive people, you must be willing to be positive too. They won't want to be dragged down or contaminated by negativity.

There is scientific research to back up the impact of our surroundings. The American developmental biologist Bruce Lipton took healthy stem cells and put them in an environment with nutrients. He found that not only did they multiply fast, but, according to the environment into which they were then transferred, they turned into muscle, bone, or fat. When he put those same healthy cells in a toxic environment, they naturally became sick. Other scientists suggested the use of drugs. Lipton, however, knew such an approach was unnecessary. Simply put the cells in a healthy environment, he explained, and they will thrive. Lipton understood that environment was the key to mutation.

My initial environment was Sudan, a war-torn country. It was responsible for my poverty and trauma. Change came when I lived in Kenya, a more stable environment full of positive people. It helped that, as a kid, I attached myself to people smarter than me. I was curious about what made them clever and wanted to know how I could be like them.

The **internal environment** comes from our density. It is a combination of our thoughts and what we hold dear in our hearts. To some degree our internal environment is organized. If we put a mixture of sand, stones, and grains into a bowl and shook it gently, similar-sized particles would organize themselves into layers. Our inner universe is the same. We have movement to maintain our balance. Love, courage, confidence, purpose, and vision all play a role. However, worry, hate, fear, and anger also contribute to our density. The key to achieving a density that works is balance, which in itself comes from beliefs and habits, the core principles that establish the chemistry in our brain and dictate either progress or inertia.

Want a better life? Then we must begin with ourselves and change our internal environment. To do so entails waking up our subconscious mind and hacking into our programs to install positive habits and beliefs. That way, the external environment, should it be negative, is no longer a threat.

HABITS AND MENTAL WEALTH

The Greek philosopher Aristotle said excellence is not an act but a habit. I would say mediocrity is the same. Everyone has talents, objectives, and dreams. Those who achieve their dreams have found the right habit and belief mechanisms. They have put them in place so that when an opportunity comes, they are in the best possible position to take it.

My Habits

My traumatic background meant that even at thirty-nine I had few boundaries. I know my experience is not unusual. Those who experience trauma are left open to exploitation. By not knowing how to create boundaries, I was also prone to hurting those close to me. Lack of organization was clearly a habit I had to rectify.

Much of that trauma was held internally, but the evidence was there for all to see. Had you come to my house in the evening at that time, you could track me by the trail of shoes, socks, and clothes strewn across the floor. Dirty dishes would pile up until a cleaner came, or until I was forced into action by the imminent arrival of a date. What motivated me to change was the discovery that organizing my environment aided my mental processes. It reminded me of a speech a general once made to his soldiers: "Your life as soldier can be tracked by how

you tie your boots, tie your belt, and the care you give your equipment."
He was right. Organization delivers order and structure, and attaining
at least the most basic level is necessary for survival. Without organization we are vulnerable.

Mental Wealth

As an activist, I got tired of asking wealthy people to donate to my
causes. While I knew millionaires and other influential individuals,
I came to understand that many of them gave so they could be perceived as generous. Their gifts did not come from the heart, so I asked
myself how I could make my own money to support the causes I
believed in.

It didn't go well. I set up record companies in Kenya, Canada, and
the U.K., but none of them worked out as I hoped they would. I ended
up owing people money, and a lot of great relationships suffered.

I also set up my superfood company, Jal Gua, and a café, which was
financially challenging. I understood that being an entrepreneur meant
working for nothing for a while, but losing money? That was never my
plan. For two nights, I slept in the basement of my café and interro-
gated the reasons why I went into business. How did I come this far?
What did I do right? What could I now add to my life to make it work
better? Those questions led directly to the formation of My Life Is Art.

While meditating, I discovered that I had the mental belief to create money but not the habit. Call it mental poverty if you like, epitomized by a lack of discipline, focus, organization, intuition, clearly
defined goals, and good decision-making. The list went on. I counted
more than fifty mental habits that were keeping me poor. It was overwhelming to discover that the issue was not the system, but me.

Our minds know our worth and our hearts know our potential, but
we are all prone to mental poverty. There are many tales of those——
athletes, musicians, lottery winners—who find wealth only to lose it
all. The reason is that self-knowledge is the most valuable commodity

in our lives. Without it, you cannot hope to achieve. A person with the mental wealth that self-knowledge brings can succeed anywhere.

When I recognized my mental poverty, I decided to do what I had done as a kid—be curious and create good habits that would serve me well. I set myself the following goals:

◘ Strategic thinking
◘ Integrative thinking
◘ Discipline
◘ Consistency
◘ Persistency
◘ Energy management
◘ Collaborative thinking
◘ Positive thinking
◘ Focus
◘ Strategic planning
◘ Organization
◘ Financial literacy

Within twelve months, I raised $400,000, which saved me from being buried under a mountain of debt. Every month I saw progress and committed myself to self-development through My Life Is Art. The program gave me spiritual wealth, which I then turned into physical wealth to lift others.

THE GENESIS OF MY PROGRAMMING AND REPROGRAMMING—SUGAR AND MILK POWDER

My mother always warned us children not to eat our stock of sugar and milk powder. One day she came home to find I had broken the rule—not that I was going to own up to it. She told me she saw me doing it, that she had a third eye which she would leave roaming around the house.

"I didn't touch it," I insisted, even though the evidence was there for all to see on my cheek.

Again, she asked me to tell the truth. "Mum," I told her, "even Jesus will say I didn't do it."

I thought she was going to explode.

"Listen to me, young man," she said. "I don't want to say terrible things to you because you are a good child. I know you have taken sugar and milk powder. But I believe you are not a thief. Tell me the truth so that we can forget about this incident and carry on."

She looked silently into my eyes. I confessed.

"Yes, Mum," I said. "I stole."

I thought she was going to beat the hell out of me. Instead, she thanked me for my honesty.

"If you want something," she explained, "ask, and if I say 'no' there is a reason. You might not understand now, but you will thank me in the future. Promise me you are not going to steal again, and I will tell you a secret that will change your life."

Mum had never told me a secret before, and I wanted to know so badly. This is the first time I have passed it on.

"If someone ever says anything bad to you," she revealed, "inside your head, say something good to yourself—and believe it." (Try it—say something good to yourself ten times.)

She was right. Her secret did change my life, and it didn't stop at words. I would write letters to myself too. Both transformed me. I was reprogramming myself to think in a different way. I still use the method even now.

After my mother had gone, I used her words to get me through my time as a child soldier and to apologize and explain to those I hurt by talking to their souls. I would remind myself, too, that if we raided a village or burned it down, I had not acted in that way because I wanted to, but that my situation had forced me into it.

I don't know where my mum learned psychology. I believe, like all mothers, she just had it from the word go.

Ask yourself: Have there been moments in your life where you have said good things to yourself? Is it a practice you could use more often?

HABIT CREATION: THE THREE PILL METHOD

There are three ways we can hack into our minds and reprogram ourselves: curiosity, hypnosis, and repetition.

Curiosity is when we just go out and acquire knowledge. We can do this by reading books, observing the environment, or listening to motivational speakers. It's a slow process to program our subconscious mind, but many people use this method.

Hypnosis is guided meditation by trusted, experienced individuals in which we completely surrender to their direction in an attempt to recover repressed memories or modify our behavior by implanting new belief systems. The process is especially effective if the subject has a supportive network to embrace them and support their growth.

Repetition—the Three Pills of Red, Blue, and Yellow

To address malaria, sufferers need to take a combination of medicines. If you only take two and not the third, the treatment won't work. The same goes for habit and belief creation through repetition.

Red Pill—Subconscious Learning

The subconscious mind learns through repetition. Pick the right mantra—what we would like to be, or what we are—and say it over and over, two to three hundred times a day for thirty days, until it becomes a belief. That mantra could be "I am confident," "I am curious," "I am worthy," "I am calm," "I am forgiving," or anything that comes from a short period of self-analysis. The statement reinforces the belief, the belief reinforces the habit, and it's all held together by the reptilian brain, the part of the mind that deals with instinct, survival, and motivation. The reptilian brain holds our built-in motivations, both positive and negative. The repetition of mantras hacks into our subconscious to create positive beliefs, which are then responsible for our daily motivation and become reinforced by experiences.

Taking this red pill of repetition and motivation becomes our inner guide in daily activities. Stories about future, present, and past act as advisors, keeping our hopes alive as we become curious to learn better ways to find solutions.

Blue Pill—Conscious Learning

We know the conscious mind learns through curiosity. It is vital that we feed that curiosity with new information. We must look for those who have encountered similar challenges to us and learn how they overcame them. We should invest an hour a day for thirty days to seek answers and solutions. This slow process of data-gathering can become information, knowledge, and wisdom. Our brains learn better through heard stories and new experiences. It's easy to lose curiosity as you age and, therefore, fail to upgrade. But remember, our internal engineering is self-guided. Nature created us perfectly. It is then up to us to remain in sync with ourselves and prosper, to learn from others who have overcome negative beliefs or habits, and to visualize how we, too, can instill positivity before putting those thoughts into action every day.

Yellow Pill—Incremental Steps of Action

After investing in learning every day, we should then take incremental steps to change our behavior. Do this and the brain will release neurotrophins, a family of proteins that create new dendrites to store the knowledge and wisdom we have gathered in both the short term and the long term.

Take all three pills for thirty days and the process will create the neuron insulator myelin. The thicker our myelin, the more our life is changing. It denies access to our old pathways and pushes the benefits of new pathways.

To transform our lives, we require long-term commitment, a daily practice that becomes part of our lives, part of us, rewiring our brains and cells and weakening old, negative pathways.

CELEBRATING OUR ACHIEVEMENTS

Every time we adopt a new habit, we should celebrate our transformation and share what we have learned with others, before picking another habit we want to take on board and repeating the process. That way changing habits and beliefs becomes a lifestyle.

Connecting with Our Inner Being

We will never find the answers about who we are or what we want to do in life until we create time to connect with our inner being. We can find wisdom, knowledge, and understanding in the outside world, but the answers we seek about ourselves come from within.

Self-Analysis

Watch, listen, and feel both your negativity and positivity without passing judgment. Think of yourself as an observer, or someone doing research. Look especially at your peers, environment, fears, worries, and perceived defeats and failures.

To conduct self-analysis, find a quiet place and breathe in and out while looking within. When you find a positive habit, try to locate what motivated it and acknowledge its presence with gratitude. When you find a negative habit, ask where it came from and what its effects are.

THE FIVE STATUSES

To probe deeper into our beliefs and habits, we need to examine our five statuses.

Social status is how we relate to people and how we carry ourselves. What do other people think of us? How are we treated by others, and vice versa? Our social status has the power to affect all the other statuses on this list.

Emotional status is the summation of the feelings we generate every day, affecting the habits and beliefs we are looking to generate. Feel hopeless and it will manifest in all aspects of your life. Feel hopeful and you will perform better and commit to an end goal. Emotional status has a tremendous effect on our outcomes. It is the driving force for anything to happen. It makes sense, then, that we should learn the art of generating positive emotion. Our future depends on it.

Physical status refers to our health, our wealth, our organs, and our body. It can affect our mood, energy, and actions. The physical body requires food, shelter, water, clothing, and exercise before it can generate the emotions that affect our mental status positively.

Mental status takes in the conscious and subconscious, imagination, intuition, and memory. It affects everything and it can destroy everything. Fear, poverty, death, and worry all damage us in the mind before they manifest themselves in our physical selves. If your mind is occupied by negative habits, your actions will show it. Negative thoughts generate negative feelings; positive thoughts generate positive feelings.

Spiritual status measures matters such as joy, peace of mind, kindness, love, courage, and patience. Ask yourself, are you growing spiritually or are you stuck in a rut?

After observing each status, mark your current position out of ten. See what you really want to change in your life, and how you can redefine who you are based on your talents, gifts, and purpose.

Then ask yourself what negative habits you would like to change and why. Think again about your vision, your purpose, and the person you would like to be. Ask what you would like to change in your external environment, what positive beliefs and habits you would like to create.

◘ Write ten "I am" statements that describe you.
◘ Write twelve life changes you would like to adopt.
◘ Write twelve mantras for your meditation.

Can you see an image of your inner being? That vision is made true by great habits powered by positive beliefs.

Takeaway Steps to Reprogram Your Mind

1. Write down your purpose statement (see page 284) and learn it by heart.
2. Write down your vision and mission statements (see page 284) and learn them by heart.
3. Analyze your internal environment, observing yourself without judgment. Pretend to be an investigator. Find out what negative habits you need to change. Pick positive mantras to replace those habits.
4. Write down your limiting beliefs and substitute them with positives.
5. Commit to creating a positive environment that supports the creation of your habits and beliefs. Analyze your inner circle, the people who are lifting you up and tearing you down. You may have to make tough decisions and lay down strong boundaries to protect your environment.

6. One at a time, for each habit you wish to address, write down a mantra and recite it two to three hundred times a day for a month, either out loud or in your head. Repetition will train your mind to adopt the habit in your statement.

7. Visualize a positive habit and imagine the impact you will create by behaving that way.

8. Educate yourself about positive habits from different sources, be they people, podcasts, or books. It will create a priming effect that will lead to positive action.

9. Practice habits, set goals, and act immediately.

10. Share your knowledge with friends, family, colleagues, and strangers.

11. After thirty days of reprogramming, have a small gratitude ceremony with yourself or a few others, a day of reward where you celebrate and congratulate yourself for your hard work in instilling new habits.

12. As you close your month, pick a new habit to create for the next one.

PROGRAMMING MEDITATION

Through programming meditation you can create self-worth by hacking into the subconscious through I-statements to define (or redefine) who you are. This is done by shifting the paradigm in your mind to create new habits that you can use to manage your thoughts, ideas, thinking process, problem-solving abilities, skills, talents, and strategies to achieve your goals.

Action: Self-Analysis

Pause for a moment of silence, then do a self-analysis by checking your five statuses—thinking or writing them down:

- **Social status:** How is your relationship to people you meet throughout your day? How are the relationships in your life? Do you think you need to improve your relations to people?
- **Emotional status:** How is your emotional stability? Do you feel joy? Are you calm? See what areas need improvement and take a note. Give yourself an overall rating on a scale of one to ten—ten being *amazing*!
- **Physical status:** This relates to your financial status, assets, health, and physical appearance. Give yourself a rating. How can you improve the situation?
- **Mental status:** Have you developed the five faculties of your mind: the conscious mind, your imagination, intuition, memory, and perception? Do you own your mind? Do you have peace of mind?
- **Spiritual status:** How are you doing spiritually? Do you have joy, peace of mind, kindness, love, courage, and patience? Are you growing spiritually or are you stuck? Rate your spirituality and consider next steps.

Meditation: Programming

After considering each of your statuses, think through what you are programming yourself on. Recite this in a simple sentence and think through the possibilities that this new habit you are creating could provide.

- Visualize the habit and belief you want to bring into your life.
- Make ten "I am" statements, out loud or in your journal, that support you in your programming of self.
- Say who you are.
- Say your dream and connect with it.

*Closing Wea**

With your voice or in your head, continue the programming wea to close this bead.

I am programmed to succeed.

I have programmed myself to succeed.

Thank you, creator, for programming me to succeed.

I am programmed to succeed, I have programmed myself to succeed.

---

* *Wea is a term I use to mean "mantra."*

8

—

PURPOSE

MEDITATION PILLAR 6

Only purpose can give our life a new understanding, a new beginning, and meaning. When we are overwhelmed by our suffering or cannot find meaning in our suffering, we exist to suffer.

On my long trek to Ethiopia as a refugee I arrived in a village in South Sudan. Around me were a thousand starving children. Bodies were everywhere. The stench of death dominated the air. All we had to eat was boiled sorghum grain every other day.

One morning, a Dinka woman turned up.

"I have food for one child," she informed the soldier guarding us.

"Pick one," he told her.

We were lined up in rows of three. I began to speak to the woman with my heart and mind.

"The child you are going to feed is me," I told her. "I want to eat this food so I can stay alive and tell this story. I want to eat this food so I can be part of the solution.

"But," I added, "if there is another child who has a greater desire to tell our story and can make a greater impact than me, let that child have your food."

The woman passed me as she walked down the long line of pleading faces. She turned and walked back.

"I want that child," she said. I looked up at her huge smile. It was matched not just by my own but by those of the other kids. They were happy for me too.

I went back to her home to eat. "Do you know why I picked you?" she asked. "I have been praying to pick a child who would not forget, who would not give up easily. I have been praying to feed a child who will be part of the solution one day. When I passed you, I felt different to how the other kids made me feel. I felt you are going to be great."

They were kind words, meaningful, but in all honesty, I just wanted to eat the food. I was too impatient from hunger to think deeply about anything. I also knew I needed to share the food with others. When she looked away, I put some in my pockets to take back with me.

Why do I tell this story? Because it is all about purpose. My purpose that day generated my luck.

What Is Purpose?

Purpose is the conscious awakening of self—a realization that the world does not revolve around us, but around everything, the physical and the nonphysical. Purpose is surrendering to a cause greater than us. In a real sense, it is up to us to find our place in it and then to work for the greater good. It is recognizing the call to serve. If we want the world to change, then we must lead the charge to generate the change we want to see.

Remember, each of us is here for a reason. There is something that only we can do—nobody else can do it better. Our contribution is what the world needs to restore balance. Purpose means we offer that contribution without expecting anything in return. And in so doing, we find greater joy than we could ever experience from receiving. Joy has no price. It can only be earned by being part of a greater good. It is the painkiller, the anti-inflammatory that keeps the body at peace and repels depression, anxiety, and stress.

By facilitating the creation of joy, purpose becomes a motivation unto itself, giving us the strength to carry on with our daily lives. It gives our lives meaning and direction. When we have purpose, we have joy in our hearts, because we are a giving, sharing species.

A poor person who doesn't have purpose will live their life blaming others. A poor person who knows their purpose will be a beacon of hope, a dwelling place and sanctuary of peace and joy for many. They may have little, but their hearts will forever be rich. If we are wealthy but don't know our purpose, then our lives will be empty, a void of fake joy provided by possessions and riches. Being wealthy with a purpose, on the other hand, means we can use our riches to have a global impact on others.

Don't Know Your Purpose?

Listen to your heart. If there is a need in your neighborhood, volunteer your free time. See for yourself how your input helps others through difficult situations. Save wildlife, campaign for a charity, feed the homeless, foster a child.

When we work for the betterment of others, we surrender ourselves to a greater cause. Pursue selfish agendas, and we give in to personal desire. We show ourselves as having a heart not grounded in purpose, one that beats with a negative rhythm.

Purpose Delivers Courage and Ideas

As a child, all I wanted was to be part of solutions, be productive, and give without expectation. I spent most of my childhood living in a hell of frustration, devastation, confusion, and desperation. Suffering and pain were the order of the day. In the middle of this mess, I would find respite by losing myself or hiding in a place I created in my mind, a place of milk and honey, where I helped feed those around me.

Such visualization refocused my mind away from my suffering. To that extent, I was filled with peace, hope, and joy. But of course, the reality was there were still kids starving next to me, groaning and crying without tears. Dead. I had to ask myself a question that affected the real world. What could I do to help us stay alive? My mind gathered thoughts like driftwood. From these bits and pieces ideas would form, then solutions. I would, for instance, eat the leaves off a tree. If they didn't kill me, I would pick some more and share them with other kids.

"Hang around with Jal," kids would say, "and by the end of the day you will have eaten something."

Of course, the risk was always there. One day I ate a plant that dangerously dehydrated me. And then those other kids saved me. They found water and comforted me until I felt okay. In that moment, they, too, showed their purpose.

As individuals, we should always think about being part of a solution. That is where my thoughts took me when I saw those leaves. "If this tree doesn't kill you, then you can share its leaves with others." It is only through imagination that we find a purpose, a way to help ourselves and others.

Purpose Gives Birth to Vision

After I was smuggled into Kenya, my life as a child soldier receded from my daily experience. But I still encountered challenges as I tried to acclimatize to a new life. I felt I didn't fit in. My existence changed, but it remained difficult. I was in a war of the mental, not the physical.

I needed purpose and found it in the form of organizing education scholarships for former child soldiers. I became a voice in the community. I set up car washes and garden cleanups with friends in the church. We used the money we collected to put a youngster in school. I also approached schools and colleges directly in search of scholarships.

I widened my purpose by reaching a broader audience through rap and used my platform to shine light on the things I cared about. My purpose was the genesis of my becoming a musician. A music career allowed me to raise funds and meet influential people of all kinds, which led to founding the Gua Africa charity to help families overcome the effects of war and poverty. Gua Africa filled my heart. I felt true joy to see another child get an opportunity to transform their life. You never know the potential of anyone unless that person is provided with an opportunity. Each of us has a chance to be that provider.

The surrendering of self to a greater cause has made my life better. Helping others is, quite literally, helping yourself.

My purpose now defines my vision—to share my experiences for the furthering of social, emotional, and intellectual learning through arts, business, and philanthropy. My vision can change due to challenges that may arise, but the purpose always remains the same. That purpose is to spread acts of kindness, be part of solutions, and contribute to the world's balance, without expecting anything in return. My purpose is to create experiences that give people joy.

Purpose is my compass, the guardian angel that has brought me this far.

Purpose Takes Us Beyond Our Threshold

I wanted to build a school in honor of Emma McCune but was struggling to raise funds. To raise awareness, I came up with the idea of a modified hunger strike. I would eat only one meal a day. I thought I was well known enough that my stunt would generate the money I needed in just thirty days. It took 662. I felt suitably humbled.

When I finally returned to my normal eating habits, I developed health issues. My body couldn't get used to the extra meals. The day I had my first breakfast in two years, I was performing on stage in Washington. I kept falling down. I was totally off-balance. The crowd thought it was part of the dance. A few days later in New York the wind blew me off the sidewalk.

When I returned to the place where we intended to build the school, some young kids started talking to me. I told them about my hunger strike to raise the money. One kid put up his hand.

"Jal," he said, "what are you talking about? We eat one meal a day anyway."

Again, I was humbled and embarrassed. I told the child how where I lived people had so much food they could choose not to eat, and that some even died of fatness. The kid's eyes popped out. He urged others to come and listen to me. They gathered with excitement and curiosity, and one raised his hand.

"Do people really have so much food that they die of fatness?"

"Yes." There was a long silence. I saw the shock in their faces and could only imagine the thoughts they were processing.

A kid spoke. "That is the coolest death ever!"

All the other children cracked up, and I did too.

It was my purpose that brought me to these children, my desire to be part of a solution, to collect new experiences, to try different ideas. Together we supported one another and together we built our shared vision.

THE THREE TYPES OF JOY

Purpose joy comes from giving without expectation—forgiving somebody, showing gratitude, volunteering, sharing our gifts, talents, and wealth with others.

Fake joy is derived from wanting and being given material items.

Higher purpose joy comes from gratitude, praise, and worship given to an infinite intelligence, a creator, without expectation.

We know that there are five key factors behind the existence of our universe: matter, space, time, energy, and the creator. But without the creator everything else crumbles.

Take a moment every day to recognize the beauty around you, to give gratitude to the creator without expectation, and you will experience joy beyond all joy.

Purpose Is . . .

The ability to rise above and beyond in a way we could never have imagined.

Knowledge we are not alone; that we are in sync with others.

A painkiller.

A guiding light.

Working in partnership with the creator.

Having joy 24/7.

Forgiving those who cause us harm.

Giving without expectation.

Living to transform our lives and those of others. What can we do that gives others and ourselves joy?

A resource to ourselves and others.

Being grateful for our existence.

The life force fueling the light that glows within us.

When you walk in your purpose with clearly defined goals and a burning desire to act, success will follow you like your shadow.

PURPOSE MANTRA

Out loud or in your head, say the purpose mantra.

Purpose is the conscious awakening of self, when you come to a realization that the world does not revolve around you, but around everything. In that realization, you surrender yourself to a cause greater than yourself and contribute to restore balance. Purpose is giving without expecting anything in return. Purpose is spreading acts of kindness. Purpose is what you do that gives you joy. Purpose is what you do that gives others joy. Purpose is being in sync with everything. We can buy momentary happiness, but we cannot buy lasting joy. Joy comes through purpose.

Action

Pause for a moment of silence. Think through your purpose and feel your purpose.

Ask yourself, "What gives me joy? What do I do that gives others joy?"

State your purpose.

Allow the joy in your heart to flood your body. Let it flow. Glow in your joy and smile.

Remember, there is no single template for your individual purpose. Cultivating it takes work.

Closing Wea

Out loud or in your head, state:

I am purpose. I have purpose.
Thank you, creator, for giving me purpose.
I am purpose. I have purpose.

9

CALM

MEDITATION PILLAR 7

CALM IS THE ABILITY TO CONTROL YOUR EMOTIONS AND allow your thoughts to fade away. You remain cool and confident when everything is erupting around you, whether positively or negatively. Staying calm is being present and demonstrating leadership.

An eruption of positivity and of negativity. Of joy and of sadness. Of love and of hate. How do we contain such bursts of emotion? How do we allow our thought waves to become calmer so that instead of crashing on to the rocks, they once again lap gently at the shore? How, when tested, pushed, sometimes to the very brink, do we stay cool and confident?

These are questions that have challenged me across the years. My mind is a battleground. Within its confines rattle past defeats, current quandaries, and worries of a future that can only ever exist in my imagination.

At times, there is only one way I can function. Experience tells me I must surrender all thoughts, desires, hopes, and dreams. Within this mental void I must place nothing. It must exist as a vacuum. I call this place Matahala. I must do nothing, think nothing. Just allow the air to flow into and out of me. With every life-giving breath, I am putting my mind to sleep. It, and I, need rest. Recalibrate, reboot, start again. On such occasions, time becomes meaningless. It could be any hour of the day or night.

When thoughts are particularly intrusive, I will lie on my bed for hours. I will not allow myself to think. At that point my mind is a cinema screen, and I am in the front row. I can see neither entrance nor exit. I needn't turn around and look behind. I know I am the only person watching the reel. Like cars on Broadway, flashbacks from my childhood pass by.

Breathing is life. It takes up to sixty days to starve to death. The average person will live for two to fourteen days without water depending on their environment and body. But after only sixty seconds without oxygen, the cells in our brain begin to die. After three minutes without oxygen the brain is seriously damaged. Ten minutes and it is unlikely to ever recover. Five minutes more and we are gone.

Breathing is the ultimate weapon in our armory, and we are going to use it to train ourselves to be calm. When eruptions occur, when our plans don't seem to work, when we face attacks from angry individuals, whose tongues are sharp and words come with barbs, or when we stare from our windows into an economically unjust world that appears to have simply forgotten our existence, breathing is our power.

Fear, worry, anxiety, depression, anger, hunger, jealousy, and a thousand other emotions sit, sometimes active, other times dormant, in our brains. Manage these emotions in a positive way and we achieve calm. How? By digging. Buried deep in the human brain is a type of wisdom that can only be found in the state of calm. Uncover that wisdom, and you will move on at peace with yourself. Leave it unfound, and you will encounter a wall. Believe me, I know. Take the following three stories. In two, you will see a man who enacted a now deep-seated plan of calmness. You will see also how that approach reaped rewards. In the final story, however, you will see a person who stepped off that path. In the undergrowth he found himself a different person—one who wasn't calm, one who hissed and spat out his words.

THREE STORIES

"I am going to f*** you and your mother."

When I was in the U.K., my calmness was tested all the time. A storm might erupt from any direction. Cold winds could arrive in an instant in the form of fragmented relationships or difficult encounters involving colleagues, family members, lawyers, businessmen, or strangers. Problem scenarios were equally unpredictable.

One time, I was in London meeting two women who were kindly helping with me with Gua Africa. The charity was dedicated to promoting education through academic sponsorships to refugees who had survived war and genocide. The charity, and therefore the meeting, was of huge importance to me. We were grabbing a bite to eat in a pizza shop when a Black man, tall and strong, confronted me.

"Where are you from?" he inquired aggressively.

I was shocked, but nevertheless answered, "South Sudan."

He put his face right into mine. "It's you Africans who sold us as slaves. And now you're hanging out with these f***ing white bitches."

I couldn't believe what was happening. From nowhere, a positive day, a meeting to push forward Gua Africa, to help children in the direst of circumstances, had met a hailstorm of venom. And the downpour wasn't going to end anytime soon.

"I am going to f*** you and your mother," the man continued. "Plus your f***ing bitches."

By now the two women, understandably, felt threatened. They were visibly scared and trying to get away from an increasingly volatile situation. They weren't alone. Even the staff was hiding at the back of the restaurant.

My mind went into overdrive. I was well known as a peace activist, yet every instinct told me to stand and fight, to respond to each vicious comment with an equally nasty one of my own. Then a small voice whispered inside me.

Choose your battles, it told me. *You didn't come to England to fight. There are laws here. You are not in the jungle. You will end up in trouble.*

Yet I was still becoming increasingly heated, angry with myself that, as a man, I was failing to protect the women alongside me. This "opponent" might not have hit me, but my pride was taking a beating. I was being humiliated.

Another voice came into my head. *You are a soldier*, it stated. *You have fought for your people, your survival. You have seen things this man will never see, experienced hardship he will never feel. Are you going to let him dominate you, get away with this? No. Show this civilian you can kick his ass.*

It was a strong voice, urgent and hard to resist. But the first voice battled to make itself heard.

Forget your pride, it reasoned. *You have nothing to gain from taking this man on. There is no advantage to be had from doing so. You will suffer. He will not learn.*

I remained silent. I controlled my emotions and let the man run out of gas. Only then did I speak.

"Brother," I said. "I was a child soldier. I have been at war. I have seen many Black people die. I myself have created situations where people died. My hands are not clean." I looked him in the eye. "If killing me will make you happy, go ahead. I will die loving you. You are my brother."

He said nothing, didn't move an inch. Instead a tear hung from his left eye. "No man has ever said such words to me," he said. We hugged. In a matter of seconds, we found the heart of calm from the edge of war.

Two minutes later, I was buying him a pizza. My charity colleagues wondered how I pulled off this amazing trick and became friends with a man who, seconds earlier, appeared intent on ripping my head off. As we spoke, he revealed his own background in gangs, and how it was a matter of routine for members of such groups to confront and intimidate other young Black men, basically as a recruitment tactic, to see what they are made of.

Thankfully, I was wired differently. My past, so long my tormentor, had in this circumstance actually saved me. My mind knew that the answer to this fraught scenario was calm, not violence. Wisdom, accrued sometimes in the starkest of circumstances, rescued me. Composure rescued me.

Calm rescued me.

"Tonight you are dead meat."

It was 2012, and I was excited to be back in South Sudan to take part in a peace concert alongside some incredible names, including Darryl McDaniels from legendary hip-hop outfit Run-DMC. All was going to plan. I felt excited and invigorated to be part of such an event. When we talk about peace in South Sudan, we know its significance better than most.

Then, out of nowhere, a security officer approached me. "We don't like activists here," he told me. "When they don't keep their mouths shut, we remove their eyes, and then we put their beaten bodies in a bag and throw it into the Nile."

He said it as if joking, but his eyes conveyed a different message. Those eyes were still boring into my skull when, three days later, I was stopped by a junior security officer on duty with his colleagues at a checkpoint. They wasted no time in making their intentions known, pulling me from my car by my hair.

"Nigga, nigga," barked the junior, as he scrambled to find a piece of broken glass with which to shave my head.

"I am here for a peace concert," I managed to tell him as he hauled me from the vehicle.

"Shut up!" he spat. "F*** you and your peace concert."

He slapped me before talking to his radio. I knew what he was trying to do. He was trying to get together a mob of his colleagues to give me a beating—or worse.

I had to act. As he talked, I jumped back in my car and grabbed my phone. I rang the first contact I could find. Breathlessly, I told him my perilous situation and where I was. Barely were the words out of my mouth when the door was nearly yanked off its hinges by the guards.

"Hey! Are you trying to run away?"

"No." They pulled me from the vehicle and grabbed my phone and wallet.

"You are Nuer!" They had heard me speaking the Nuer language on the phone, giving away my origins. To these men, Dinka, I was the enemy.

"Tonight you are dead meat."

It seemed the young officer's promise was true. His fists made contact and kicks came flying in from the others as I fell to the ground. They forced me into a seated position and stood behind me. Taking turns, they hit me two-handed on both sides of the jaw, a tried and tested torture method which causes untold pain and, quite literally, makes you see stars.

I could see no way out of the situation. I was outnumbered. Escape was impossible. Then, amid the pain and the violence, I heard a voice.

"The time to kill Nuer people has not come. Let him go!"

Another man spoke. "I know this man. He is Emmanuel Jal. He is harmless."

"Shut up!" the junior officer snapped. Another blow thudded into my head. A boot smashed into my stomach. I felt half dead, the pain almost absent as I slipped toward unconsciousness. My brain searched for something, a gesture, a word, anything, that would save me.

And there it was. *Speak in Dinka. Say your mum was Dinka.* From somewhere in its deepest recesses my brain had dragged up a jewel of knowledge. My use of the Dinka language would show my wider connection to the peoples and cultures of the region. That I was more than an object, a Nuer, to be brutalized.

Somehow I managed to get the words out. Immediately I felt a change in the group. The beating stopped. The junior officer was pulled back and held down by other men. Two carloads of national security officers turned up.

"What happened?" one of them asked, looking at the half-dead form before him.

"He attacked us," claimed one of my assailants. "He almost killed us."

At that point, another of the national security guys gave me a slap. His more responsible colleague restrained him.

"What's your name?" he asked.

"Jal."

"Tell me the side of your story, Jal."

The officer listened intently. When I finished, he apologized to me and promised to investigate the incident fully. Then he insisted on escorting me on the rest of my journey.

After the intensity of my ordeal, there was still part of me that wanted to display my anger, shout at and curse those who had inflicted such pain on me. But I knew silence was the better way. It had served me well. Let them take from it what they wanted. I had acted with dignity. Maintaining my calm delivered me to the point where I found the perfect word—"Dinka"—that saved my life.

South Sudan, it seemed, was not a place wholly ready to embrace a peace concert. Even the mosquitoes welcomed me with a beating— when I finally climbed on stage, not only did I perform with pain coursing through my body, but with full-blown malaria coursing through my veins. Yet somehow, none of it mattered. In fact, the roof nearly came off as Darryl McDaniels, reggae star Original Ras Korby, and I performed together. Immediately afterward, however, as the adrenaline seeped away, I collapsed, grateful to Susan D. Page, the United States ambassador to South Sudan, who ordered that I be rushed to the American embassy for treatment. A woman of great passion and intelligence, she also encouraged me to continue the good fight.

It took me two months to recover from malaria, a year more to get over the beating. I still to this day carry side effects of ongoing pain and discomfort. At least I am still here. One wrong word that night and my life would have been at an end.

"You can bark as loud as you want so long as you don't bite."

It was a yellow New York cab like any other. Or so we thought.

My English manager Tania Campbell Golding, South Sudanese actor Ger Duany, and I were heading to a business meeting in Brooklyn. All was going fine until we pulled up outside our destination, at which point the driver demanded payment and a tip in dollar bills, no coins. We checked our pockets, purses, and wallets. No good.

"We don't have enough dollar bills," Tania told him. "Can we pay partly in coins?"

"Bitch," snarled the driver. "What are you talking about? English f***ing c***, you are so disrespectful."

The driver's sudden aggression was as shocking as it was frightening. Ger stepped in. "Don't talk to the lady like that."

"Nigger, shut up," the driver shouted. "This is an Asian and white world."

I was astonished. "Why are you like this?" I asked.

"Nigger, suck my dick," he spat.

By now we were boiling. Where had the driver's rage come from, this outpouring of sheer prejudice? How had three people just going about their business been dragged into a world of such violent and putrid hatred?

We weren't going to allow ourselves to be steamrollered with racism. Again and again we repelled his barbs. We tried, and failed, to make him see the disgraceful error of his attitude, how unreasonable he was being.

His response was to call the police. Their first instinct was to believe the driver, until Tania spoke, at which point the officers began to see the truth of the situation.

"So can you pay the driver?" they asked.

"Yes," we replied. With no shortage of satisfaction, Tania began giving the driver coins, one by one. No dollar bills. He flared up again, revealing his true self to the police.

"Officer," I pointed out to one of them, "This taxi driver has been very nasty, aggressive, and humiliating toward us. What are you going to do about that?"

"Welcome to America," he replied. "It's called freedom of speech. You can bark as loud as you want so long as you don't bite."

I was offended by this response. So someone could racially abuse another person and just get away with it? How could this possibly be?

I turned to our tormentor. "You are one very lucky taxi driver," I told him. "Today you met two good Black guys. Next time you will meet a Black guy who will punch your head and it will go down your throat and out through your asshole."

One officer looked away smiling, another asked what I was saying.

"I was just giving the driver a few words of advice," I explained.

I look back to that day and still feel how ready I was to punch that man in the face. I lost my calm. I also learned the meaning of freedom of speech, or a variation of it. For Ger and me, the driver's words were a trigger. We had survived prejudice of the most barbaric kind—genocide. But for all our anger and rage, it was Tania's oh-so-British calmness that cut through the waywardness of the driver's hatred. She did so by barely raising her voice. I didn't hear a single swear word. It was another lesson, and after that day I stepped up my calmness meditation to prepare for the future challenges that I knew would come my way.

THE UNIVERSALITY OF CALMNESS

Calmness can be applied in all aspects of life—business, military, family, personal, whatever—to build relationships and support well-being. Some are lucky enough to be born with calmness in their genes, or maybe they were raised in an environment where they gained the habit. Others may not be so fortunate. Whatever the level of our calmness, it is vital we rein in any instinct to react. We must surrender that desire, take a deep breath, and allow our challenges simply to be, as if we are an observer watching them, allowing us to experience a scenario untainted by intrusive thoughts. Once we have set ourselves into a natural calm state, then we can react to the challenge on our own terms and with the right decisions.

I have seen firsthand how those who have conquered the heights of their own passions and desires have used calmness as the silent engine propelling them forward.

I love watching sports, concerts, and speakers, to observe how participants perform. In boxing, outwardly the most aggressive and explosive of sports, I was amazed to discover how integral calm is in attaining focus. A boxer prepares intensively for months ahead of a bout. What will win them the fight is courage, planning, and strategy. But after their opponent has landed a few blows, only those who remain calm are able to remember those three elements. Let instant reaction intervene and all that training, all that planning and strategizing, goes to waste.

Life is a game and each of us has been placed in the ring to play. For us to win our battles we must remain focused, be calm, and trust our plans and strategies. Only then can we punch through the walls in our way.

The wisdom to overcome arises from a mind with a broad bandwidth. When the brain is cluttered with worry, fear, and anxiety, it can't access its most beneficial assets to support us. Without calm, only the louder, more dominating voices and thoughts will respond. The advice those voices will give is ill-considered, desperate, and ineffective. True creativity comes from the part of the mind that is quiet. In that sacred place, neuron activities access life lessons and memories hidden on our mental hard drive and combine them with new and recent experiences to formulate positive solutions beneficial in both the short and the long term.

I know this to be the truth. At school I was expelled numerous times for fighting. Why? Because words—vicious and abusive—sparked a vigorous internal reaction. I couldn't continue along that reactive path if I hoped to accomplish my goals. A change of approach was not only necessary, it was vital. I trained myself to manage my thoughts, flashbacks, and emotions. The single most important element in that training was breathing. On a bad day I would find a dark place, find a gentler rhythm to my breathing, and observe my emotions without reacting. I found myself a place of calm. Doing so would bring on the most peaceful sleep, and I would wake the next day bursting with joy.

I reached that point through the gradual understanding that when I react to unwanted emotions or thoughts in an instinctive, negative, or aggressive way, my life can turn miserable for months. I created different methodologies for different times in my life. In my late teens, music and dance meditation not only brushed away intrusive thoughts but also applied a sheen of joy. In my younger childhood, I explored visualization and prayers as relaxation formulas.

The value of those calming exercises never left me. In my twenties and thirties, I upgraded them with ancient Egyptian techniques, yoga, and Buddhism. The ultimate goal is to achieve a state of nothingness, to let go of all desires and surrender myself to that Matahala. When we attain a state of flow in our breathing we feel like we are in heaven. Worry, stress, anxiety, fear, and other negative thoughts and emotions occupy a lot of space in the mind. No wonder we struggle to find solutions or access wisdom to make the right decisions. Yet, as I have shown, there are many methods we can apply to manage our emotions and clear our thoughts.

The use of breathing allied to meditation, freeing of the mind, is simple and effective, and that is important because in times of stress people do not want, nor do they have the headspace, to deal with complex techniques. Remember, whenever you feel knocked off your feet by a wave of overwhelming thoughts, there is an easily accessible answer:

calm. You can clear your mind simply by applying measured breathing. Any time your mind drifts toward a place that spells danger, bring your entire being back to your breathing. Imagine your mind to be a dog you are walking in the park. Every time your dog loses focus it will pull on the lead, but if you pull it back, after a while the dog will learn to walk alongside you without your ever having to worry about it. Breathing is the lead on which you keep your mind.

The calm meditation I so love was boosted when I met a lady named Paige Elenson, founder of the Africa Yoga Project. A New Yorker, Paige was on safari in Africa in 2006 when she saw young men doing handstands. She decided to join them. She was invited back to teach them yoga, which was the catalyst for her project to train young, marginalized Africans to become yoga teachers and professionals, creating new economic opportunities for them and making yoga's wellness benefits accessible to lower- and middle-income communities.

Initially, I thought Paige was a devil worshipper. When I walked in on her class, I encountered a lot of loud breathing and bending in different positions. But then I had another thought—"Wow!" The last time I had done anything like this—bending, movement, exploring the possibilities of the body and its capacity for relaxation—was when I was a kid. Not that I saw it in those terms back then—I was just a young boy messing around. Certainly, there was none of the structure, detailed instruction, and understanding I saw now with Paige.

She and her class were practicing Baptiste yoga, a holistic approach to transform the mind, body, and spirit, said to provide a foundation for physical prowess, mental acuity, and spiritual growth. I could see straight away the impact it was having.

"If the devil is making people's lives this good," I told myself, "then the devil is good!"

From that moment on she had my absolute trust. I was familiar with what she was teaching from a mental and movement point of view, but the more intricate techniques were alien to me. I wasted little time in incorporating them into my existing calmness practices.

CREATING MENTAL SPACE THROUGH CALM MEDITATION

Find yourself a comfortable place. This could be sitting upright or lying on a bed or mat with your belly facing the sky.

Now bring yourself to the moment. Visualize yourself as a calm person for thirty seconds. Then, out loud or in your head, say the following mantra:

Calm is the ability to control your emotions. Calm is allowing your thoughts to fade away. Calm is remaining cool and confident when everything is erupting, positively or negatively, around me. *Staying calm is being present and demonstrating leadership.*

Action

Pause now. You need to settle into a period of meditation to find calm in your body and mind.

- Enjoy a moment of silence.
- Bring yourself into the moment.
- Notice your environment.
- Notice what you are wearing.
- Notice your heartbeat.
- Notice any noise around you.
- Notice the sensations in your body.
- While counting to twelve, inhale and fill your lungs. Then count to fifteen while exhaling. Repeat three times.
- Let your breath return to normal and focus your attention on it as you do so. Breathe in and out through the nose.

- ◘ Find your flow and rhythm as you inhale and exhale.
- ◘ Allow thoughts to fade away. Every time your mind drifts, bring it back to your breathing.
- ◘ Let go of everything until it is just you and your surroundings.
- ◘ Continue in the rhythm of your breathing.

Closing the Session

Out loud or in your head, deliver the following mantra:

I am calm. I have calm.

Thank you, creator, for giving me calm.

I am calm, I have calm.

10

COURAGE

MEDITATION PILLAR 8

What Is Courage?

- Courage is the power, the strength, the force within us that helps to overcome fear. While courage makes us see opportunities, fear makes us see obstacles.
- Courage is the force that allows us to stand up and protect what we believe in. To gain courage we must have a belief in which we can invest. When what we believe in becomes more important even than our own life, then we have courage.
- Courage is understanding that fear is the beginning of knowledge and wisdom, and that failure is an infinite source of intelligence.
- Courage is the force that allows us to spend time with those we don't know and who may be a threat to us.
- Courage is the force that allows us to hunt, to battle through storms, believing we will come back safe, and to provide for our families, loved ones, and communities.
- Courage is the force that allows police, firefighters, and armies to carry out duties that they know might end their lives.
- Courage is the force that allows us to swallow our pride.

- Courage is the force that allows us to perform with confidence in uncertain situations.
- Courage is what make us socialize and share our experiences with each other.
- Courage is as simple as walking out of your house to meet a friend without worrying you will be eaten by a lion or kidnapped.

Any human being who says they have no fear is lying. Nelson Mandela put it perfectly when he said, "I learned that courage was not the absence of fear, but the triumph over it. The brave man is not he who does not feel afraid, but he who conquers that fear. It always seems impossible until it's done."

Nelson Mandela was one of my heroes. I had a wish to meet him. One day it happened. I was performing in Hyde Park in London for his ninetieth birthday celebration. He shook my hand and encouraged me to keep fighting the good fight. We will all, at one time or another, ask ourselves if we can overcome the fear of something put in our path. The key is remembering we can all find the courage to do so. That courage may come from loved ones, friends, the community, or even encouragement from strangers. It also comes from taking confidence in what we have learned and understanding that on occasions it may be incumbent upon us to show courage to others. An army commander, for instance, must not show signs of fear because if they do, their soldiers, too, will be afraid. Children look for similar signals from their parents. If you lie, they will lie; if you cry, they will cry; if you are afraid, they will be afraid.

Of all the many different types of courage, the two most challenging are finding the courage to look within ourselves and finding the courage to give to others. Yes, we can go out and fight for something, but to then share what we have with others takes another level of courage.

The Need for Courage

Past defeats, current conflicts, and future worries can overwhelm and damage our hearts and minds, bringing forth illnesses such as depression. That doesn't just apply to humans. There are examples all across the animal world. Dolphins, for example, can become suicidal at times of severe stress. They, like us, can fall victim to trauma.

The future, in particular, can give rise to anxiety, break a person's will, and make them lose hope. My own suicidal thoughts were triggered by just such a situation. I could think of nothing but an uncertain future. That, along with unanswered questions from my past, produced a combination that was choking me to death.

"When are my problems going to stop knocking at my door?" I would ask myself. "When are all these negative issues going to stop calling my name? When are the nightmares and flashbacks going to stop? Who has given my name and address to the problems that keep coming at me?"

Just when I thought it couldn't get worse, another layer of hell would descend, hotter even than the previous one. My future would go from blank to pitch black. I would be surrounded by a desert of darkness, tormenting me to kill myself.

Only by surrendering to hope would I find courage. At that point, the darkness would crack. A path would appear for me to walk through.

THE SIX PILLARS OF GAINING COURAGE

Courage comprises six pillars. These pillars are Belief, Understanding, Fear, Knowledge, Wisdom, and Failure.

Belief—accepting something as the only truth.

On one of my childhood survival treks across the desert plains of South Sudan, the situation became intense. With no food or water, we were left to drink our own urine. Everyone was exhausted. One child soldier was left under a tree with the promise we would return to pick him up later. I was fifty meters away, looking straight at him, when he shot himself in the head. It planted a seed—maybe I should do the same.

My left little toe was severed, hanging off, rotten. Every step caused sharp searing pain across my body. I felt like my head would explode. At one point I stopped. Multiple thoughts rushed into my mind. I zoomed in on my past—it was depressing. I did the same with my current situation—unbearable. Zooming in, finally, on my future, I could see only a thousand miles of emptiness without light and hope. We were dying. There was no sign that we would survive.

I took hold of my gun and tried to cock it with my hand. No good. I didn't have the strength. I used a foot instead. Looking straight down the barrel, knowing for sure it was aiming straight at me, I closed my eyes and pushed the trigger with my toe. The gun fired but no bullet came out. In that moment I didn't know if I was dead or alive. But I had a voice whispering in my head.

You are here for a reason, it told me. *You are alive for a reason.*

I thought about what that reason might be and concluded it was so I could tell my story. It was something only I could do, and I had to stay alive to do it. My old childhood beliefs sprang to mind. As a kid I would tell myself I was going be part of a solution. I began again to visualize myself in that way.

I repeated the mantra "I am going to be part of a solution" over and over until I felt possessed by it. I lived entirely in my head, disconnected from the rest of my body. I took one step, then another, and another, all the time holding my dreams and positive words in my head. The pain receded. When I settled down to rest that evening, I experienced the best night's sleep of my life—so sweet, no worries. I was completely filled with joy and assurance, confident in a way I never had been before that I was here for a reason.

I don't know if anyone realized what was going on in my head. I didn't share the experience with my companions. It took me a long time to share the story at all. The next day, however, I felt my toe was healing. As the journey continued, the feeling that I was going to be part of a solution only grew more intense. Belief is power. Everywhere I go I carry my beliefs with me.

After discovering the power of belief, I wrote many belief statements. Here are my top fifteen:

- I believe in justice, equality, and freedom for all.
- I believe in the power of gratitude, a forgiving heart, faith, a positive mindset, the programming of self, purpose, calm, soul food, and love.
- I believe there is a creator who made all things.
- I believe I am here for a reason.
- I believe in the power of education.
- I believe goodness and kindness exist in all human beings.
- I believe all men and women are created equal.
- I believe any problem that comes my way is a present, a special gift designed especially for me with my name printed on it.
- I believe storms will always blow themselves out.
- I believe purpose generates luck.
- I believe as I walk in my purpose, I can rise beyond what I could not possibly imagine.
- I believe as I walk in my purpose, I am in partnership with the creator.
- I believe as I walk in my purpose, I am in sync with everything.
- I believe as I walk in my purpose, I am not alone; every soul I touch has my back.
- I believe as I walk in my purpose with clearly defined goals and a burning desire to act, success will follow me like my shadow.

Understanding

Understanding shapes us and shapes our world. It is impossible to understand something if it is not inside us, just as it is impossible to do anything if we don't understand it. When you understand something, you are in control of your destiny.

Those who influence the planet are those who understand themselves and what they are great at. Those who understand the importance of financial freedom value education, knowledge, and wisdom. They have a burning desire to achieve that freedom because they also understand the devastating effects of poverty. Those who understand justice, equality, and freedom will go beyond the call of duty to sacrifice their lives to attain freedom for all. Those who understand the importance of planning and creation of habits to achieve success will take time to plan and create those habits.

How can we impact our lives and bring meaning if we don't understand that we have a role to play in the universe? That we are important and have worth?

Recently I watched a documentary about high school students in the U.K. It made me laugh. One student was doing exams and came across Pythagoras's theory and pi. She was so puzzled. What is pi, and where did it come from? She was lost and confused. It took me back to my own struggles with mathematics. It took me nine years of failing before I really understood the subject. It made me almost hate mathematics when, in reality, I loved it. If we can't understand something, we must seek to understand it. Understanding is the absolute key. Try to love somebody who has never experienced love and it will be a challenge for them. Until they understand love, their reaction will always be contrary to what you desire.

Fear

Fear tells us if something is going to cause us pain, suffering, or death. It is a prophet, advisor, and storyteller. But it may be a bad advisor and poor predictor. However, listening to the advice, stories, and prophecies fear brings us gives us options and room to prepare for what is ahead.

Fear Can Make You a Champion

Floyd Mayweather is one of my favorite boxers. He won fifteen world titles, so I wanted to know what made him a champion. The bottom line was fear. Fear made him train harder than other boxers. Fear of losing or of being humiliated made him hit the gym again and again. When other boxers were asleep, Mayweather was training. Floyd retired a multimillionaire without losing a fight.

Fear Drives Creativity

In 1957, Russia launched their Sputnik satellite. When the Americans heard this, they feared Russia was going to bomb them from space. The country would have to act urgently to save itself. It did exactly that, recruiting the smartest scientists and creatives and providing an enormous budget to come up with innovations and solutions. Fear of Sputnik would give birth to computers and microchips. It spearheaded the technological advancements that we enjoy today, from the internet to smartphones. Fear makes us think laterally. It is fear that makes us create at times when we cannot countenance failure.

Fear Drives Intelligence

As a very optimistic person, I have in the past ignored fear, an approach that has caused me to make terrible decisions. Too much optimism can blind us to reality, at which point we fail to ask the right questions. Great generals, great businesspeople, and great scientists all understand that fear is not an enemy—it drives intelligence. We should welcome our fear with gratitude, and we should look at it in three ways: the fear we know, the fear we should know, and the fear we will never know. If we know of a fear but don't act upon it, that is our fault. If we should know about a fear, but fail to make an effort to find out more, then that, too, is our fault. A fear we will never know is out of our hands; we should never worry about it.

We all have fears, causing anxiety, worry, and mental illness. Fears come in levels and waves—job insecurity, failing exams, losing loved ones, death, divorce, crime, war, climate change, animal attack. You name it, we fear it. Fears are infinite. But they are also what lead us to action. Fears are encoded in us by nature to protect us from danger.

Fear, then, is good. It prepares us and, hand in hand with courage, makes us act. It is the beginning of knowledge and wisdom. If courage is what makes us fight, then fear is what makes us act. One is the proton, the other the electron. Together they illuminate us.

There are three types of fear: fear that can make you fight, fear that paralyzes us, and fear that can make us run. I have experienced each of these fears, and the fear that I hate the most is the one that paralyzes me.

Before we got trained as child soldiers, there was an animal called Nyanajuan that came in the evening to snatch children away. We were all familiar with it on our journey. It was famous for eating children. We even sang songs about it. *Lele lele Nyanajuan ah cham ran / lele lele Nyanajuan ah chum ran.* Which means "Nyanajuan eats humans." One evening, one kid shouted, "Nyanajuan." I was caught between the fence. The kids with me stormed off, but I was paralyzed by fear and collapsed. I couldn't run away. I was done. I thought, "This is it, I am now Nyanajuan dinner." Luckily for me, Nyanajuan took another kid instead. When I came to my senses, I got a burst of energy and broke through the fence. I made such a racket screaming that everybody thought I was Nyanajuan, but I was screaming, "I am alive. I am alive. Thank you, God."

Knowledge

Knowledge is knowing and knowing is power. It drives our skills, talents, and thinking. We can lose everything, but if our skills and talents are powered by knowledge, we can survive and thrive anywhere. Wealth is not money in the bank, houses, or cars. It is our ability to solve problems. Knowledge holds the key to unlocking our potential.

I never knew that a girl could take my heart without my permission, but when I was in school one girl did exactly that. I used to dream about her. I couldn't concentrate in class. She was in my mind all the time.

If I heard her speak, my heart would beat faster, I would sweat, and my legs would begin to shake. I would feel good and yet also afraid. I would dream of her, and when I heard her sing in the school choir, I thought I was listening to an angel. She didn't actually have a great singing voice, but she sounded beautiful to me. Sometimes I would wake up in the morning and try to fight her away from my heart and my mind. I felt as if I was bewitched by her and that her influence on me wasn't good. I was justified in this view. It transpired that she was deliberately trying to distract me so I could not concentrate at school. She wanted her sister to beat me in class.

An adult once said to me that love is strange. The heart of every man he knew had been stolen by a woman without their permission.

"Jal," he told me, "the sad part is that sometimes it takes a lifetime to get over it. Some don't recover from it at all."

That freaked the hell out of me. "How do I get my heart back?" I asked.

"Get busy," he advised. "Study, play sport every day, and don't think about her. Just think about your future."

He made me understand the situation, but still I could not believe how losing your heart could just happen like that. It took me a while to recover. I had to tell myself that I came to school to study, not fall in love with girls, and that was how I overcame the feeling.

Later, as I grew with new knowledge and understanding in my high school years, I fell in love again. This time, I had an opportunity to take the girl on a date, but I lacked courage. I didn't know how to kiss. A friend told me to watch French movies.

"I don't speak French," I told him. "I will watch American movies instead." We both laughed.

"The French kiss better than Americans," he advised me.

In the end, I watched both, before practicing in my bedroom with a pillow. Sometimes I would watch couples kissing in the park, going closer and closer to see how they did it. Eventually, the guy would give me a look that said, "Get any closer and I will kill you!"

"Please continue," I would say innocently. "I am doing a science project." The couple would storm off, calling me a strange kid.

Strange as my methods may have seemed, they allowed me to find the confidence to take the girl for a date. It was wonderful. I gave the greatest performance of my life. The girl was impressed, and we kissed until we were drunk with love. No alcohol, just burgers, chips, Fanta and Coke, and lots of kissing.

By gathering knowledge and putting it into practice, I recovered from my broken heart. I discovered a way to handle my fear, which led to my gaining confidence.

Wisdom

Wisdom is the ability to use the knowledge we have gathered in our lives, supported by intuition, to solve complex problems. Wisdom allows us to plan and think with depth. It gives us a 360-degree view of problem-solving.

King Solomon

King Solomon, ruler of the United Kingdom of Israel from 970 to 931 B.C., was renowned for his wisdom and the ability to solve the most complex of problems. He was brought a complicated case. Two women who shared a room had babies. One night one of the women fell asleep next to her baby. She rolled over on to it and it was smothered. When she woke, she swapped it with the other child. Nobody could definitively prove to whom the living baby belonged—who was telling the truth. No judge was able to solve the case, so it was put before King Solomon. He listened intently as each woman gave her version of events. He concluded that the baby should be cut in two and each woman given half. One of the women agreed, the other pleaded for the baby to be spared.

"I will have more peace with my baby alive," she said, "even if it is raised by that woman. God will provide me with another child."

Solomon now had his answer. The child's true mother was the one who called for the child to be spared. The case was solved. As ever, people were amazed by how he had managed to do it.

Each one of us will encounter difficult situations. But we, too, have the ability to use our experience combined with our knowledge and intuition to make decisions. We learn through practice and by listening to wise people around us. Knowledge is expansion of ourselves.

Failure

Failure is an infinite source of intelligence. Those who succeed fail many more times than those who do not. Detach emotion from the pain failure brings and soon you see its true value.

Thomas Edison

Thomas Edison was considered a stupid, troubled child in his early life. Teachers didn't like him, and he was bored by school. His mother had an idea. If the school couldn't teach him, then she would do so instead. Instead of a formal education—primary school, high school, university—Edison's mother allowed her son to explore his imagination. As Thomas's skills improved, he began reading books that were scientific. These inspired him to create an electric light bulb. Time and again he tried and failed. Yet he never gave up.

"I have not failed," he told his fellow scientists. "I have just found ten thousand ways that won't work."

Finally, of course, Edison found success. He is credited with inventing the electric light bulb.

For any of us to succeed, we will have to fail. To reach my current point in life, I have failed, in one way or another, around three hundred times. But I have come to welcome failure as my most hard-core critic. It delivers the most straightforward feedback. It comes with no sugar coating. If you are doing something and you haven't failed yet, be careful, it's coming. We can always become wiser, smarter, and more creative.

IS COURAGE WITHIN US?

I became a refugee in my own country. I was eleven years old and, like thousands of others, slowly dying of starvation. I hadn't eaten well for weeks and had no energy left. It was then I saw a food compound. I worked out that the only people allowed to eat there were aid workers, security guards, important visitors, the blind, and the disabled. A thought occurred to me.

"Let's go and eat that food with those kids," I told the boy I was with.

"What are you talking about?" he replied. "The guards will beat the hell out of us."

I weighed up the options. My fear worked with my courage to create a plan.

"Let's go down to the river, put dirt and mud in our eyes, and pretend we are blind." We did just that, but when we got close to the compound my friend backed out, fearing getting beaten. I, however, continued, walking close to the gate acting blind. My eyes stung from the dirt and tears rolled down my face. Within minutes, somebody grabbed my hand and took me inside. I was put with the blind children. Finally, I was able to eat, even putting some extra food in my pocket. But the fuller my belly became, the more I forgot I was blind. It was obvious I could see clearly.

"This kid is not blind!" someone shouted.

I tried to run but was grabbed by a guard. My punishment was to be thrashed across the buttocks with a stick. Back outside the compound, the other kids laughed at me. I didn't care. I was happy. My belly was full, and I hadn't hurt anyone in the process.

"I wish I had come with you," the other boy told me. I had boiled grain mixed with beans in my pocket and gave him a little. With the ensuing energy, my friend and I managed to walk to the forest and find plants to eat. We searched for animals to trap. While so many others were starving, we found a way to have two meals a day, always sharing our finds with other kids.

CAN WE GET COURAGE FROM OTHERS?

When the British army came to Sudan in colonial times, the Naath warriors had never seen such advanced weaponry. They couldn't understand how something could be pointed at a human, make a loud bang, and then that person would fall and die. The Naath were used to fighting with spears, or men attacking them with arrows and swords. It was a challenge like no other they had ever faced. Every time they confronted the British army, hundreds would be gunned down. Many tribes surrendered. Rape, genocide, destruction of property, and terror were prevalent.

The Naath women called a meeting with their warriors. "Who are these men you are running away from?" they asked. "Do they have two legs like you? And do they have penises like you?"

"Yes," replied the warriors.

"Take courage then," an elderly woman told them. "A man is respected if they die for what they believe in. If you believe this land belongs to us and we have a right to benefit from it, then you must take courage so our children and our children's children will know it is important to fight for their rights and that it is noble to die for what you believe in."

The women told the warriors they would accompany them to the battlefield. "We shall not fear death," they told them, "because it's reunification with our ancestors."

The warriors thought it was a joke, but the women were true to their word. They removed their clothing and told their men, "If you run away, we will sleep with the enemy."

They sang songs and marched behind the warriors. If a man tried to run away, they would catch him, beat him up, and tell him to move forward.

Many died that day, men and women, but finally the Naath managed to defeat the British. History was made. There were great celebrations. And all because the women had given courage to the men.

COURAGE MEDITATION

This meditation keeps me grounded and focused. I hope it can support and ignite similar thoughts in you.

Setup

Find yourself a comfortable place. Bring yourself into the moment. Notice your environment, what you are wearing, your heartbeat, the sensations in your body.

Fill your lungs to a count of twelve, exhale to a count of fifteen. Do this three times. Let your breath return to normal. Breathe in and out through the nose. Find your flow and rhythm.

Allow your thoughts to fade away. Every time your mind drifts, bring it back to your breathing. Let go of everything and continue in the rhythm of your breath.

Courage Mantra

Courage is the power, the strength, and the force within me that helps me to overcome fear. Courage will make me see opportunities, while fear and worry will make me see the obstacles. To gain courage, I must have something I believe in. I must understand that fear is the beginning of knowledge and wisdom, and failure is the infinite source of intelligence.

Action

Pause after these words. Think about what makes you feel and act courageously. State ten beliefs dear to you that elevate your courage.

Closing Mantra

Out loud or in your head, say the courage mantra.
    I am courage. I have courage.
    Thank you, creator, for giving me courage.
    I am courage, I have courage.

11

SOUL FOOD

MEDITATION PILLAR 9

WE NEED TO FEED OUR SOUL. STORIES, IMAGES, SOUNDS, lyrics, and poetry keep us motivated, rejuvenated, educated, and fired up to live by our purpose. They also increase our imagination, sparking our creativity and problem-solving abilities. Feeding the soul gives us the tools and raw materials we need to maintain and improve our internal engineering.

What I love most about soul food is positive priming, the fact that it sits not in the stomach but in the mind, so we can be nourished by it at any time. Its influence sits beneath the surface, reinforcing and encouraging positive new experiences.

I first became aware of soul food as a young boy. I loved stories with positive endings. Such stories drove me forward. They empowered me to keep hope alive. If there was no one to tell me a story, I would take sustenance from imagery, walking for hours looking at plants, flowers, bees, clouds, anything that caught my eye. In Kenya, I would often make a stop on my way home to buy roasted corn on the street. The sellers had very little, but they always had jokes and stories in abundance. They were broke but joyful. I asked one, Kamau, who his hero was. He told me of John Commando, a man who came from a poor background but worked hard until he was a hero to thousands.

"Where I can I find him?" I asked.

"Over there," he said, pointing. "It will cost you five shillings."

I looked to where he was indicating—the cinema. Long lines of kids and adults queued at the door. I needed to get the money together to get in there myself. Two days later, I returned clutching five shillings.

I should explain that even at age fourteen, I had no concept of acting. I used to think all movies were true, even cartoons, even Bruce Lee. John Commando was the ultimate hero—a man who could beat hundreds of others on his own. I was hooked. When I got home, I would reflect on how my life could be like his, but not in a violent way. "How did he become so powerful?" I pondered. "How come he is so smart?"

Every chance I had, I would go to see Kamau. He would make me laugh and sometimes give me free corn.

"How come you are always happy?" I asked him.

"I love stories," he explained. "Every day I make sure I hear one and then it keeps me going. The more stories you know, the better your life becomes. I am now selling corn on the street, but if you look for me ten years from now, I will have a big shop and a happy family."

I believed Kamau would change his life. I don't know if he realized he was changing mine too. Either way, the stories he told me gripped my imagination so that by the time I got home, my traumatic experiences would have been pushed right to the back of my mind.

I understood. Our lives are shaped by the stories we hear, and our success depends on the stories we were told.

Self-Experiments on Priming

I am a person easily influenced by words. Conversations, articles, movie dialogue, lyrics—they all stick in my head. In 2019, living in Canada, understanding the value of priming, I decided to conduct an experiment. Along with my usual practices, such as meditating, checking my social media, and following news about South Sudan, for one month I would seek content far outside my usual boundaries. The first week was fine, but then I found my words started to change; my mood was affected. I was less patient, finding it hard to listen, as if my focus and attention were being snatched away. My positive thinking evaporated, my eating habits were affected, and I began buying things I didn't need, such as new clothes and a new iPhone, even though I had a perfectly good one already. My behavior was changing, and not for the better. I was rude to my manager, and while I had joy in my life, I began worrying about the future for no reason. I started comparing my lifestyle with those of others.

I realized the content I was consuming was tricking me into believing I was alone, that nobody really cared about me. It made me feel as if everyone was after something from me. Then, when they had it, they would tear me to pieces. I noticed also that I was getting tired easily, like I hadn't rested even though I'd slept well. My brain was working through the night, preoccupied with fears and worries. Some days I wouldn't want to meditate. My heart yearned for it, but my body wouldn't cooperate. I noticed an influence on my eating habits. I developed a sudden interest in cookies, bread, pizza, chocolates, alcohol, and fizzy drinks. Ridiculously, I had dreams about smoking cigarettes and cigars, surrounded by models. The toxicity in my body was affecting my mind. When the month finally ended, I was relieved.

The next month I did things entirely differently. On Sundays, I wrote my goals for the week. At the end of each day, I would write my goals for the next one, and then on Saturday I would review my performance. I intended to maintain a tight structure. On weekdays, I would wake at 5:31 a.m. and meditate until 6:12. I would then make my bed, use the bathroom, drink warm water, and start on the goals I had set the previous evening, including further meditation, taking in positive content, and ten hours volunteering on initiatives close to my heart.

I was excited to start this second month, but I was sluggish. In the first week, my meditation lacked focus. I also had to force myself to feed my soul with positive content. My mind craved negative news and negative media. My goals were a challenge, too, as I was all too easily captivated by other diversions. Only discipline and persistence took me back into the state of flow where I could focus on purpose, vision, and mission, with clearly defined goals.

The experiment told me everything I needed to know. We become what we hear, we become what we eat, we become what we smell, we become what we touch, and we become what we see. We are all prone to priming. The key is finding the words and stories that influence our thinking, behavior, and productivity in a positive way.

It is through feeding our souls that we unite our hearts and minds. It is through feeding our souls with positivity that we overcome our challenges. Research shows that our brains collect negativity, so we must actively look for positive content to restore balance. Our brain can only grant us our wishes when we give it the raw materials to do the work. It needs positive words, inspirational stories, beautiful things to smell, touch, taste, and see. Reading scriptures or inspirational books, looking at art, walking in nature, or listening to music can uplift us and set us up for success, as can finding common ground with others, listening, and talking with respect.

We can only give what we have. If we don't have love in us, we will not have love to give when the time comes to do so. The same goes for respect. If we don't have it, we can't give it. It is by feeding our souls that we gain the priming effect and relearn who we need to be. That works not just for individuals but for communities. Every positive story told provides unity and purpose. The experiences we have are the experiences we are going to give to others.

The Bully Bull

One day in my village, a boy turned to me.

"Jal," he said, "your father is a coward. You are the son of a coward."

"Why are you saying that?" I asked. "How do you know?"

"Because," he replied, "your bull is a coward."

I was angry and punched the boy in the face. We started fighting before some other kids jumped in to separate us. But I couldn't get his words out my head. The truth was that our bull was indeed a coward. It didn't roam with the rest of the cows. It stayed by itself and came home early.

My grandmother was upset when she heard what the other kids had said about my father. She understood how it disturbed me. One evening, the bully of the herd, a white bull with short horns, a fierce fighter, was terrorizing the other animals. Our bull, as usual, was staying out of the way, having come home early. My grandmother set about performing a ceremony. First, she removed her traditional cowskin skirt. Then she took some hot ashes and burnt cow dung from our altar.

"My white bull," she said to our bull, "our white bull, our pride. When you go out there to face your fears, you are not alone. We are with you. You are our spirit, our strength, and our work ethic.

"Gatwitch Nyak," she added, "has a son who is a warrior represented in this family by you. I want you to stand your ground and do your best. This is your territory. Put up a good fight and that bull will not want to come here again."

All the time, my grandmother was massaging the bull's neck and singing songs. Finally, she hit it with her skirt.

"Now go out," she told the bull. "You are ready."

Our bull went straight out. It was ready to fight. The bully charged. It was a tough fight, and our bull suffered a stab wound to its neck. Initially it retreated, but then continued the fight. By now, every kid in the village had come out to watch.

"Jal's bull is fighting!" they shouted.

It was a tiring battle, almost to the death, but eventually our bull came out on top. I cried tears of joy. Never again would a kid tell me my father was a coward. Even if our bull had lost, it would have been respected for picking up the challenge. It represented the courage of our family.

What my grandmother did changed my life. I couldn't believe what I had seen. On that day I discovered the power of words and motivation.

Knowing Ourselves by Words

I take time to think about words: whom I listen to, what books to read. The more positive words we have in our lives, the better. Negative words will, if we're not careful, combine to destroy our lives and those of others around us. I should know—on one occasion, a person I very much respected said some words that almost split me in two. This man was presenting me with a peace award (I won't mention his name, as he still does good work that I wouldn't want to undermine). I was seated at the same table as him, enjoying our conversation, before he was called upon to make a speech and present me with the award. The words he said on stage touched many souls. We hugged and I accepted the award before performing and delivering a speech of my own. Back at the table, we continued our chat. I told him how I love going into schools to share my experiences with students and asked him if he had any thoughts I could carry with me. I was not expecting what he said.

"Emmanuel," he told me, "your story is old and irrelevant."

I took a deep breath and walked away. I needed to shake off the shock and keep myself together. I returned to my hotel room with a body boiling like a volcano. I felt like a grenade with the safety pin removed. It was a bad night. His negative words triggered flashbacks and nightmares, and I couldn't sleep. Every good thing he said to me was erased in a second. From that point on, every time I spoke in a school or at a conference, his words followed me on stage. His voice repeated itself—"Emmanuel, your story is not relevant"—again and again, like a broken record. Every time I received another award, his face, and that same line, would appear. He stung me like a bee and tore me apart like a puff adder.

Had I not been grounded in my purpose and practice of feeding my soul, reminding myself that my story is relevant, it would have been the end of me as a positive influence. I can't help but wonder how many people have had their confidence, and future, shattered by something similar. The truth is that words have the power to build us or break us. They can generate strong emotions that lead us to positive action, or they can wield great destruction.

Don't be complacent. Ask yourself every day what words you are using to communicate to yourself and others. Remember what you are saying has influence and power beyond anything you might imagine.

Some of the Positive Words and Phrases I Use in My Daily Communication

Gratitude, purpose, joy, love, positive mindset, kindness, peace, courage, feeding of the soul, calm, focus, vision, competence, loyalty, humility, strategy, amazing, excellence, exuberant, powerful, destiny, beautiful, forgive, learn, meditation, motivation, health, desire, innovation, endurance, persistence, intuition, wisdom, action, faith, I can, I will.

Steps for Priming Yourself

- Read only positive content in the morning.
- Recite three positive quotes every day.
- Read at least one book a month.
- Listen to positive stories every day.
- Look for positivity every day.

SOUL FOOD MEDITATION

Find a comfortable place. Bring yourself into the moment by visualizing yourself as a calm person for thirty seconds.

Notice your environment, what you are wearing, your heartbeat, any noise around you, and sensations in your body.

Fill your lungs to a count of twelve. Exhale to a count of fifteen.

Do this three times. Let your breath return to normal. Breathe in and out through the nose. Find your flow and rhythm.

Allow your thoughts to fade away. Every time your mind drifts, bring it back to your breathing.

Out loud or in your head, say the soul food mantra:

Feeding of the soul is about providing myself with positive content to keep me motivated, rejuvenated, educated, and fired up to live by my word and purpose.

If you have time, read a scripture or listen to a motivational speaker. There are so many books, podcasts, speaker series, and social media accounts to choose from. Explore what's out there and what inspires you.

To end, out loud or in your head, say the soul mantra:

I am soul, I have soul.
   Thank you, creator, for giving me soul.
   I am soul, I have soul.

12

LOVE MEDITATION

MEDITATION PILLAR 10

What Is Love?

PEACE. KINDNESS. ENERGY. PATIENCE. JOY. TRUST. CARING. Sacrifice. All these things are love. Love is never destroyed but transforms from one form into another.

From my own experiences, and in my own language, I believe there are seven types of love:

Tuon—The love we give to our close family—brothers and sisters, fathers and mothers.

Mar—The love we give to our extended family.

Tribe—The love we give to those with the same beliefs and perspectives; those who we would lay down our lives to protect. The type of love that builds communities and nations.

Reaw—Friendship love, extended to those whom we are not related to by blood, but whom we can trust with our lives, and who trust us in the same way.

Wuon—Selfless, purpose-driven love, unconditional and with no expectation, applied to anyone from family members to friends and strangers, even someone who may profess to hate us. This love works best when a person is in sync with the creator.

Rom—The love between two people who have decided unconditionally to give love to each other. Romantic love is demanding, with a lot of expectations and pain.

Kel—Self-love. A person looking out for themself and their well-being in order to be more productive and serving.

The seven types of love fall into two main categories: love for the self and love for others. My relation to both is run by emotion. When I am sad, I am mean to myself and others. When I am happy, I am kind to both. Basically, I give out whatever is in me. This realization gives me a view of love as the art of generating positive emotions, which can then manage our mental and physical states. If we feel prolonged sadness, it smothers our happiness and joy. If we become depressed, it seriously impacts ourselves and others. Feel energetic and hopeful, meanwhile, and we impact those same lives positively. When we are joyful and happy, we want our loved ones, friends, and communities to feel the same. Kindness, patience, joy, and empathy—emotions all based in love—generate positive feelings in our bodies. It is vital to understand that emotions play a huge role in running our lives, because emotions inform decisions. The summation of emotions we generate makes our decisions, and the summation of decisions we make every day creates our future.

Three Ways to Generate Positive Emotions

Spiritually: through prayer, reflection, and meditation. Faith, yoga, hope, dreams, forgiveness, and programming and reprogramming of self are all ways to generate positive emotions, as is the application of all ten principles of meditation in My Life Is Art.

Mentally: by generating positive emotions through what we hear, read, smell, taste, and see. Allowing our minds to absorb positive content puts us in a strong mental state.

Physically: through exercise, sport, sleeping, rest, dancing, and a healthy diet. It has been shown scientifically that exercise and a good diet both generate positive emotions.

Be warned—often people turn to outside influences to change their emotional state. Alcohol is a case in point. It is able to affect our emotions negatively or positively. People drink to gain confidence so they can socialize and forget about their problems, focusing on just having fun with friends and family. But overconsumption of alcohol can create a reaction in the body, which can influence emotions in a negative way, resulting in behaviors undesirable to ourselves and those around us. Also, when negative situations arise, alcohol can become the God we run to for help. Addiction is then a possibility, with its plethora of harmful medical conditions and emotions. Alcohol is just one of many drugs that pose this threat. Tobacco and marijuana generate a calming effect, but they, too, can be addictive and have a tremendous health impact on our lives.

LOVING OF SELF AND LOVING OF OTHERS

These are the two forms of loving that have transformed me beyond imagination. Loving of self is about providing ourselves with the basics of what we need. Food, shelter, clothing, water, rest, meditation, exercise, a sense of community, and spirituality are all essential for our well-being. Give ourselves what we need and not only do we benefit from that love, but so do others. Give ourselves what we want, and we lack fulfillment.

When I came to Canada, I didn't understand why I got so tired during the day. I was taking a lot of painkillers to address the body aches associated with my history of physical trauma, and I also suffered from migraines. I had early symptoms of diabetes and serious high blood pressure. I collapsed several times on tour and was hospitalized for three days, a time when I genuinely thought I was going to die. The medical staff tried to get to the bottom of my condition. One doctor told me it was genetics. Another said it was related to my experiences as a child soldier.

On another occasion, this time in New York, I was almost paralyzed. Luckily my manager, Tania Campbell Golding, is intuitive. She sensed something was wrong and stormed into my room where she found me in bed, body shaking and eyes rolling like a dying person. She put ice on my hands and a cold towel on my head. Those interventions brought me back to life.

The real problem was that I was so focused on activism, campaigning, and music that I had lost touch with loving myself. I never took the time to take a deep look into myself and think about what was making me feel ill. I stayed up late, woke early, and hardly rested. I ate fast food and my favorite drink was red wine and Coke. I hardly ever drank water.

In my culture, everyone dreamed of being fat. The more fat on a person, the more they would be respected. If a man was fat, chances are a woman would be interested in him. If someone was skinny and yet sought a powerful position, they wouldn't be trusted. People would believe they just wanted to get fat by stealing from them. This mentality was lodged firmly in my brain, so when I moved to the city, I ate all the foods that would make me fat, waking every morning with the hope of seeing my belly popping out. It wasn't that difficult. One time, I stayed in an apartment above a KFC. Breakfast, lunch, dinner—everything was KFC. I was such a regular they gave me a free meal every day. I became "skinny fat"—skinny with a hard belly. After a big feed, I looked like a snake that had swallowed a frog. As my eight-pack disappeared, so my one-pack began to emerge. Just what I'd always wanted! A big one, to show my friends back in Kenya, and that would earn me respect in my own country. It frustrated me that I couldn't get beyond "skinny fat." But in the end, I also understood that my pursuit of a big belly came at a cost. I could either love myself and live longer or try to get fat and die young.

I knew I had to address the root of my high blood pressure. I was reminded how, as a kid, people with high blood pressure from the city would come to our village. They would eat the local food, and after a few months would be well again. High blood pressure was a city disease, not a village disease. I decided to eat simply once again, like a poor person in the village. I would drink only water and eat fresh fruit. My city habits were hard to break. Fresh produce didn't taste great because I had become accustomed to processed foods. I forced myself to eat healthy but realized I needed to create the correct environment for the change to work properly. I made sure there was no junk food in the house. I also cut down on eating out, because when I did so I would eat like a pig, like there would be no food tomorrow. I shut off the triggers that sparked bad habits, such as negative environments and people who complain a lot. Again, meditation played a huge part. It supported me in creating an environment to help me persist with eating healthy. Instead of the old fast, processed food, I ate porridge and drank smoothies in the morning. Grains, beans, and vegetables formed my lunch or dinner. My health improved exponentially. I found more energy and my blood pressure returned to normal. I invested in loving myself by giving my body what it needed to give me more mental clarity and energy. In fact, the process of eating healthy led me to create my own superfood, Jal Gua, a blend of African ingredients that provides consumers with seven essential nutrients and vitamins. I always want to give what is in me, so I will always pass on knowledge, just as I hope others will pass it to me.

To truly conquer fear, worry, and poverty, we must first love ourselves and walk in gratitude for who we are, our talents, our skills, our lives. Loving ourselves plants positive seeds in our lives. We can then take time to watch those seeds grow, bearing fruits we can eat and share with others. When others say bad things about us, self-love creates a defense mechanism to protect ourselves from their negative attentions. Quick gratification is rarely the answer—chances are it will impact us in a negative way ten years down the line.

Loving others is the good that comes from our doing good for people. Do one good thing for someone and they will want to do ten good things for us. Do something bad and they will try their best to get us back a hundred times over.

Remember also that love is very different from want. Provide people with what they need and they will love us for life; provide them with what they want and, once we stop, they will not want to know us.

Loving is providing opportunities for friends, strangers, and enemies so they can enjoy the same benefits as us. Giving need not be a grand gesture. It can just be words—in fact, positive words are the most powerful gift of all.

GIVING CAN CHANGE THE WORLD

Two of the greatest gifts I ever received were **opportunity** and **forgiveness**. It is no exaggeration to say they changed my life, setting me on a path of enlightenment that would allow me to make a global impact.

Opportunity came to me via my savior Emma, who believed that education could transform a country and an individual. She worked with communities to set up classes in the shade of trees. Kids would sit there and learn how to read and write.

Emma rescued more than 150 child soldiers. I was the only one she smuggled to Kenya. She saw me standing with a gun almost bigger than myself and told me that if I put my weapon down, she would take me to school. It was like she read my mind. It was always my dream to have an education. Emma traded my gun for pen and paper. In so doing, she became my turning point, an angel sent to take me in a different direction.

No one can know the potential of a child until they are given an opportunity. The change of environment and gift of education set me up for success. It also set me up to give more and more.

Being able to read and write exposed me to more knowledge, and forgiveness was the biggest lesson I learned. When I was trained as a child soldier, my desire was to kill as many Muslims and Arabs as possible. Only later did I come to understand the real reason why people were being asked to kill each other. It wasn't ideology. It was gold, oil, free labor, and land. It happens all the time. The population of a certain area increases, meaning resources become scarce. At that point, elders justify invading the spaces of others by recasting them as monsters. The Arabs came to Sudan believing the land was theirs. Europeans, meanwhile, came to Africa armed with the idea that Africans were a subhuman species, justifying acts of terror on an unimaginable scale. The biggest threat to human existence is not the nuclear bomb. It is poverty—whether of food, land, or resources—which has always been our biggest enemy.

When I discovered this truth, I had the option either to forgive or to continue being the same. It was far from easy, but I decided to forgive those who caused me and my loved ones the greatest harm. I forgave myself too. That forgiveness could never have happened if I hadn't had a chance to go to school. To forgive was the greatest gift I was ever given.

LOVE MEDITATION

Setup

Find yourself a comfortable place. Bring yourself into the moment. Notice your environment, what you are wearing, your heartbeat, and the sensations in your body.

Fill your lungs to a count of twelve. Exhale to a count of fifteen. Do this three times. Let your breath return to normal. Breathe in and out through the nose. Find your flow and rhythm.

Allow your thoughts to fade away. Every time your mind drifts, bring it back to your breathing. Let go of everything and continue in the rhythm of your breath.

Out loud or in your head, say the love mantra:

Love is energy; love is power; love is kind; love is patient; love creates; love is about providing yourself what you need and also providing others with what they need. Love is the art of generating positive emotions that can manage our mental and physical state.

Take a moment to meditate on love. Feel it, enjoy it, glow with its energy. Become it.

Ask yourself how you can love yourself. Imagine the impact it will have on you.

Ask yourself how you can love others. Imagine the impact it will have on you and them.

Action

We can generate love physically, spiritually, and mentally. Consider the day ahead and incorporate some or all of the following elements to cultivate love.

Physically: exercise, movement, touch, dance, and eating healthy food.
Spiritually: prayer, yoga, faith, God, breathing, and vision.
Mentally: positive thoughts, plus what you see, hear, and smell.

Speak the following sentences to cultivate love:

- Today I will make sure I eat something healthy.
- Today I will exercise or dance.
- Today I will listen to something positive, read something positive, or watch something positive.
- Today I will meditate or pray.

- Today I will leave somebody ten times happier than I found them.
- Today I will rest my mind and my body and sleep well.

Closing Mantra

Out loud or in your head, deliver the love mantra:

> *I am love. I have love.*
> *Thank you, creator, for giving me love.*
> *I am love. I have love.*

13

MY LIFE IS ART

PRINCIPLE 2:

Yearning

YEARNING—FALLING IN LOVE WITH AN IDEA OR HAVING A burning desire to achieve a goal.

In South Sudan live the Naath, known as the Nuer tribe. Tradition states that when a boy reaches the age of twelve, he has six lines etched into his forehead with a tiny knife. A boy will bring something of great importance to him to the initiation, something precious he owns, or perhaps a girl he admires, to give him comfort and increase his pain threshold. The process is slow and if the young man moves his face slightly the lines may not come out straight—a negative result that will haunt him for the rest of his life. If the lines are crooked, it will affect how well he is respected. To a Nuer woman, straight lines indicate persistence, endurance, courage, trust, and every other basic principle that makes a man.

Initiation is every young man's worst nightmare and biggest dream. It yields great pain but delivers transformation into adulthood. What drives a young man to accept the ritual are the opportunities it brings—the self-discovery, purpose, and freedom to do whatever he wants with his life.

Those six lines define a man. But more than that, they are the six commandments that govern the tribe, which is again why the lines should not veer from a straight path. Those commandments are:

- **Courage:** A Nuer willing to die for their beliefs is respected. Such a person has no fear of death as it will unify them with their ancestors.
- **Control:** Emotional strength is key. A Nuer must show patience.
- **Respect** of peers and elders.
- **Loyalty** to those around them.
- **Justice,** equality, and freedom for all.
- **Seeking** a partner out of the family.

After a young man completes his initiation, he spends time with elders and warriors to learn warfare strategies and the wisdom to apply them. Young Nuer men dedicate a lot of time to training and preparing to fight. When they reach the age of eighteen, they become part of a group of three hundred young men with a self-defined and shared goal—raiding another tribe to steal their cows, perhaps, or taking new territory. They take this goal to family members to receive their blessing. Armed only with spears and shields, they set off to songs of praise and encouragement from their fellow villagers. There is only one rule—NORUS (no return until successful). Should they meet a challenge, retreat is not an option. They must fight to the last man. No get-out clause—win or die.

These characteristics defined the Nuer as fearless in the eyes of British invaders. The Nuer mentality was always "If you want something with a burning desire, you will give your life in its pursuit." The sadness is that some, naturally, never return.

The Nuer's all-or-nothing approach is an extreme example, but nevertheless it embodies the power of yearning: the thirst, hunger, fuel, and passion it provides. Yearning, like love, is a hunger that cannot be resisted, a desire that never goes cold. When somebody yearns, they do so with persistence and passion. They won't rest until they find what they need. Only then will they be free.

Think about it: a person with a full belly wants to play, rest, and party. A person with an empty belly desires only one thing: food. They might break the law to find it, but whatever they do, it will be with an intense sense of urgency. They will waste neither time nor energy, and they will continue looking until they are successful. Yearning will focus their mind to find the best idea. It will produce the positive feelings that create the necessary chemical reactions that support them in bringing that idea to fruition.

YEARNING PILLARS

Courage: The boldness that makes us knock on doors and ask for help. Sharing an idea with somebody is courage, as is the pursuit of what we desire.

Hunger: Anyone who misses breakfast knows what it is to get to mid-morning and feel like they could eat a horse. The chosen snack will probably be a Snickers, but you get the picture. Hunters in the wild are the same; the only difference is that they must find, rather than buy, something to eat. But hunger can be for a vision or an idea as much as for food, especially if it is something a person has put their heart and soul into achieving, because it will guarantee security for themselves and others far into the future.

Urgency: Most people fail in life because they don't have a drive, a sense of urgency. Most successful people will meet their deadlines. In doing so they improve channels of communication and trust. They also build a reputation for being reliable. Action is vital in getting things done.

Fuel: As long as a dream remains dear and important to us, it keeps fueling the fire that burns within. Whenever we think about it, we add more fuel to the fire. Stop thinking about it, and chances are the fire will go out.

Faith: We must believe we will find what we're looking for. Through faith, we can do things beyond our imagination. Lose faith and the project dies. Faith is the force that creates luck for us.

Persistence: We must generate the ability to break resistance, both within us and without; to do things even if they prove difficult.

Becoming a Rapper

"You can't rap," the producer told me. "You can't follow the beat. You lack passion and flow."

The first time I stepped into a studio, I was kicked out. I tried elsewhere and was kicked out again—and again—until I met two producers who showed me some support, Chris Adwar and Junior. Both shared one thing in common—they recognized my passion and respected my persistence. I gave them no rest until they gave me a chance, one time even jumping the fence at Junior's house and being attacked by his dogs for my trouble.

"I am not a thief, look at me!" I told one dog as it clamped its jaws on me. "I just came here to make music. I am Junior's friend."

Junior came to the rescue. The dog stopped barking and we sat down. I ignored the pain of the bites and concentrated on the music. A few dogs were never going to outweigh my desire to take my skill to the next level.

Dream-chasers have one thing in common. They understand that those who wait on God for opportunities to come their way will end up like vultures battling for leftovers. The hustlers will have grabbed everything. For dreams to happen, you must sleep like a soldier, with one eye and one ear open, and be fast and persistent. Yearning is one of the basic ingredients for greatness. It hacks new habits into the subconscious, transforming thoughts into ideas and onward into reality.

YEARNING MEDITATION

Setup

Find yourself a comfortable place. Bring yourself into the moment. Notice your environment, what you are wearing, your heartbeat, and the sensations in your body.

Fill your lungs to a count of twelve. Exhale to a count of fifteen. Do this three times. Let your breath return to normal. Breathe in and out through the nose. Find your flow and rhythm.

Allow your thoughts to fade away. Every time your mind drifts, bring it back to your breathing. Let go of everything and continue in the rhythm of your breath.

Action

Ask yourself what it is you are yearning for.

Can you visualize the desire?

Is what you are yearning for worth the input of time and energy?

Are you able to give up everything for this desire?

Is your goal one where you will not look back until you succeed?

Yearning Mantra

I yearn. I yearn for a positive change.

I have a burning desire to lead with a positive change.

Yearning organizes my mind to create positive thoughts and emotions.

It helps my body and organs generate the energy to holistically support me toward achieving my goals and dreams.

Thank you, creator, for I am yearning.

14

MY LIFE IS ART

PRINCIPLE 3:

Leading

I WAS VERY CURIOUS GROWING UP. THERE WERE NO LIMITS to my search for knowledge and my desperation to satisfy it, which was how I found myself in the company of generals.

One day, Dr. John Garang, the leader of the Sudan People's Liberation Army (SPLA), turned up to my camp to make a speech. We had been ordered to sit in our groups and I was so far away I could hardly see him. I was determined to get closer. My mind soon conjured up a plan. When he started speaking, I inched my way forward through the rows, unnoticed but for the odd slap, until I was sitting right in front of the esteemed visitor. I was in awe as I listened to a speech that was both funny and captivating. Dr. John used stories, metaphors, and poetry to emphasize his points. The crowd was cheering, crying, and dancing. Several women and boys fainted, so overwhelmed were they. It was as if he were a god talking to his congregation.

"Why is this man this way?" I asked myself. "How did he reach this position? How come he sounds so different?" I didn't have the answers, so I turned instead to a nearby soldier.

"Why is John Garang so powerful?" I asked him.

The soldier considered my question. "Because he cares about us more than we ourselves do," he answered. "He works harder than us and has a pure heart, which drives his intelligence. God chose him to lead us, the same as he chose Moses to lead in the Bible."

Later we had another high-ranking visitor, Dr. Riek Machar, a high commander in the SPLA. This time I took my chance to actually ask him questions. I wanted to know his views on leadership.

"We can all lead," he told me, "no matter where we are from. When we are true to ourselves and do our best to serve others, God will elevate us."

Growing up, I would seize any chance to quiz those with knowledge. Occasionally it got me in trouble, but the wisdom I received became my secret strategy for survival. I realized so much that is important in life comes from an individual showing the way, and that it can be any one of us, in any given field of life, who does so.

A true leader is a person willing to die so others may live. A soldier in the battlefield is a leader, but so is a street cleaner sweeping away a mountain of bacteria-riddled rubbish in a street in Ghana, or a fisherman in Haiti. Think about it and you will find we are all, in one way or another, leaders.

REQUIREMENTS FOR A GREAT LEADER

The Foundations of Leadership—AORAE

AORAE stands for:

- **Attention:** Gaining the attention of others is vital. It is how we present our vision to the public.
- **Opposition:** There will always be those who oppose. They are useful. Their presence delivers balance.
- **Reviewers:** Those who offer criticism, revealing areas for improvement and urging us to do our best.

- ▫ **Appreciators:** Those who love what we stand for and who will give us their all.
- ▫ **Enemies:** People who want us dead to make their own lives easier. Also people who, when they find common ground for survival, become our friends.

Leadership Characteristics—How Different Types of People Behave as Leaders

Purpose-driven individuals: Kind, hardworking, and caring, purpose-driven individuals have hearts that power the planet. They give without expectation and work harder than those around them. They express gratitude and calmness and blame no one. They hold nations together and are positive to the last.

Grabbers: Skilled at taking from others, grabbers prey on purpose-driven individuals. They give less, expect more, complain a lot, and are always self-promoting. They love nothing more than to bully those at the bottom of the food chain. Grabbers hold grudges. They never forget those they perceive to have caused them harm, waiting until the balance of power is in their favor, then punishing those who "wronged" them. Utterly merciless, grabbers believe in the survival of the fittest, the strongest, and the smartest. They are incredibly adaptable and will mimic others to worm their way into their lives. Once entrenched they will then exert control.

Justers: These people believe in love, equality, justice, and freedom for all. Society, and everything in it, should be fair. Help them and they will help you. Justers love protecting and supporting purpose-driven individuals. They never forget good deeds, so even when a grabber does something good, they will reward them. When things go wrong, they blame themselves. They harbor regrets. They believe things went wrong because they didn't do better.

Purpose vision-driven individuals: With purpose, ambition, and audacious goals, these people come up with creative ideas that raise the standard of the collective. They are community builders, selfless, goal-oriented, and humble, putting others before themselves. At the top of the food chain, they raise the standards of humanity and, if they create wealth, they share it with others. In politics, they advocate for laws that are good for people and the planet. Because of this, they are looked down upon by grabbers, but enemies respect them.

Just vision-driven individuals, or Justers driven by a vision: These people never forget. When they rise to the top, they remember everyone who has ever done them good and reward them accordingly. They are tough on crime, obedient, and set up systems that are fair to all. They can detect a grabber from a mile away and will confront them. Just vision-driven individuals reside in the middle of the food chain and are good and law-abiding citizens, often advocating for human rights.

Vision-driven grabbers: Highly competitive, vision-driven grabbers have big ambitions, can outperform everybody, are adaptable, and never take their eyes off the goal. They don't need a Plan B; they have a Plan A—to win. They prepare, work hard, and are highly intuitive, logical, and strategic, driven by both achievements and power. They want everyone to sing their name and praise them. Everything they do is large scale—and in their own interests. When they find power, they instigate laws that protect their interests, not those of the people.

The Five Stages of Leadership—PARGO

PARGO stands for:

Position: When a person is first given a leadership role, they face many challenges. They lack self-knowledge, so the jury is still out on whether they will become authoritative, a dictator, or an honest and humble leader. Those working with the leader, meanwhile, may lack direction and passion. They are still digesting the new leadership and may feel fearful of losing their jobs and security.

Acceptance: If people connect with a leader, they are willing to invest in their vision and, therefore, cooperate. An unconnected leader, meanwhile, will struggle to motivate those below them. They may have the wrong team or simply not be equipped to do the job, lacking the skills to get their vision across. They might not yet have discovered what they are truly great at. In this case, the leader must increase their mental power to create great leadership habits.

Reverence: At this stage of leadership, a leader knows what they are good at, delivering outstanding results with a team that is energized and motivated. The leader's motivation comes through devotion to their work and the love of their job. The negative comes if, having reached this stage, a leader turns their back on taking a company, community, country, or organization forward, preferring instead to make history and glory for themselves. If self-centered, often this kind of leader can become authoritarian.

Grant-masters: Having mastered their skills and talents, a leader identifies key talent in the organization whom they can train and prepare to fill their role. Everyone is passionate and knows what they are doing.

Optimizing: When a leader reaches the position of optimum leader, they can spend time developing other talents outside their organization and contributing their vast experience and skills to serving humanity. Such leaders often enjoy serving people for free.

Heart Power—Leadership and the Heart

The heart is like a king or queen. It has desires and wants to dominate and conquer. Only the mind defines its limits. To realize our ability to lead, we must understand the power of the heart. One of the first organs created, the heart knows all our potential. Therefore, if we don't live up to that potential, the heart will never give us peace. There are three sources of heart power—bitterness, purpose, and self-interest.

Bitterness

There was a time when I was terrified on the battlefield. Government forces were shelling us with artillery and bombing us from jets and helicopter gunships. The stench of rotten bodies blew on the wind. The wounded groaned in pain. Three soldiers, overcome by fear, shot themselves dead. My head created story after story of how I was going to die. It was totally and utterly terrifying. What kept me from giving up was not prayers, but bitterness, a desire for revenge.

"If I am going to die here," I told myself, "I want to do so with dignity. I will not just let the enemy come for me. I will take down as many as possible."

In doing so, I found strength. I understand that a heart powered by bitterness is toxic, but in war, on the field, it delivered the power for me to carry on in my hardship. It made me feel like a man.

Purpose

We have already learned that purpose can make us rise beyond what we couldn't possibly imagine. It is why I believe a purpose-driven heart has the power to bring peace to the whole world and make our planet sustainable, because it is driven by the well-being of others. The courage to give, forgive, and let go is the greatest attribute we have. When my first opportunity came to go to school through a scholarship, I happened to be spending a lot of time with other former child soldiers, one of them named Mayiel. One voice told me to take the opportunity. But another said I should give it to Mayiel.

"I have given too many opportunities away already," I pointed out. "If I give Mayiel this opportunity, what is going to happen to me?"

Mayiel's success will be your success, the voice told me. *When your opportunity comes, your heart and mind will know.*

I gave the opportunity to Mayiel. I felt drunk with joy, and a year later, as the voice had signaled, my chance to go to Brookhouse School came along. It proved to be a stepping-stone to my music career. The owner of the school became a mentor and funded my first video.

Purpose allows us to put others first, outweighing our fear of being left behind. It allowed me to discover my vision and open my mind to infinite possibilities. To this day, this singular and deeply rewarding type of heart power sustains me. It makes me understand that I have an opportunity to be part of a solution, to restore balance, and to surrender to the greater cause. It is what I value the most.

Self-Interest

Those who believe their heart is there only to cater to their own needs and desires are driven by ego, blind to the needs, wants, and feelings of others. Inevitably, they hurt people along the way.

As a soldier, there came a point where I decided to hide food from my starving child comrades rather than share it. I blocked any empathy for a week, but in the end I couldn't bear the emptiness in my heart.

Something similar happened in the refugee camp. I would go to the UN hospital pretending to know a sick patient. Being able to read meant I could read names over beds. I would tell the patient a story and then, when they closed their eyes to sleep, I would take their biscuit rations, protein bar, and whatever other food they had been given. Not everyone was taken in. The kids may have been ill, but their intuition hadn't been dulled. They knew I was there to rob them. However, the nurses couldn't understand their protestations. They saw me only as a likable young boy visiting his friends. Eventually, I was caught. My punishment was to be locked in a store full of biscuits.

"Eat them all!" I was told. "Shame on you!"

I didn't touch any of them. I felt only disgust for myself. I am grateful for the actions of those who caught me. If they hadn't corrected my behavior at that early stage, I don't know how my life would be today.

Sadly, self-interested people are all around us. Such people would betray a whole village for a glass of wine.

MENTAL POWER

I used to ask questions. *How do white people fly in the sky? How did they manage to conquer the world? How do they make tanks? How come Arabs can enslave us in millions? Why are Black people on the bottom of the pyramid? Where is the food dropping from the sky coming from? Are white people fallen angels or are they aliens? Why is my life going round in circles? Why do I repeat the same mistakes? How come my problems keep following me wherever I go?*

Such questions drove me crazy. However, the more I was exposed to learning, the more I came to understand mental power, which set me on a path of positive self-development. Nowadays, I blame no one for being a barrier to what I want to achieve. Previously, when I hired someone to help me in my music, or as an entrepreneur, and they had failed to perform, I would complain about how poorly they were working. Now I think differently. I hired them, so it was my lack of mental power that meant I didn't get the right person for the job. Mediocre people hire mediocre people, and great people hire great people. Mediocre people hire quick and fire slow. Great people hire slow and fire quick.

To increase my mental power, I spent a year learning about the five faculties of the mind—consciousness, intuition, imagination, subconsciousness, and memory—analyzing where I needed improvement. By doing the same, you also can improve your lives, training your brain to find what you need and want.

The Five Faculties of the Mind

The Conscious Mind

One night a vision transformed my life completely. I was asleep in bed in Toronto when a huge light appeared. It was so strong that even with my eyes closed and covered with my hands, I could still see it.

Three entities appeared. "Everything is looking for attention and collaboration," one told me. "Pay attention!"

The entities carried me away to far-flung galaxies. It was freezing, but they kept me warm. When my eyes became accustomed to the brightness, I saw beauty in incredible detail going on for millions of miles.

"Everything is looking for attention and collaboration," repeated the entity.

I was told to look at the moving space particles and to pay attention to one in particular. Initially, I struggled to focus on any single particle as they were moving so fast. When finally I managed to do so, it stopped.

"Give it your full attention," I was told. "Connect with it with all your heart, mind, spirit, body, and soul." I did as I was asked and the particle became much clearer. Inside it were yet more particles buzzing around.

The entity told me to talk to the particle. I asked it to make my face, which it did immediately. It was as if I were looking in the mirror. Later, back in my bedroom, I wondered just what had happened. Had I died? Met angels? Been abducted by aliens? I was excited and shaking, wondering how I was going to apply the knowledge I was given. It set me on the path to learning about the conscious mind, the source responsible for deep thinking, planning, reason, logic, organization, strategy, and programming and reprogramming. It is also responsible for manifesting our dreams and managing our resources, energy, and time to create positive outcomes. It makes 5 percent of our decisions every day.

The more I discovered, the more I came to understand that my conscious mind was weak. I needed to make it strong. I found that the conscious mind learns through curiosity; it becomes more powerful by accessing information. More than ever, I opened my eyes to the world around me.

Intuition

To make the right judgments, we must be able to discern situations. Intuition comes into play when logic and reason do not provide an answer. When a conscious mind and intuition join forces, making correct decisions is even more under our sway. We will learn more about intuition in the coming chapters.

Imagination

Imagination is a creative faculty and learning institution rolled into one. It captures thoughts and turns them into ideas, expanding them to become better, clearer, and more memorable. Imagination also delivers visualization of concepts, plans, and visions. It brings perception, consciousness, and intuition. Increasing our imagination allows us to enter into new ventures, explore new opportunities, and see possibilities where there appear to be none. It brings harmony where previously it didn't exist.

As a child, imagination was my friend. When the pain of reality became too much, I escaped into a world where I would see myself dancing happily, playing, and jumping around. I would even fool my senses. In my mother's tongue there is a tree called *thou*. It has bitter seeds and leaves with a nutty punch. This tree became our food source for months. We ate it morning and evening, and I hated it. The only way I could manage was by fooling my sense of taste, imagining the seeds were nuts mixed with beans, cow butter, and sorghum grain. Now I enjoyed this bitter tree.

As I grew older, I began to see that my imagination was dying out. I didn't use it as much. While I had the desire to be imaginative, the reality was a challenge. I was taken back to a game I used to play in my head as a child soldier. I called it the "thought game." When a negative thought came into my mind, I let it pass. When a positive thought—playing with baby sheep, seeing my mama smile, being part of a solution—popped up, I would not only capture it but let my imagination complete it for me. Often I would laugh out loud at where my imagination took me. The game stopped when I went to school, but I was inspired to bring it back after stumbling across the inventor Nikola Tesla, a man wholly driven by imagination, whose many electrical innovations, most notably alternative current, paved the way for the technology we enjoy today. Tesla had the ability to see with his eyes closed. He could visualize exactly what he wanted to create in his mind. I thought of others whose imaginations had changed the world. Martin Luther King Jr., for instance, whose vision of equality brought us his "I Have a Dream" speech. Such external output reflects our internal creation.

After thinking about those whose imaginations have changed the world, the revival of my childhood game made sense, so now when a negative flashback comes into my mind, I don't react to it. I just let it be. That way it cannot have a significant impact. I stay still, silent, and wait for other thoughts to pass through my head until a thought I like comes along. When it does, I react to it quickly and allow my imagination to build it into something that will make me smile, be joyful, and be hopeful.

The thought game has played a huge role in my life. At various times it has banished fear, trauma, anxiety, and worry from my head. It has given me peace where none otherwise existed. But I am not special. All beings possess the ability to create.

The Subconscious Mind

Whenever I lived in a peaceful environment, I always saw myself as right and thought everyone else was against me. I would often make wrong choices that got me into trouble. It was only later, while studying psychology, that I came to realize that my subconscious was at the heart of this disastrous pattern of decision-making.

My background, as ever, was at the heart of the actions of my subconscious. War, poverty, and hunger were just part of the accumulation of trauma in my mind. My subconscious saw my childhood as a reason to lead me into situations that would bring even more "drama" into my life. A traumatic event can hack into our subconscious at any age, but whatever slips into our subconscious mind at a young age will dominate us when we grow up.

Science backs this up. Long-term research on a group of children in New Zealand found that predictions made based on their behavior, health, and well-being at age three mirrored their lives at age twenty-three. The subconscious is massively informed by what we see and hear as a child. And what we see and hear we will put into practice. We will find it difficult to correct subconscious behavior, because learning and trying new things becomes harder the older we get.

As someone still dealing with my own childhood setbacks, the research resonated with me deeply. Had I not found loving human beings to give me second chances and guidance, I would have been doomed. Dealing with my past made me committed to reprogramming my subconscious mind, adding habits and beliefs to govern me and create my future. I know also I was lucky. A lot of adults are effectively walking children. Their "failures" in life can be directly attributed to their upbringing. The subconscious runs 95 percent of our daily lives. Habits, beliefs, productivity, you name it—the subconscious directs it all, acting so fast in its decisions we don't even notice. The conscious mind does the stuff that requires deep thinking while the subconscious hums away in the background, a software constantly absorbing and saving information for future use, the accumulation of which builds a person's character and personality and affects their day-to-day decision-making.

It makes sense, then, that a child raised in a violent atmosphere would have difficulty with learning, self-control, focus, and discipline. They would be enormously troubled, and their difficulties would be exacerbated by the fact that the conscious mind is not activated until they reach the age of seven, meaning their perceptions of the world would be well set by that time.

In Africa, a child is seen as being raised by their village, so growing up I was beaten by both strangers and family whenever I was considered to have done something wrong. The worst time came when I was between seven and nine. I got in trouble on a weekly basis and was hit by seemingly every adult around. I couldn't understand how and why other kids got it right and I didn't. Force was deemed the only way I could obey orders and do my duties well. I wonder how different my subconscious would have been had beliefs and habits been implanted in me in a more positive way. If we provide our subconscious with the right habits and beliefs, it will grant us our wishes and dreams on a silver plate.

Ask yourself: Do you think your subconscious requires an upgrade?

Memory

Memory collects and stores information for short-term and long-term use. Words, language, numbers, friends, enemies—everything we know is stored in our memory. Everything we do depends on it.

My interest in memory was heightened by my brain's inability to absorb information when I really needed it to, a situation at its worst when I was in high school. I would walk into class, sit down, and listen to the teacher, but afterward, I was unable to remember anything. As other kids discussed what they had learned, my own academic experience left me with an inferiority complex, planting a belief in me that I was not intelligent. I even developed a negative mantra—*I am not smart, I am doomed, I am a failure.* I often wonder, when I pass people in the street, what is going on in their heads and what false and destructive beliefs they harbor about themselves.

No matter how hard I tried, I just couldn't figure out why others could remember better than me, why I had to work ten times harder. This challenge haunted me well into my thirties. On stage I would forget lyrics or come in on the wrong beat. The only way I could keep on track was to perform the whole set in my head before the show.

As an entrepreneur, storyteller, activist, and actor, I needed to figure out how to improve my memory so I could achieve my goals. I read and watched so much about the subject. One fact I discovered was that one of the greatest thinkers of all time, Albert Einstein, had challenges with his memory. He struggled, but managed to overcome the issue with purpose, getting smarter and smarter all the time. The more I read, the more my mental belief that I was slow and stupid was dismantled. My ability to absorb information increased exponentially. I could remember most of my dreams vividly.

I came to understand that I could rewire my brain by creating new communication pathways. I ate a well-balanced diet and challenged my brain in ways that were unusual to me. The approach backed My Life Is Art and made me even more committed to my daily practice. It confirmed My Life Is Art as a 360-degree approach to life.

Tips to build your memory

- Eat super brain-foods such as almonds, peanuts, avocado, and blueberries.
- Meditate to relax the brain, create mental space, and relieve stress.
- Create positive habits and beliefs.
- Manage your environment to support your well-being.
- Eliminate negative self-talk.
- Be curious.
- Sleep well.
- Exercise or play games.
- Do yaya, yoga, or dance.
- Practice gratitude and appreciation.

- Do everyday things differently—for example, walk home a different way.
- Protect your brain from radiation emitted by devices such as phones and computers.
- Practice visualization.
- Look at and memorize a picture.
- Listen to your surroundings—pick one sound and give it your full attention.
- Make your bed with your eyes closed.
- Identify spices and fruits only from taste and smell.
- Identify objects only by touch.
- Challenge your brain to do something important when you really don't feel like doing so.
- Eat ghee butter and fish.

Remember:

Memory doesn't disappear with age. Like a muscle, it can grow with proper nutrients and exercises.

A great memory will set us up for success.

A great memory is the power that drives creativity and productivity.

Mental power is best illustrated in terms of the entire self. If the human body is a country, then the heart is the monarch, the conscious mind is the prime minister, the subconscious mind is the government, the cells its citizens, the imagination the creative industries, and memory is the land upon which everything is constructed. Intuition, meanwhile, delivers policy provided by the intelligence and counsel of advisors.

When the heart wants something, it communicates its desire to the conscious mind, which then discusses the matter with the imagination, intuition, subconscious mind, memory, and cells to see if it is possible. The conscious mind checks the resources available and its capacity to perform the task before delivering its answer back down the line.

Most of the time the heart is like a baby. It doesn't understand reality and puts want over reason. If it is persistent, the subconscious will see if it can deliver its request. If it can't, it will pass it on to the conscious mind for consideration. If again the answer is no, all other avenues fail, and the heart continues to make demands, the mind will impose its force. It must do so in order to stop the heart from using valuable energy and resources. If the heart refuses to accept reality, and the conscious and subconscious mind do not act, the result is conflict. The kingdom will be divided, resulting in anxiety, worry, loss of hope, and depression. It is not wrong for the heart to push, because it knows our potential. But for our own good, the mind may need to impose limitations.

The key to moving forward is exposing ourselves to more learning, setting up routines that prepare us for future challenges, and going beyond the limits of our imagination.

What we put in our mind is what will grant us our wishes. That is why we must commit to self-improvement. The more habits and beliefs we accrue by accepting challenges, the more we create a new us.

15

PRINCIPLES OF LEADERSHIP

VISION

IT RAINED FIRE AND THE RIVERS TURNED RED.

In the Sudanese Civil War, hell came calling. No matter how fast or how far we ran, it always caught up with us, taking aunties, uncles, and my mum to a place of no return. Hell took my innocent soul and replaced it with one tainted by death. Witnessing such suffering made my heart bitter. Every cell in my body hurt. There was no letup. Every day brought new challenges. All I could do was bottle up the poison and hope it didn't kill me as well.

As a child, I wondered how the suffering could be stopped, driving adults crazy with my questions. At times, I was lucky enough to escape reality by slipping into dreams. I would be fighting the enemy alongside my father, handing out food to hungry children, or be surrounded by so many cows that when I climbed a tree, I was unable to see the end of the herd in the distance.

In my dreams I possessed superpowers. I could fly, fight ghosts and demons, or turn myself into stone or water. One time, I even went to the moon. These dreams may have been weird and wonderful, but they also gave me energy and made me feel special. The challenge was how to turn my dreams of a better life into reality. Mum always told me that education was the answer. But schools barely existed in rural Sudan. So, to lift my spirits in those dark and perilous times, I turned to mantras.

"I am going to acquire education," I would tell myself. "I want to be part of the solution."

From that point on, I used nightmares as a lesson on how to avoid life's perils, and beautiful dreams as a guide to making a better world come true. In my imagination, I would get drunk on the possibilities and joy of the future.

I wanted to become a doctor, a teacher, a pilot, or even a priest. Christianity was a strong influence, and I imagined myself born again, baptized as Peter, Abraham, or John Jal. One day a traveling preacher told me about Mary Magdalene, one of Jesus's most celebrated disciples. Afterward, I approached one of his assistants and told him I, too, wanted to be called Mary Magdalene. He laughed—"That's a woman's name!" I didn't see why it mattered. It was her character, her strength, that fascinated me.

I tied myself to anything that might give me the strength to become part of the solution to the desperation that surrounded me. My desire was such that my father sent me off to school in Ethiopia, an ambition that would end instead with my becoming a child soldier. The journey to Ethiopia was hellish. I watched children as young as six years old leave or bury their own dead who had been unable to survive the drought and starvation. It was too much to take in. The only refuge I had was my imagination. I saw myself flying an airplane, bringing food and water to my people. Instead of the featureless plains, I would lose myself in a heaven of honey, water, and milk. Instead of suicidal thoughts, using my imagination I found peace of mind and was able to sleep well. I believed that what I saw in my head could come true, and that belief kept my heart joyful.

Okay, I didn't become a doctor or a pilot, but one element of those childhood dreams remains. I always want to be part of the solution, not the problem. With the support of some great individuals, I have created three companies, founded a charity, and rebuilt a school for two thousand children. Yes, I might not have yet arrived at the 100 percent beautiful place of my imagination, but I will always pursue that dream. Travel that path and you will witness many good things along the way. A vision clears psychological blockages in our mind.

What I saw in my head and believe in my heart has brought me this far. My vision kept my hope alive, made me curious, made me a hustler, and attracted those who changed both my life and that of so many others. That vision now has evolved to sharing my experiences in the cause of conscious global awakening through the arts, business, and philanthropy.

A vision is something we see in our minds and feel in our hearts. It is the ultimate force that keeps hope alive; a visualization of something imagined and created in the mind. It is an energy of thought, transformed into an idea with a clear, distinct purpose, backed up by imagination, strong emotion, faith, enthusiasm, and a burning desire to achieve.

When we have a vision and begin to believe it, live it, and breathe it, we radiate a strong electromagnetic field that attracts others toward us. We are designed to help one another achieve, to manifest our dreams and desires. Have a vison that benefits only yourself and you will end up hurting others in its pursuit. Have a vision that benefits others and you will be joyful in life. Even in our hardest times, we can still try to grow an orchard to feed others.

Act selfishly and you will experience short-term gain and long-term pain. We are created for the betterment of one another. Ignore that aim and anxiety, stress, depression, unworthiness, lack of confidence, and illness will be your long-term companions. People who seek just to give themselves pleasure are doomed, a boat drifting inexorably toward the rocks. If we don't know where we are going, how can we have direction?

We all have the power to create the future we want to see, but first we must picture it in the mind, feel it in the spirit, and believe it in the heart. A single thought can create connections and possibilities.

INSPIRATION

In the pursuit of our own vision, we can take great heart from the actions of iconic individuals who have achieved so much down the years. Many of those I admire came to my attention via the woman I call my "Kenyan mum"—Mrs. Mumo. She talked of Mahatma Gandhi, whose vision was to see Indians govern themselves, a right to be acquired through nonviolent means. Gandhi overcame the might of the British Empire and led his country to independence without firing a bullet.

William Wilberforce's vision, meanwhile, was to end slavery. As a Christian and a man with integrity and high moral values, his conscience would not allow him to die without having challenged the enslavement of his fellow man. Learning about Wilberforce planted a seed in my heart. Kindness and the willingness to do good can overcome the odds.

Martin Luther King Jr. dreamed of a United States of America where people would not be judged by the color of their skin but the content of their character. He was assassinated for his beliefs but not before rallying millions behind his cause, an unstoppable force that ushered in a new wave of equality.

To enjoy life fully, every one of us must have a vision. A dream has the capacity to reprogram us to aim higher in life and in so doing discover our best selves.

COMMUNICATION AS A PRINCIPLE

We must be able to articulate our message clearly to ourselves and others. If we don't understand it, how can we expect to communicate it to others? Poor communication is both careless and disastrous.

To be most effective, we need a 360-degree approach to communication. What we wear, how we walk, how we talk, how we feel inside ourselves, our daily actions, and how we present ourselves can all affect us or others positively or negatively.

One Saturday morning, I meditated for five hours. By the end, I was drunk with joy. At that time my businesses were not doing well, and I had personal, political, and family issues occupying my mind. My meditation provided me with so much energy that I felt I was floating. I threw some clothes on and stepped out of the house. My shoes, hoodie, and jacket were all black. I looked like a teenager about to rob a convenience store. I jumped off my train and a young woman approached me.

"Can I talk to you for a moment?" she asked.

The woman was beautiful and well-dressed. I was dreaming of finding a wife at the time and wondered if I'd been sent a gift from heaven. Then my thoughts turned darker—perhaps she'd been sent by an enemy to poison me for something I'd said about the conflict in South Sudan. So many things were running through my head. I even thought maybe she was looking for marijuana.

I stepped closer to her. "Go ahead," I said.

She looked me in the eye. "I had a breakdown this morning," she told me. "I just wanted to talk to someone outside my usual circle of friends. When I saw you, I was confused. The way you dressed freaked me out, but your face and body communicated a different energy that was calming and peaceful. I felt safe sitting opposite you."

Her honesty was remarkable. I told her my name and she told me hers was Alexandra. We walked to a nearby food court and sat down to talk.

"I have two jobs," she said. "Mainly I work at a restaurant. My side job is prostitution."

My jaw dropped. I couldn't swallow my food.

"I am married with two kids," she explained. "My husband and I are immigrants in Canada. He had a great job at a bank but was paralyzed in a car accident. Doctors say he will recover with time, but because we are immigrants, we cannot access the family support system. I get paid peanuts in the restaurant, whereas as a high-end prostitute, I can earn up to a thousand dollars for four hours' work. But such a lifestyle has eaten away my confidence and dignity. The only way I can comfort myself is that I am doing it for my husband and children. My husband doesn't know how I made this money, and I will never tell him. You are the first and only one to know."

The woman was in tears. Our food sat uneaten and cold.

Her opening up, communicating in such an honest manner, moved me. I reassured her that what she was doing did not make her a bad person. I talked about the demons in my own past.

When the time came to go our separate ways, I asked her to give me her number. She told me there was no need.

"We are now connected," she said, "and your story will live inside me, like my story lives inside you."

She thanked me for not passing judgment on her. "Sharing my story with you has given me freedom."

"When the universe allows," I told her, "we shall connect again."

It is said by some communication experts that 45 percent of a message comes from tone of voice, 45 percent from body movement, and 10 percent from the actual words we say. I believe this is true. When this woman opened her mouth, her tone demanded my attention and made me trust her immediately. Her body, hair, eyes, tears, posture, and hand movements spoke louder than any words. When she did talk, her words made me think. She connected with my heart, made me smile, made me want to cry. It was as if she were directing my emotions, keeping me glued to my chair. She was a great storyteller, and I hope she goes public with the terrible situation she was placed in someday.

Communication with clarity is the key to achieving. It is a skill that can make us—or, if absent, destroy us. It is the key to our survival.

Through it we can make friends or enemies, encourage people to stick together or fall apart.

KNOWING YOUR LISTENER

Knowing our listener is vital. Whether as an entrepreneur, artist, activist, or performer, I got along with some people very well. With others, it was a head-on dogfight. Not understanding the type of person I am talking to has caused me breakdowns in business, political, and personal relationships.

I have encountered four types of listeners in life: those who are talkative, those who are thinkers, those who operate visually, and those who feel. Know our audience and we can adjust according to their needs and wants.

Talkative people like to dominate situations. They process their thoughts as they talk. Put them in an environment where they will have to do the listening and they won't enjoy it; they'll get bored. Such people want you to get straight to the point. I am in the talkative category, but I have learned to adjust my brain so I can listen more.

Most talkative people are good at showing initiative, but when it comes to long-term projects, they often rely on others to see them through.

Thinkers like to know where they are going and how they can succeed. They talk little and are interested in facts. They apply reason and logic and are great at building strategies. They see danger coming because they are naturally cautious. Such people take time to process their thoughts before they open their mouths. When they do speak, they have evidence to back up what they are saying. Talk to these people and they expect you to take the same approach.

Visual people see pictures when we speak to them. Highly imaginative, they don't want facts; they want a story. Visual people like to win and love to plan things big. They can envisage the future and make great communicators and listeners. Detail oriented, they use both intuition and logic to make decisions.

Those who **feel** seek the deepest meaning in words. They want to understand and are not ashamed to ask questions. Like worker bees, they have a lot of energy to accomplish goals. They don't waste time, are well organized, and are detail oriented.

ASSUMPTION

When I was a soldier, communication was everything. We had to be like meerkats, observing, listening, smelling. A single error in communication could cost thousands of lives. There can be no assumption when it comes to communication between generals, officers, and soldiers. When a general gives a command, the officer should listen carefully and attentively. If the officer instead makes assumptions about the message, and the subsequent action goes wrong, then they face being heavily punished. Similarly, if the general assumes clear communication but the orders are then carried out wrongly, they, too, will be accountable. Naturally, those charged with carrying out the orders, the soldiers, will lose trust in their command. Their viability on the battlefield will be affected.

If our message is not articulated or communicated properly, a listener may make assumptions about our intentions. Assumptions are dangerous—like crossing a busy highway without looking left and right.

CONFIDENCE

If we are to lead and expect others to follow, then we must be confident in what we are saying and doing. Confidence is faith in self. When the time comes, we are confident that we can stand up and perform our task. Confidence is also knowing that, if something goes wrong, we have the inner strength to get up and try again. It is believing that we can handle the challenge we have been set; that we have the skills and the will to overcome any situation that may arise.

Whether it's going for a job interview, raising children, or facing rejection, achieving anything is difficult without confidence. But we can all acquire confidence. Some are born with it; others learn it along the way. Every time we overcome a challenge, we build confidence and foster a belief in ourselves that we can succeed even though others may lack faith in us or project their own fears and limitations in our direction. When we then realize our ambitions, even our detractors will find confidence and enlightenment in our success. Lead a life with confidence and we pave a path for generations to come.

Confidence: My Lows and Highs

In Kenya, I felt lost at school. My work was unpredictable. Sometimes I would pass with high marks; other times I would fail terribly. I found it hard to settle, was deemed problematic, and was expelled many times. I loved education but, it seemed, education hated me.

A breaking point came when I failed my high school exams. I attempted to continue my education at a different school, Brookhouse, one of the best in Nairobi, but with no money for the fees, and low grades to my name, a scholarship was out of the question.

Even so, I sat for the school's IQ test—and failed it miserably. The principal said that my heart was willing but my head was saying no. He advised me to go to polytechnic to learn a skill.

"He has a very low IQ," he stated. "Higher learning is not for him."

That sentence shattered my confidence. My head went blank, and my stomach boiled to the melting point. In that moment, a belief was born in me that I was stupid. After all I'd been through, my internal energy, desire to live, and self-worth disappeared. The sentence kept playing back in my head, and every time it did so, I saw myself as more and more unfit.

Low IQ. Low IQ. It was all I heard. The constant negativity triggered desperate childhood memories and nightmares. I could barely function. In public, I would wear a mask of energy and excitement, not showing any sign of weakness. When I was alone, however, I felt deeply damaged.

Somewhere in that darkness, a memory nagged at me that insisted confidence could be brought to life by core beliefs. Amid all the negativity flooding into my life, I could at least remain confident about one thing: I had survived for a reason. I could make a contribution. It was my only window of hope.

That belief gave me a reboot. My confidence increased incrementally until I could tell myself, "I am not stupid, and I am not useless." I made it my goal to prove that to myself and to others. People noticed this change in attitude—including that same principal, Mr. Manze, who so affected my self-worth. A few months later, he called.

"There is something I forgot to say," he began. "Emmanuel Jal's EQ, his emotional intelligence, is far greater than his IQ, and it is clear to me he will achieve great things. We have never given a scholarship based on EQ, and I am going against my rules, but we would like to give him the opportunity to come to Brookhouse."

In terms of events that transformed my life, this was one of the most amazing. Mr. Manze had no idea of the gift he had given me. His words opened the floodgates on a tide of self-belief that washed away the idea that I was stupid and useless. At Brookhouse, I ended up winning a community service award for staging a charity concert. My emotional strength gave me the ability to win that award.

I am lucky that Brookhouse was way ahead in welcoming all kinds of students and gave me the chance to study there under the scholarship. Confidence is self-belief. It can be shattered, but it can also be gained, through one's core beliefs and knowledge, and perfected through daily practice. Confidence can be found within us or gained from others. Like a muscle, it needs to be nurtured and provided with an environment to support its growth.

Confidence will:

- give you an upbeat, forward-looking personality
- allow others to trust you
- allow others to see the true you
- provide safety and security to those around you
- make people want to be associated with you
- make you perform better
- allow you to become a star

16

FURTHER PRINCIPLES OF LEADERSHIP

LEADING WITH QUESTIONS

I WAS PLAYING CHESS WITH RICHARD BRANSON. THE GAME was fun, and we chatted as we competed. Immediately, I noticed something. He asked questions—again and again. How was I? How was my work going? What challenges was I facing? How could he help?

I was amazed. I thought someone with the life and business experience of Richard Branson would just talk. He knew it all, right? But the more he spoke, the more a realization washed over me. *Asking questions is vital if a leader is to succeed.*

However, there is more to success than just asking questions. They have to be the right questions. Great questions ignite innovation and lead to solutions. Asking such questions means we act in a forthright and positive manner.

Analyzing myself afterward, I realized that as I had grown older, I inquired less and less. The only time I could remember asking a lot of questions was as a soldier. Every day, questions, questions, questions. I asked questions, my fellow soldiers asked questions, the officers asked questions, the commanders asked questions, the general asked lots of questions. I was amazed by how intensively and curiously the senior military gave their full attention. They took notes, their egos disappeared, and they became like students again.

Questions, I learned, reveal danger, help avoid failure, and unearth hidden wisdom buried deep within us. I saw the same approach when I came into contact with great world leaders such as U.S. presidents Jimmy Carter and Bill Clinton; former Mexican president Ernesto Zedillo; South African president Nelson Mandela; and his fellow Nobel Peace Prize winners, the former Finnish president Martti Ahtisaari, who worked so hard to end numerous international conflicts, and former United Nations General Secretary Kofi Annan. Questions were also important to Jane Tewson, the British charity worker who brought about Comic Relief, a biannual event raising millions for good causes across the world; Tibetan Buddhist leader the Dalai Lama; business tycoons ranging from the aforementioned Richard Branson to Sudanese-British telecom billionaire Mo Ibrahim; female empowerment spokesperson Angelica Fuentes; Google cofounder Larry Page; and health and well-being pioneer Radek Sali. Historically, we're told, people asked questions of leaders, yet here were these amazing leaders doing exactly the opposite. What gave these people the attitude of leading with questions? The truth is great thinkers have always been curious.

Albert Einstein

Einstein is perhaps the most esteemed of scientific minds. Yet often he would escape the adult world to teach piano, violin, and science to youngsters.

"You are wasting time, Albert," his colleagues would tell him. "You should be concentrating on more important things."

But Einstein loved teaching children because they ask questions. Hearing the thought processes of young minds made him analyze his own methodology. Curiosity, to him, was the key.

It is said that, on occasion, Einstein would spend an hour formulating a question and then take just five minutes to come up with the answer. It was just such an approach that supposedly led him to create the formula $E=mc^2$, which paved the way for modern quantum mechanics.

Consequences of Not Questioning

On the long and perilous journey to start school in Ethiopia, the Nile was one of many obstacles that stood in the way of the realization of my dream of holding pen and paper and reading a book. A boat was on hand to make the crossing. The captain was ordered by the military commander who accompanied us to fill it up. A thousand children, myself included, waited. Herded aboard, we were crushed together like sheep. There was no room to breathe. The boat was low in the river. Water lapped against the red danger line on its side. The captain told the commander that the 150-person capacity had been reached. He didn't listen. He demanded the captain take more, backed up by the threat of setting armed soldiers on him. Shaking, fearing for his life, the captain allowed more kids to board. There were now 250 crammed in. The boat set off across the broad, deep, fast-flowing river. Not long after, water began to flood in on one side. Instinctively, we moved across to the other side, but it was useless. In less than a minute the boat capsized.

Only sixty of us survived.

Had the commander asked the captain the significance of that red line, chances are those lives would have been saved.

Asking the right questions is the way to green pastures. Asking the right questions shows us where the devil has laid traps.

What questions are you asking of yourself and others today?

Types of Questions

Constructive questions make us find solutions. They provide room for collaboration and allow us to build relationships. If somebody wrongs us, for example, we can approach the situation by asking, "What is the best way forward now? What can I learn from this challenge? How can I avoid this same scenario?"

Destructive questions create havoc. They absorb energy and bring fear, worry, and distrust. Instead of working toward solutions, destructive questions provoke blame and division. We can ask them of others: "Why are you so stupid? Did you even think before you acted?" Or we can apply them to ourselves: "Why me? Where did I go wrong?"

We can correct the situation by asking constructive questions: "What is the best way forward? What will make this better?"

Deep questions are difficult to answer. They can panic us if we believe we don't have the capacity to handle them. When analyzed, though, such questions make us see things previously invisible to us. They become like a torch in the darkness, a North Star to give us directions. Deep questions require us to reflect, meditate, research, and ask for help. They challenge our thinking and organize our thoughts to find the facts that will lead us forward. Deep questions bring success; they make us great.

Shallow questions are easy. We can answer them in our sleep. They don't add value or growth to our lives. They don't make us see the future.

Open questions spark discussion and create an atmosphere for ideas to flow. An open question doesn't have a defined answer. Each person has their own viewpoint.

Closed questions require a straight yes or no answer. "Did you do it?" "Do you love me?" and "Can I do this?" are all examples of closed questions.

Changing my mindset to leading with questions has given me added strength. It allows me to either focus or relax, depending on my needs. Knowing I can find answers when I need them means my brain can switch, clear of fog, worry, and fear, into meditation or the simple joy of everyday experiences, leaving me with a reserve of mental energy when I need to address more serious issues for a long period of time. But to truly succeed in leading with questions, we also need to practice humility and discipline.

The Principle of Humility

The Titanic Tragedy

At the time it was built, the transatlantic passenger liner *Titanic* was the largest man-made moving object on Earth. Its 1912 maiden voyage from Southampton in England to New York caused great excitement. At the ship's helm was one of the White Star Line's most experienced captains, Edward Smith. However, when other ships reported icebergs in the North Atlantic, urging caution, the captain neither slowed down nor changed course. The rest, as they say, is history. The liner hit an iceberg and sank, causing the loss of more than 1,500 lives. Had Captain Smith asked the right questions about how to avoid a possible collision, and acted on the answers, the *Titanic* would never have perished.

Humility gives us perspective. It allows us to value every person we meet and to walk with truth and purpose.

In the Naath culture, humility is a way of life. No man or woman is allowed to tell somebody else what to do. The correct way is to ask, "Sister (or brother), can you help me with this?" This approach reflects a way of life built on relationships, serving one another, and knowing that you are who you are only because of the love, respect, kindness, and protection offered by others: "You are who you are because of us, and we are who we are because of you."

That spirit of brother and sisterhood means the Naath serve each other with pure intention. They expect nothing in return. The spirit of humility allows them to stay deeply connected to core collective values.

Humility means controlling our temper, treating other people the way we would like to be treated, and obeying the same rules we would expect others to. It means sacrificing ego and swallowing pride so there can be peace. It means being willing to die so others may stay alive.

Humility is the highest form of respect for others. It is the ability to recognize that we can learn from everyone. It allows us to recognize those with skills we don't have and step aside for them to teach us, as they would in return. Humility is like becoming a child always eager to learn.

Isaac Barrow

Isaac Barrow was an esteemed seventeenth-century theologian and mathematician at Cambridge University, holder of the Lucasian Professorship of Mathematics, one of the most prestigious academic posts in the world. One of his students was Isaac Newton, himself a mathematical genius. Barrow was deeply impressed by Newton, to the extent he shared his student's work among other great scientists of the era. Moreover, to demonstrate his profound respect, Barrow stepped down to himself become a student of Newton's. Isaac Newton became the next holder of the Lucasian Professorship of Mathematics.

In the same position, many people would act only to protect themselves. However, Barrow's great humility allowed him to recognize that Newton would make great leaps for the knowledge of humanity.

Leadership is recognizing that other people can be better than you. To be leaders, we must also be willing to become followers.

The Principle of Discipline

Discipline is the art of managing our emotions, directing them to do what we need to do even if we don't want to.

Forced Discipline

Forced discipline may come through parents, community, law, or culture. People may apply harsh discipline to children because they fear that without it, they will stray from the straight and narrow. Coming from a culture where a child is raised by the village, I had my share of beatings by strangers to correct my behavior.

I also experienced violence from others. Before I became one myself, I admired child soldiers. While I wanted to go to school, I still revered their strength. On one occasion, I saw such a soldier in the Panyindu refugee camp. I was excited and asked him questions. He was having none of it and slapped me so hard that I saw stars. I actually blacked out.

The soldier's attitude only spurred me on. *Wow!* I thought, as I hauled myself to my feet. *I want to be as strong as that.*

Not long after, the boys of the village were gathered and told we, too, were going to become soldiers. I looked forward to the training. I imagined making my mother in heaven proud and saw myself killing people on the battlefield. It was as scary as it was exciting.

The training wasn't what I thought. We were welcomed with a beating, shouted at, and bullied. Fear and violence were the tools our trainer used. I felt like my soul was being raped. My spirit crashed through the floor. I wondered just what I had wished myself into. Every time I slipped back into my old self—chatting, asking questions, laughing out loud—the trainer would beat me. It was as if the trainer never slept. Everywhere I went, he was watching me. If I went to the latrine, he was there. I'd look up from my plate at mealtimes and he'd be staring straight at me. I assumed he was giving me special attention because I was different from the other kids, not good at being told what to do, wanting to do things my way.

At night, one of us would be assigned to guard duty. One time on my watch, I slept intentionally to see what would happen. Next morning, we were beaten almost to death. We cried until there were no more tears. The trainer told us we worked as one, and my sleeping had risked the lives of everyone. He made us do push-ups, kicking one boy who refused so hard in the skull that he vomited blood. I never saw him again. I did the push-ups, but cheated, lucky that for once the trainer didn't see me. I realized more than ever that this place was no joke. Basically, we were slaves to our masters.

Then one day a trainer spoke to me. "Jal," he said, "you hate me now but one day you will experience a real battle and then you will love me." He was right. The lesson I learned was hard, but when the time came to fight, it saved my life.

Do a mediocre job and you jeopardize yourself and those around you. The military uses force and fear to instill discipline because it is the quickest, most efficient process. Soldiers have to obey orders and do their duties. It is a matter of life and death. The chain of command must work.

Self-Discipline

Self-discipline is powered by our core beliefs, purposes, wants, and needs. With self-discipline we can enjoy our lives in full and achieve audacious goals.

Self-discipline comes from our reality, observing our parents or guardians perhaps, or the way we form an understanding of the world and how our futures could pan out. That education, if it comes, gives us the desire to organize ourselves and develop strategies.

As an activist, artist, and entrepreneur, I apply self-discipline. My drive to do so comes from the desire to create positive change. I did what I had to while in the training camp because the alternative was severe punishment or death. Now I do so under my own will. That isn't always easy. In the battlefield there is no safety net. In real life, we don't immediately see the perils that could come from not being disciplined. But self-discipline, on any level, is important. Think about it. Self-discipline allows our actions to speak louder than words. And it can be applied in all areas—dieting, finance, education, work, business, relationships, everything.

Inherited Discipline

In Nuer culture, marriage is a big thing. A person marries not an individual but their family, friends, and beliefs. Both sides want the next generation to inherit good habits and beliefs, and one of the finest qualities in a potential newcomer is discipline. Any suggestion of laziness and the marriage is off. Even a history of procrastination in a family could affect the viability of a union. In our culture, discipline is wealth.

One time, I was talking to a group of young people in Canada, including an Indigenous woman. She looked sleepy, and as I shared my story, I felt myself judging her for her lack of attention. I was astonished then when afterward she asked to talk. I found her captivating. She was so ambitious, reserved, and thoughtful.

The young woman explained that as a Canadian Indigenous woman she was at risk. "We face domestic violence and death," she told me. "Canada doesn't care about us natives, and the world has turned a blind eye."

The things she told me were horrific. Like many Indigenous women, she had been raped multiple times. Murder, she said, was common—young men and women disappeared only to be found abandoned dead at the side of roads or in the bush.

"Emmanuel," she told me, "I want to make an impact in my community, but I have one big problem. I procrastinate. I am behind in my assignments, my grades are poor, and I want to quit school. I need discipline to keep me in the game of life."

"Where do you think your procrastination comes from?" I asked.

"It is a curse passed down to me," she replied. "Jobs are hard to find for Indigenous people. My parents drink alcohol and sleep in the day, as their parents did too."

She explained how her parents had given up, and that she was going the same way, too, finding it hard to find the discipline even to make her bed.

"My heart is willing to change," she said, "but my habits are pulling me back. If I could only find discipline, I would transform my life."

My head went blank. I didn't have the deeper advice she needed. All I could say was that discipline comes through practice. Now my advice would be different. I would tell her to build discipline by reading thirty stories about the subject, by saying "I am discipline" a hundred times in the morning and a hundred times before bed, and by visualizing her self-discipline, making it a reality by completing small tasks.

That young woman remains imprinted in my mind. Wherever she is on the planet, God bless her soul. She completely shifted my thinking. Now when I speak and see somebody lacking attention, I think of her and what a curse inherited attitudes to discipline can be.

But it is a curse that can be broken.

What Fuels Discipline?

Simple—emotions. Positive or negative emotions drive us to achieve our goals; negative feelings sabotage them. Discipline builds and protects our vision. Positive feelings deliver that discipline.

Positive emotions to create self-discipline and build a vision:

- Desire for change
- Belief, hope, and faith
- Love for family and friends
- Finding common ground with strangers
- Courage
- Positive thinking driven by mantras—"I am strong," "I can make it," "I am wise," "I am smart," etc.
- Encouragement from others
- Uplifting music
- Good health generated by eating well
- The buzz of testing oneself mentally, physically, and spiritually

Negative emotions derail discipline, leading to the slow fulfillment or even death of a vision. Examples include:

- Baseless fears
- Bitterness and being unforgiving

- ◻ Unfounded worries about the future
- ◻ Envy and jealousy
- ◻ Greed and selfishness
- ◻ Unworthiness
- ◻ Anger
- ◻ Leaping to wrong conclusions
- ◻ Bad eating habits
- ◻ Lack of drive

Anyone can learn to be disciplined. It's a habit we all can create. But to do so, we should be aware of the existence of procrastination and persistence.

Procrastination, continually putting things off, is the enemy of anyone who wants to lead. To progress we must add discipline to our psyche to provide order, focus, and structure in our lives. In my case, I used my passion to create the positive emotions that gave me the discipline to drive my vision of being part of a solution.

The Principle of Persistence

To persist to stand by your truth. To follow your vision with your mind, heart, soul, and spirit, even if it proves to be difficult. It is the conscious effort to apply absolute determination to resist any negative pressure. It is the willpower, the internal force, that pushes us to find a way forward even when every avenue seems to have been blocked off.

Persistence is fueled by the condition of the heart and the mind. It is precious and must be treated with care; otherwise it can wear out. It can run out of gas. Persistence behaves like a muscle. It requires rest. Think how you might halt every few steps when you carry a heavy bag up some stairs. It's the same with persistence. When we have goals, objectives, and tasks they must be done one at a time, step by step.

Treated correctly, persistence is the force that drives us to try every possible option to get what we want. We can learn from that persistence, even if we have to wait thirty years. Remember, most people jump on an idea and then give up after a few failures. To succeed is a lifetime commitment, held together by persistence, bound by a concentration of effort, and driven by purpose.

Molai

Let me take you back to 1979 and introduce you to sixteen-year-old Jadev Payang, nicknamed Molai. Walking along the River Brahmaputra in Assam, India, Molai was in tears, shocked and dumbfounded by what he saw. Thousands of animals had washed up on a sandbar by an island. The island could have been their salvation, a place to settle and thrive; instead, it was barren and uninhabitable.

Molai reported the situation, but the authorities were unmoved. He tried to mobilize locals to help, but again they were reluctant. So he did it himself. Every day for thirty years he planted a tree on the island, creating a thriving ecosystem.

The forest now spreads across 550 hectares. It is home to tigers, rhinoceroses, apes, and all kinds of other wildlife. A herd of a hundred elephants visits every year. Jadev's work so impressed government officials that they named the forest after him. Molai Forest is now internationally recognized as an example of how people can make a huge and positive impact on their environment.

Molai's story is a reminder that if we really want to do something we should do it regardless of what other people think. We should do it because it is our purpose. It is our calling. It is our discipline. As we can see from Molai, persistence makes things happen.

LOYALTY

Loyalty is one of the greatest qualities we can ever possess. It can be applied across the board to relationships, friends, businesses, and nations. At its core it is about a sense of belonging. It is about knowing that we are there for others and they are there for us. That if we fail, people will not run away. They will be there with us, just the same as if we succeed. Loyalty is an important trait for leaders to possess.

Professional Loyalty

Working in the professional world is both challenging and risky. When an employee makes mistakes or fails to achieve their goals, an organization may well fire them. A better approach would be to find out why they didn't reach those goals. Maybe their role wasn't aligned with their strengths. Maybe they just needed motivation. Either way, a conversation would have been the way forward.

Sadly, the business world is full of leaders who are not loyal to their employees. When a company performs well, praise is thrown around. When that company dips, those instrumental in its success find themselves made redundant or replaced. A better way to behave is to understand that businesses have ups and downs. Employees should be assured they will still be on board when the curve moves back upward. Just imagine if a tribal leader behaved in that way—if a tribe was facing difficult times and so it chased some of its members away, only to recruit new members when things picked up again. Anyone watching that scenario pan out would think it was morally wrong. But what is a group of employees if not a tribe?

Employment provides safety and financial security. Loyalty to employees means thanking them for their contribution and creating a healthy and inspirational environment in which to work. The greatest loyalty of all is shown when a leader makes sure those who work hard alongside them enjoy the same benefits, be it bonuses or pay increases. Success should be shared, and if a boss won't do that, an employee is justified in looking for one who will.

The disadvantage of being loyal is that it can leave us open to exploitation from grabbers—those who manipulate us into thinking they are something they aren't. Grabbers are a virus in an organization, there only for themselves. Unless they are identified and dealt with, they drain us, grind us down. It is important we be aware.

It is complex, I know. We don't always know who is there for us, and our logic and intuition can be hacked into by those seeking to twist our will. But there is a way to measure trust and loyalty. Fail miserably and those who are loyal to us will still show their faces; those who are not loyal will run away.

Loyalty is only one factor in our relationships with people and the world we need to be aware of—there are plenty of others too.

RAPPORT

Rapport is the ability to find common ground with somebody, to leave them in a happier state than when you found them. Rapport is also the ability to read people and speak to their needs by giving them hope.

When we talk to someone, our brain is designed to look for either agreement or disagreement. Disagree and we shut down; we go into defense mode. That person then becomes an enemy. Rapport, however, brings another element into the equation. It is emotional intelligence. It is connecting with a person even if you disagree with them. Without rapport, we lose every beautiful thing that person has to offer. We paint them simply as a threat. We must be aware of being sucked into that trap.

Sociologists have shown it can take less than a minute to connect with someone, five minutes to like and accept someone, and two hours to love them. Our appearance—clothes, hair, the way we talk, laugh, and smile—plays a part in building rapport but is outshone by the revelation of our true selves. It is easy and understandable to adopt a character and hide elements of ourselves if we like a person and want to establish a relationship, but honesty from the start should always prevail. That way we know if a connection is being made on a true and open basis. Only then can trust between two people exist.

The bottom line in building rapport is giving back what we are receiving. Listening is a case in point. It shows respect and demonstrates that we value a person and are ready to help or serve them. If we have a problem listening, then we should train ourselves. For example, listen until a natural opportunity to talk arises. When it comes, don't change the topic but discuss what they have said.

Show people they are important and we create the necessary bond for long-lasting relationships.

COMPETENCE

As an entrepreneur, I began to notice set patterns. I had great ideas that started out well, only to hit a plateau. I would hire people but then they would move on. There always seemed to be politics in the workplace that made for a difficult environment. Work would be done at a mediocre level or not at all, and no one would take responsibility. I lost money and my business lost relationships.

I decided to stop and reflect on my leadership style. What I found was enlightenment. I realized that what was happening in my organization was a reflection of me. The people I hired were not at fault, I was. I was the one who chose them, after all.

If we are incompetent we reduce the productivity of those around us. I began to ask myself how I could increase my competence. That question humbled me and set me on a lifelong path of self-development. I know now that competence is the ability to achieve while maintaining focus. A competent person understands that they cannot be good at everything. A competent person keeps developing what they are great at. They seek to practice that greatness every day.

Learning about competence gave me the required skills to grow my ideas and business. The areas in which I'm not great, I delegate to others. The challenge when we start out alone is that we can't delegate, but having knowledge of our competence means we can navigate those waters until we can bring someone in to take up the oars. Picking the right person is a great quality that can be applied across our relationships, family, business, and friends. It is an exchange of knowledge, making all sides feel a sense of belonging.

The professional world is both challenging and risky. When it comes to those I work with, I prioritize the heart of a person. I want to know what they aspire to be rather than focus on what they are now. My manager, Tania Campbell Golding, is someone I respect deeply. Hers is a tough business where people have been known to backbite. Successful and very wealthy businesspeople have told me that I should change my management, that Tania isn't the right person to take me to the next level. Some have given me ultimatums, demanding that if I want their support then I must fire Tania.

To me their words are madness. Why would I ever fire Tania? She is incredible. She knows her job inside out. She works tirelessly and can be reached any time. She is exactly the sort of person who will take me where I need to be. In my culture, she is family. She has been with me through some terrifying situations, not least the peace concert in South Sudan (see Chapter 9) where we both survived multiple threats against our lives. Tania, her twin Amy, and her friend Simine refused to leave the country until the concert was done. We lost a lot of money on the back of that trip, but Tania continued working for me, on many occasions for free.

Whatever the situation in my life, whatever my mistakes, and at a point where anyone else would disappear, Tania will always say, "We are in it together." That's what comes from strong relationships. What also comes is belief, profits, and growth. I know that Tania brings values which are embedded in her core principles. It's not easy to be an activist and a rapper in a world where everybody wants rewards immediately, but Tania's actions have always demonstrated a strong belief in my work. The help she provides me and my organization is priceless.

SKILLS AND TALENTS

To be competent we must have multiple skills and talents, backed up with knowledge, practice, and leadership.

A **skill** is something a person does with confidence. Someone who practices a specific skill for a long time becomes a specialist, perhaps even a genius.

To be effective in our modern, fast-moving world, we need five skills at which we are adept and one in which we are specialized (i.e., a specific skill practiced over a period of years until we become a master). My skills are reading and writing, as well as being multilingual and academic. My final skill, farming, comes from my youthful days looking after cattle, sheep, goats, and chickens. Performing would be a good example of a specialized skill.

Talent is something a person is born with. They don't need to work hard for it to shine. They might be funny, a great singer, or an excellent communicator. Everyone has a talent, although some don't know it.

Identify your talent, hone it, and bless others with it and it will open doors for you, putting you at a higher frequency.

My talent is storytelling. It is rooted in my imagination and drives my creativity. Had I known my talent earlier, I would have invested in it at school, studying subjects that would have enhanced its growth. Now I have embraced it, I can apply it in all kinds of areas to give people joy and happiness.

DECISIVENESS

To achieve competency, we must refine our decision-making. There are several ways we can make our decision-making razor sharp.

Thinking Like a General

In 2017, I closed my Jal Gua Café in Toronto. It pained me to do so. Jal Gua was more than a café; it was a community. But the business was operating at a huge unsustainable loss. There was no way I could ride out the bad times. The good times simply weren't going to come.

I spent two weeks thinking like a general in a battlefield. I put away my emotion, subconscious mind, imagination, intuition, and memories and concentrated my conscious mind on the facts. It wasn't easy. For all involved, closure was like we were letting our home go.

With the cold, hard facts on board, I then opened the debate to the rest of my mind. There were so many random questions and statements in my head, it was as if I were on fire. But one question more than any other battled to be heard: where could I concentrate my energy, time, resources, and discipline to find less resistance and a greater return? Asking this question was the turning point. I closed the Jal Gua Café, and my focus became My Life Is Art.

Thinking Clearly Under Pressure

Each of us will face hard and easy decisions. There is no escaping that truth. Some decisions will be life or death, while others will be as simple as deciding what movie to watch. But to progress in our daily choices, we must bear in mind that some decisions require logic and reason, others require intuition, while still others are heuristic.

Making decisions shapes our lives. Each one helps to write our history. Knowledge, then, is vital if we are to avoid pitfalls. The subconscious mind goes through its decision-making process at warp speed. If we are to make good decisions then we need to program the subconscious with the right habits, experiences, emotions, and beliefs. What we feel about the past, present, and future will strongly affect how we act given any challenge or opportunity.

The ability to make the right decisions is an art developed over time. But in the end every decision can be pared down to applying focus, whatever the source.

When we are in a survival state, we often don't make smart decisions. An example of poor decision-making was when I was auditioning for the film *The Good Lie*. The process was something new to me and I didn't understand why I had to keep going back to audition over and over again. It was tiring and confusing, so when they asked me to fly to America for the final audition (which I didn't realize was a live screen test alongside Reese Witherspoon), I nearly declined, opting to go give a talk to a school instead. My manager and friends rallied around and explained to me calmly, many times, the bigger opportunity I could be losing. Thankfully I finally took their advice and went to the audition. If I hadn't taken a moment to reassess my position, I wouldn't have starred in the film and benefited from the amazing opportunities that happened as a result.

The gift of decision-making is one we all have. Research indicates that an adult makes around thirty-five thousand decisions every day, many without even realizing, as they come from our subconscious. Children, meanwhile, make roughly three thousand decisions every day. Most of their decisions are made for them by their parents, guardians, and community.

I was blown away by this news. Had I been spending year after year wasting energy? After all, making fewer decisions in the day has its advantages. Armies wear uniforms and are constantly drilled specifically to minimize decision-making. I knew I had made many terrible decisions in my life. How could I make better decisions? Who could I learn from? I wasn't going to reprogram myself to make better decisions overnight. We make decisions about food, drinks, clothes, social media, jobs, friends, relationships—the list has no end. The ability to make the right decisions is an art and a skill that is developed over time.

Intuition and Logic in Relationships

A man decided to look for a wife. He wanted a marriage that would last a lifetime and decided to use logic to aid his search. He wanted a woman with a master's degree in psychology, a good job, focus, ethics, and who had been raised in the countryside. He drew a line down the middle of a piece of paper and, according to his criteria, wrote down the positives and negatives relating to each woman he met. When he found a woman where the positives exceeded the negatives by 80 percent he asked her to marry him. Nine months later they divorced. The man had used logic and reason—math—to find a wife. But math is an illogical way to choose a partner. There is no calculator that deals with relationships.

Another man didn't care for positives and negatives. He wanted to make an intuitive choice. He and his wife had little in common, yet the relationship worked. Did this man get lucky? Probably not. When it comes to building relationships, intuition makes the best decisions. At a cellular level, intuition tells us whether or not we will always love the person in front of us.

But there is no such thing as a "perfect relationship." Success depends on each half of the partnership finding personal, spiritual, mental, and emotional growth and commitment to face uncertainties and find solutions to continue in a common purpose.

There is regret when an instinctive decision goes wrong. But that may be because the decision has been made in either the heart or the mind. Combine them both and together they operate well.

A Forest Siege

A besieged commander in the Sudanese Civil War was brought news by an officer that much-needed reinforcements had been ambushed. Casualties were heavy and survivors were being hunted down like antelopes. Ammunition and food supplies had been captured. The officer said the enemy would reach the commander's position within the next four hours and was already covering any possible escape channels. The commander gave no reaction. He stared blankly ahead. Eventually, the officer touched him. There was no response. He had no pulse. The hopelessness of the situation had killed him stone-dead. When we are unable to make a decision, it puts us in a paralyzed state. Our system is overwhelmed. Making a decision creates activity.

The second-in-command was now faced with the same bleak scenario. He gathered his soldiers.

"Look, gentlemen," he said, "we are losing the battle, but our cause remains worth dying for. Let us show our enemy that our cause is our life. Let us concentrate our energy and take down as many enemies as possible. No retreat. No surrender. We will fight hard and if we don't make it through alive, we will still write history."

It was a tough battle, but the soldiers gave their best, eventually breaking through the enemy defenses and gaining the upper hand. Not only did they survive, but they retook control of the area.

When I heard this story, I was reminded of a young South Sudanese woman, known as Captain Nyapuoch, faced with a seemingly impossible challenge when South Sudanese government forces pounced to raid her village. Tanks and troops were heading straight for her community. She knew their intentions only too well—genocide.

Captain Nyapuoch had two options. The first was to join her fellow civilians running for shelter. But she had a newborn baby. No way could she run fast enough. In fact, even had she been alone, the chances of reaching safety were slim. Instead, as the government forces got closer, she grabbed an RPK machine gun from a man who had frozen with fright. She had a single thought: "If I can finish off the soldiers, then my baby can survive." She hoped also that the example of a young woman taking on the might of the government forces would give hope to others and spur them into action. Without hesitation, she fired on the soldiers. Taking them by surprise, she wiped them out. But the tank still came at her, firing shells indiscriminately. It seemed her fight was over. Yet the shells failed to explode, sliding and slithering instead in the mud. Diving into a bunker, Captain Nyapuoch found another villager and a soldier, this time with a rocket-propelled grenade. The soldier, too, was paralyzed with fear. She took the weapon and fired the round. It was the deciding factor. The tank took off and the village was saved.

Hers is a great example of an intuitive decision (she was under attack and had to do something to survive) based on logic (taking on the advancing forces was the only way to survive).

Heuristic Decision-Making—U.S. Airways Flight 1549

Chesley "Sully" Sullenberger was captaining U.S. Airways flight 1549 when it left LaGuardia Airport in New York on January 15, 2009, with 155 people on board. Shortly after takeoff, both engines were disabled by bird strikes. Air traffic control gave him the option of three airports at which to make an emergency landing. Sully felt sure he could not reach any of them. In that moment, with absolute calm, he made a decision to land in the city's Hudson River. Air traffic controllers were shocked, but immediately rallied behind his plan. Minutes later, the plane touched down on the icy cold water. Everyone was saved.

How did Sully reach this remarkable decision? He applied heuristic thinking—a practical answer, a combination of logic and intuition, that may not be perfect but is sufficient to achieve an immediate goal. He used his logic to estimate the distance to the nearest airports and saw he couldn't make it. The option to land in the Hudson didn't guarantee safety but was better than anything else. That delivered his heuristic decision—the outcome would ultimately decide the wisdom of the choice.

Such challenges dig deep into our psyche. Sully's mental power, his heart power, and all his leadership qualities and experience were put to the test that day. The result was that he became a hero. He made history. By applying heuristic thinking, he achieved a focus that saved multiple lives.

It is very important in decision-making that we choose the right process—logic, intuition, or heurism. One plus one requires logic. A relationship requires intuition. A stricken plane with nowhere to land requires both.

Before making a decision, ask yourself these questions:

- What exactly is the decision I need to make?
- Is it an opportunity or a problem?
- Is it hard or easy?
- What information do I have?

- ◘ Is there anyone who can help me?
- ◘ Do I have enough time to think?
- ◘ What does the negative impact look like?
- ◘ What does the positive impact look like?
- ◘ What do I want to achieve with this decision?
- ◘ Does this decision require logic and reason?
- ◘ Or is it intuitive?
- ◘ Are my heart and mind united in making this decision?

TIME

We need to reflect on how we spend our time. We have created a system where everyone thinks they are free, when in fact we have been programmed to accept being chained to the system. Some work hard for little money. Others make loads of money but create little or no time for their loved ones.

My three children, Nyakang, Jal, and Shang, have all been raised by their mothers. I never created as much time to be with them as I should. I was wrapped up in my activism and, ironically, seeking a way to live outside the modern Western system that mentally destroys people. Sometimes I wished there were thirty-six hours in a day. It was the only way I could do what I felt I needed to. And that was without the mental, political, and emotional challenges that also form such a major part of modern existence.

The Western attitude to time was such a mental shift for me. Where I come from, time is not something people take seriously. If somebody tells you, "Let's meet in ten minutes," it means an hour. It took me a while to adjust to this new way of keeping time. I had issues at work because I would turn up late for important meetings, but my worst experience came when I visited Finland for a major event hosted by President Martti Ahtisaari. I spoke and performed and then later there was a dinner. My manager Tania told me to be on time. I, however, saw myself as someone who goes with the flow.

"There will be important people there," she reiterated.

In my head I thought, *Okay, that means they will be late too.*

I was wrong. By the time I arrived, everybody was already seated, including my hero, Kofi Annan. My chair was the only one empty— and dinner was not going to be served until I was in it.

As I sat down, I felt that every eye was judging me. I tasted nothing but embarrassment. I wanted to bury myself alive. Even later, back in my hotel, the same feelings of shame consumed me, although no one else who had been at the dinner even mentioned it.

From that night on, my conscious mind told me always to respect time. My subconscious mind, meanwhile, sought to reprogram me by asking questions of my behavior. Why was I always late? Why was I so disrespectful? What was so important to make me late?

Only eight years on, when I sought to find out what else is important to me apart from my vision and purpose, was I able to fully understand time and my relationship with it. After deep meditation, I realized time is a gift that I have been given, just like everybody else. Just as the Earth never spins backward, I can never get it back.

I wondered if, forty years on, I would look back, happy and joyful at how I used my time. Such thinking changed my perspective, prompting me to invest more deeply in relationships with colleagues, family, and friends. Without relationships, I realized, I am doomed. Relationships cannot be traded. They have no price tag. The only currency with relationships is time.

TI^2—Time, Impact, and Income

My new relationship with time allowed me to develop a formula. Whenever I am asked to do something, I ask a myself a question: "What is my TI^2?"

When, for example, we give our time to sleep, the impact is rest, and the income is energy, health, dreams, focus, healing, and rejuvenation.

When we give our time to a job, the impact is productivity, and the income is shelter, clothes, food, protection, and other needs.

When we give our time to family and friends, the impact is care, kindness, and presence, and the income is the same, plus peace of mind, self-worth, and emotional and spiritual support.

When we give our time to education, the impact is productivity, skills, and value in the marketplace, and the income is a better job, better payment, respect, and other benefits.

I used to spend so much time on social media, scrolling, flipping from page to page, hour after hour just gone. The time consumed, without purpose or clearly defined goals, gave me stress, migraines, insomnia, and unproductivity. When I go on social media now, I first ask, "What value will this give me? What is my TI^2?" When I go for a meeting, I ask the same questions.

Time has a value of its own. If family is important to us, we should create time for family; if friends are important, then we should do the same. This is an unchangeable truth.

Time and Love

I fell in love Daniella, a beautiful South Sudanese girl. She was tall with smooth skin and was a better rapper and lyricist than me. I admired her for her intelligence and how she challenged me to deliver quality work.

At the time, major media outlets such as *The New York Times*, BBC, and CNN were covering my activities. I was getting paid for making music. The fact that creativity could sustain me was truly amazing. Opportunities were flooding my way and I was at a junction. One way offered more time with the woman with whom I had fallen in love; the other offered travel, excitement, and money. I tried to go both ways at once. I would turn down gigs to spend time with Daniella, loving our time together, but then I would regret missing out on my purpose and vision. On tour, meanwhile, I would miss her terribly. We tried a long-distance relationship for a while, but it didn't work out. My heart was broken.

Thankfully, I had a system to help me through such periods of personal trauma. I fasted, prayed, and meditated for three days. Having purpose in my heart, vision, and mind put me in a better place, like entities living inside me.

Questions also fast-forwarded my healing.

Are you able to love Daniella without expecting anything in return? Yes.

Are you able to let her go? No.

My meditation conversed with me. *You chose to give your purpose and vision more time than Daniella, and that's why she has to find somebody who values her more than that.*

More conversations followed. It took a while to get myself completely together, but those internal questions gave me a head start. I learned the greatest-ever lesson about time. It is a finite resource. You give it to something and equally it is lost elsewhere.

My son asked me once, "Dad, do you love me?"

"Why are you saying that?" I asked.

"Because you are busy and never around," he replied.

Those words took longer than they should have to sink into my head, but I came to understand what really is important in life and tried to create a balance where it could exist.

In this precious life, balancing our time is what delivers 360-degree success. Those who give time to building wealth above time for their family are those whose relationships become broken, whose bonds of loyalty are snapped. Those who give more time to their loved ones have relationships that stay strong.

Remember, each minute is a gift. Yes, we can sell it, but we can also give it for free to those who mean the most to us.

How are you using your time? How is it affecting your relationships? What is your TI^2?

17

MY LIFE IS ART

PRINCIPLE 4:

Ideas

IDEAS COME TO US IN THE FORM OF THOUGHTS. WHEN WE react to a thought, it attracts others in the creative faculty of our mind to form an idea. Apply more ideas to support that initial idea and we can form a big idea. If it is super-big, it becomes a vision. When we imagine the impact of that big idea and can see it in our minds, it means we can create it. All a person needs in life is one good idea. That idea might transform both their life and those of others. It might transform a community, a country, the globe. Ideas are what structure our world. They are in the air around us. Angels deliver them to us every day, as do demons, and the cells within ourselves.

IDEAS: THE SOURCE OF BETTERMENT

Research by the National Science Foundation, an independent agency created by the U.S. Congress to advance health and welfare, shows that the average person has between twelve thousand and sixty thousand thoughts per day. Of those, 80 percent are negative and 95 percent are repetitive. When I read this research, I was relieved. "I am not mad after all!"

The same research shows that 85 percent of what we worry about never happens and that the other 15 percent more often than not makes us stronger, smarter, and more knowledgeable, creative, and purpose driven. In essence, 97 percent of our worries are entirely baseless, a pointless source of stress, tension, and exhaustion not only for the mind, but also for the body. The truth is we have the capacity to use lessons learned to take care of future needs and to climb out of peril.

The Magnification of Ideas

We can learn a lot by immersing ourselves in thought.

A thought entertained for more than thirty seconds soon morphs into an idea. Our imagination then magnifies it, increasing the chances of it becoming a reality. The source of an idea can be positive or negative. Stress, success, religion, teachers, our environment, and experiences all provide scope for enlightenment, bringing with them spiritual and physical wealth. A thought does not exist in the physical world, but if we invest belief in that thought, it can become real and impact people's lives.

Capturing the right thoughts can transform our lives in incredible ways. In ancient Naath, or Kemet, now known as Egypt, someone came up with the idea of building the pyramids as the final resting place for the pharaohs. In more recent times, the Wright brothers designed a working aircraft; humans have journeyed to the depths of the oceans, the heights of Everest, and into space. All these ventures were once just ideas.

Sometimes we don't even have to come up with an idea from scratch. We can draw inspiration from what already exists, innovate, and take it to the next level by applying our own creativity. Through innovation we are able to push the bar higher.

Evolution of an Idea

I was elected to become a youth leader for the Consolidated Association for Sudanese Youth, an organization set up to help the young people of my homeland work through the endless challenges they faced after years of violence, oppression, and war.

A youth leader for thousands? It was a huge responsibility and one I wasn't sure I was prepared to take on. Hundreds of young people shared their problems with me. Some struggled with mental health issues and suicidal ideation. Others had issues with the police. Many had no money or hope.

My own issues were buried as my mind was swamped by the trust these young people placed in me. I was selected for the role out of the blue. Some friends had invited me to a youth summit in Nairobi, and the next thing I knew I was listening, jaw dropped, as a group of youth leaders revealed they were stepping down and nominating me to become secretary general of the organization.

The pressure to go along with their plan was intense. "Jal," one of them stated, "we know you and how creative you are when it comes to finding solutions. I know that anyone who comes to you will find peace of mind."

Their words were encouraging. My heart told me to accept the role, even if my mind felt ambushed. From that point on, I faced an endless stream of young people. I would have sleepless nights as I tossed problem-solving ideas around in my head. I was exhausted, to the extent that eventually three ideas, potential solutions, formed in my mind.

The first was to become a gangster, creating an underground movement to kidnap corrupt African politicians and businessmen, steal their wealth to share with the poor, and then leave them dead. The idea was so powerful that I even began to research how it might be possible. There were others equally as desperate as me, after all, many of whom knew how to use guns. I began planning, wondering who to share the idea with. The root cause of such an outlandish idea was my disdain for those who accrue personal wealth by taking innocent lives. I wanted God to send those people to hell. And I wanted him to do it sooner rather than later. I couldn't understand how there could be people with so much and yet others with so little. Kenya's poverty was breathtaking. Even the refugee camps I lived in were better than the Nairobi slums of Kawangware, Kangemi, and Kibera. At least in the camps, I knew food was eventually coming.

Thankfully, my purpose, asking myself what I really wanted, how I could truly effect change, meant I could never go through with such an idea. While I was undoubtedly excited by it (evil thoughts are seductive and captivating), I asked myself a question: Could I ever be proud of such work? The answer was no.

Another idea cropped up. It told me to pursue a military career. If I reached the top of the pile, I could wield enormous influence against those individuals who wrought so much damage. But the idea was virtually impossible to process. Even if it were viable, it would take many years to make it happen. Also, the use of violence didn't sit easy with me. I knew ultimately I lacked the motivation ever to pursue such a plan.

But there was one idea that seemed to have potential. One day after a youth meeting, I was listening to Puff Daddy on a minibus. A thought came to me. It told me to rap. At first I laughed. But after a while, I allowed my imagination to work with my courage to create stories about the challenges faced by both myself and others.

If you rap, you can create a bigger platform to tell those stories. That way you can support many people using your talent.

That single thought set me on a path I never expected to travel, discovering a talent I didn't know I had. It set me on a path of curiosity that made me an international artist and provided me with more opportunities than I knew existed.

Ideas grow through imagination. Therefore, the strength of an idea depends on our imagination.

Twelve ways to expand ideas through imagination

Be open-minded

Coming up with ideas is easy. What stops us from taking an idea to the next level is fear of both judgment and failure. Allowing our minds to be open to criticism and advice is a skill. Being open is crucial for us to thrive and create. It may be that the opinions of others are the spark that makes our idea truly great. The input of others has the power to ignite our imagination; to discover our own flow.

Read

Imagination is a faculty of the mind. A thought is an ingredient. What sparks thought is information, constant learning. Reading is powerful. It generates new knowledge and creative thinking and makes us more versatile in our approach to solving complex problems. Every time we read, we attract a diversity of thoughts.

Tell stories

Before we could read and write, we learned by listening to others tell stories, which created images, tastes, smells, and characters in our minds. Stories remain important throughout our lives. Invent our own and not only do we produce stories for the kids of the future, but we hone our imaginations. Everyone has a story to tell. What's yours?

Childlike curiosity

Children are curious. They have a strong imagination and are willing to try new experiences. We should think like children. Learning an instrument, for example, or swimming in the sea will take us mentally to places we have never been before.

Want

Deciding what we want in life gives us a burning desire to expand our imagination, a burning desire that fuels the creative process.

Self-development

We all have skills and talents to make us shine like stars. When we polish those skills we increase our imagination.

Find creative people

The saying goes that if we hang around thugs, we become a thug; hang around wise people, we become wise. It follows then that if we hang around creative people, we become creative—so long as we are willing to learn.

Indulge in creative content

Watching great drama, visiting museums, immersing ourselves in nature, listening to music, dancing, or exploring art—experiencing the creativity of others oils our own.

Meditate

When your imagination fails to fire, take a walk or find a quiet place to relax your mind.

Visualize

Look at an image, then close your eyes. Train your mind to recall the exact picture. Do this again and again and you strengthen your imaginative faculties.

Challenge

A challenge tests our strength. Wanting to succeed makes us raise the bar of creativity, in the process learning new techniques and stretching our imagination.

Brainstorm

Engaging in constructive debates challenges our imagination to come up with solutions. We also benefit by learning from others.

18

MY LIFE IS ART

PRINCIPLE 5:

Focus

WHAT WE GIVE ATTENTION TO, WE CAN CREATE. WHAT WE give attention to, we can become. What we give attention to can exist.

Focus is like the sunlight that helps plants make their food, the water that allows seeds to germinate, the oxygen that gives life to everything. It is impossible to do anything, achieve anything, without focus. A focused brain is like a missile—only with direction that is true can it hit its target. Important then that we develop habits to focus our brains. The ability to manage our focus will help us perform both simple and complex tasks.

LEARNING FOCUS

Had I truly understood the importance of focus, I would have taken it seriously growing up. In Naath culture, children are trained to focus from a young age. A child is assigned certain tasks, and if they don't perform them well, it impacts their family. In my case, I was assigned to look after a week-old calf. I was told not to allow it to suckle its mother. If it did, the family would be without milk.

To start with, I gave that calf my full attention. Wherever it went, I went. But after a while, I got bored. My attention wandered and I kept having to drag it back to the calf. At one point an eagle flew by. It stole my attention completely. I ran after it screaming, "*Shuor! Shuor! Shuor!*" ("Eagle! Eagle! Eagle!"). When I returned, the calf was gone. My legs weakened and my stomach churned. I knew I would be beaten for losing the calf. Finally, it appeared with its mother. At least it was alive, but I knew I would still be punished. I was right. That night I was given a beating before we all sat down to eat our meal without milk. Every time I heard someone ask why there was no milk, their words pierced through my center. I felt so bad for failing everyone.

The next day, a neighbor was asked to look after the calf while I watched. The day after, I was charged with the task again. This time I was determined the calf would not reunite with its mother. Occasionally, I was momentarily distracted, but my focus was good. As the evening approached, I got so excited. I began celebrating by dancing, singing, and giggling. When I stopped, I saw the calf was gone. It was a hundred meters away—with its mother. I ran as fast as I could and grabbed it by the neck, desperate to stop it getting the milk. But it wanted its prize and threw me to the ground. I managed to get up, but it kicked me in the mouth. I was dizzy, tears running down my face. I had failed again. The calf drank the milk. At least I was not beaten for my failing, but again everyone went without milk. It took me close to a week to be able to take care of that calf.

What prevented me from watching that calf was not lack of skill, but lack of focus. Given any task, my mind would wander. Even when I was given more calves and more responsibility, I would still occasionally be careless. My guardians eventually decided that I would be the one eating food without milk until I had mastered the art.

Failing to focus and pay attention has haunted me into my adulthood, getting me in trouble many times. Throughout my life, and during my childhood especially, multiple challenging events have affected my thinking, attitude, and outlook, creating habits that have distracted me from the goals I have set myself.

Lack of focus drained my energy and exhausted my emotions in both primary and secondary school. My mind would wander; I would talk with other kids and get in trouble. Over time, I came to see that others also struggled with focus and were unable to commit to jobs, goals, relationships, or opportunities that came their way.

It became clear to me that gaining focus is a lifetime lesson. To be great at it, we have to make it our daily practice. Look at the natural world. Animals can't afford not to focus. The price they pay is starvation or death. When wolves hunt, they identify their prey and then focus as a pack on that specific animal. To do otherwise would be a poor use of their resources. Acting alone would much reduce their chances of making the kill.

But we humans are easily distracted. We have our thoughts, our families, and now the added temptations of TV, phones, and social media. Too easily we end up doing what offers us comfort rather than what we should really do. We then become anxious and depressed at not achieving the results we desire.

To be focused means saying no to the thoughts that bombard your head, focusing instead on the important ideas that will deliver the results you are looking for. It is also learning how to say no to those seeking a slice of your time.

Snipers and Sharpshooters

To become child soldiers, we were taught how to be snipers and sharpshooters.

My trainer came close. "Soldier," he said to me, "your ability to hit a target depends on your focus. The target requires your full attention. Your breathing has to flow, you must be still, every part of you as one with your target. When that moment comes, hold your breath and fire."

I understood his words, but putting them into action was a challenge. I didn't have the discipline to be truly focused. I never hit any targets.

I soon wished I had taken the trainer more seriously. On the desert trek we were forced to endure, starvation was a constant threat. One evening, I found the energy to hunt. Out of ninety bullets I took only three, because I didn't have energy to carry more. A mile into my search, I encountered a wild turkey. I stopped and leaned on a tree. Remembering what the trainer told me, I did my best to focus. I fired—and missed. That sunny evening, I had two more opportunities to bag a feast—another bird and a warthog. I missed them both. The result was several days without food.

Recently I heard an athletics coach state that he can predict the performance of an athlete from their ability to focus. I can see where he is coming from. Focus saves us time, energy, and resources. It helps in decision-making, gets work done, and delivers the force we require to create.

The lessons the Naath nation presented to me were great lessons, as was that handed me by the trainer. Our greatness can be measured by our ability to focus. To be focused, we have to make it a lifestyle and daily practice.

TRAINING YOUR SELF-FOCUS

- Write down important thirty-minute goals.
- Go through them one by one, setting yourself up for success by not doing anything else, however long it takes. Practice it.
- If your focus lapses, train it by lighting a candle. For the next six minutes, focus your eyes on the flame, following it wherever it may flicker or swing.
- Programming and reprogramming of ourselves helps to hone focus.

Meditation

- Find a quiet space. Take a deep breath and allow your mind to settle. Every time it drifts off, bring the process back to your breathing.
- Close your eyes and listen to the silence, or quietest sound, in your environment. Forget any other sounds that are present. When your mind drifts away, bring it back to that sound.
- Whenever you are doing something important, give it your full attention. When your mind drifts away, bring it back to the goal you want to accomplish.
- Allow your mind to wander only when you are doing nothing.

19

MY LIFE IS ART

PRINCIPLE 6:

Endurance

CLIMBING MOUNTAINS

I WAS FIVE YEARS OLD WHEN I SPOTTED THREE LIZARDS heading toward our mud hut. The two largest reptiles climbed the wall quickly. Behind them was what I took to be their baby. It tried to follow, only to fall to the floor, its tail breaking off in the process. I felt sorry for it and wanted to help. But a voice whispered in my head—*Don't interfere. Just watch.* I did as I was told, looking on as the baby lizard tried and failed to climb the wall six more times. It seemed a hopeless task. And then, at the seventh time of trying, it stopped, stared, and made a sprint to the top of the wall. The way all three reacted, twisting, intertwining, was like a lizard celebration.

The experience didn't just leave me happy, it embedded a message of endurance in my soul and spirit. Every time a challenge came my way, the baby lizard would pop into my head, encouraging me not to give up without trying. At my lowest points, when death appeared a certainty, I would see the lizard, accompanied by my mother's voice telling me to take heart from its endurance—"My son, remember the lizard, don't give up." It was all I ever needed to keep going.

Each one of us will face several mountains in our lifetime. On occasion, we will fall, but it is vital we start at the bottom and try again. Watching that baby lizard made me realize there are situations in life only we can conquer. Others can only watch and encourage us to do so.

Endurance is the ability to swallow pain in the pursuit of gain. It is a place to experience hell, but also the magical shine of the stars. The place we get to die and be born again. Through endurance, we are blessed with skills, talents, knowledge, strength, and wisdom we never knew we had. The journey may be hard, conditions harsh, but it has to be if we are to truly appreciate our value, truth, and purpose. Endurance is the place where our dreams are tested. We either lose faith or realize we truly possess the strength to realize them.

Every human has a vision, but when hit hard by challenges it's easy for that vision to disappear. When we are overwhelmed by our circumstances, we can forget who we are. But endurance acts like a shell. It protects us, reminds us who and what we are, and allows us to get up again and again. When I watch a boxing match, the fighter who inspires me most is the one who drags themself to their feet after being knocked down, who tries to resurrect their dream even when it seems dead, who always finds the strength to carry on. Staying hopeful, keeping our dreams alive, is one of our greatest attributes as a species.

Every one of us will be tested by the universe. Those who don't quit, keep working, and maintain belief will reap the benefits of their endurance.

Why People Give Up

- Lack of willpower and drive
- Lack of discipline
- Lack of focus
- Deeming other areas of life more urgent or important
- Slow progress—failing to understand the need for hard work over a period of time
- Insecurity or fear of failing

- Feeling overwhelmed
- Lack of support
- Perceived lack of brainpower to solve a challenge
- Lack of faith that better times will come

All these scenarios can be overcome if we embed endurance within ourselves. Endurance allows us to adapt to all situations and environments. Without endurance we can be rigid and break easily.

SURVIVING PERSONAL CRISIS

The first person I ever saw take their own life was a thirteen-year-old boy. I was eight and had just arrived in Ethiopia as a child refugee when I saw the boy hang himself from a tree. We all watched helplessly. I didn't know what suicide was at that point. It never crossed my mind that someone might want to kill themselves. But, without me knowing, the seed was planted in me.

The second time I heard the word "suicide" was in the refugee camp. Several women were talking about a friend, how she had gone through so much but was now at peace. She had died a peaceful death (one of them said) by overdosing on anti-malaria pills.

"All that is keeping me alive is my children," said one. "Each time I want to end my life I think about who is going to take care of them. The gods and devils can end my life, but not me."

A week later, I got sick. The doctor prescribed me a course of anti-malaria tablets to last a week. Remembering how the woman had escaped her life of pain, I took them all at once. At first I felt dizzy, then I wanted to throw up. But I couldn't. A searing pain took over my head, like my brain was turning to mush and dripping through my ears. I could make out women gathering around me to pray. They had no idea what was making me so ill. It was the afternoon—doctors were only around in the morning.

The women did what they could, some massaging me, some

singing songs that were soothing, some praying, others applying oil. One woman took control, directing others to look after me and checking on me when she had a chance. Nyahon DK was her name. She was a powerful influence in the camp. For every problem that arose she had a solution. Her name has remained with me.

The pain I felt that night was like nothing I would ever experience again. At times, it felt as if my feet were burning, my skin was on fire, and my eyes were going to explode. I wanted to cry out but could find no voice. The next day, thankfully, the pain began to disappear. I had failed to kill myself.

On another occasion, when being a child soldier had dragged me not toward salvation but into a pit of pain and death, I pointed my gun at myself. I fired—and the gun failed. That day, I discovered I am here for a reason. I made up my mind that I wanted to stay alive to make a difference and be part of a solution to the world's ills. From then on, every time I had suicidal thoughts, I had purpose, vision, and core beliefs to protect me.

Escape to Hell

My two failed attempts to end my life laid the foundation for an endurance that would be tested on many occasions, but most of all when we sought to escape from the Sudan People's Liberation Army, fearing for our lives if we remained close to its heart. The organization had splintered into opposing factions, and to be in the wrong one meant certain death.

Two hundred of us escaped, but freedom was many weeks and miles away across unforgivingly barren and inhospitable territory. For the first month of our journey, we had enough food, but then the rations, like the water, ran dry. We ate anything we could lay our hands on—vultures, snails, bugs—and drank our own urine to survive. But exhaustion often overcame me and I would lag behind the others.

A thought entered my mind—*End it now and it will all be over.* But there remained one part of my brain telling me differently—that I was on this Earth for a reason.

Hold on like the lizard, it told me. *Twice you attempted to take your life, and twice you failed. That's a sign that the gods are with you.*

My internal structure was stronger and more prepared this time. It grounded me in my purpose, vision, and beliefs. I would not seek to take my life again.

"If I am to die," I told myself, "let it happen naturally. It will not come by my own hand."

Soon the arid landscape turned to swamp. I struggled through water above my chest. Mosquitoes swarmed around my head. I let them land on me, piling up on my face, and then wiped them off, grabbing them as I did so, and eating them. Each handful would, I hoped, give me the energy to get through the swamp. I also found some snails floating in the mire. I saved them as a reserve for later. I was surviving, but plenty of others weren't. Every so often we would see a comrade slip beneath the surface. There was nothing we could do. We had seen someone try to rescue a drowning child, only to be dragged down to die with them. The only bleak evidence either of them had ever existed were the bubbles vanishing away to nothing on the surface. Strength, what little of it any of us possessed, had to be preserved for ourselves.

Back on dry ground, and denied whatever nourishment was offered by the swamp, extreme starvation kicked in. I felt my physical senses change. My comrades began to smell not like people who had suffered the most unimaginably awful of journeys, but like food. I watched in mental torture as other soldiers started to eat the bodies of those who died around us. But I was no different. I realized that to live I might have to eat a dead body myself.

I hoped to avoid such apparent depravity, so the next day, when another comrade died, we placed a small amount of explosives around the body. We hoped a hyena might come scavenging and by detonating the bomb we would harvest some meat. The animal came as predicted, the explosives went off, but when the smoke cleared the hyena was nowhere to be seen, no sign even that it had been hurt. I was back to my dark plan. I looked at a comrade, who also happened to be my friend. He was dying. He looked back at me and said nothing.

The following morning, I crawled under a tree to see if I could locate any pieces of my comrade's dead body, but all I found were flies, which carpeted the ground. To sleep, to blank this misery out, was appealing, but I refused its invitation. For a starving person, sleep appears sweet. But to take its hand is to risk never waking up.

I lay down instead. Flies crawled over me, in my eyes and ears. I hung my mouth open and as the flies entered, I chewed them.

That evening, I prayed to my mother's God. "If you are there," I pleaded, "give me something to eat. If I survive, I will always thank you. I will always give you credit."

I waited the whole night. If God didn't answer, then I would have no choice but to eat my poor departed friend. One part of my mind told me it was the only way to survive; another insisted that to do so would disturb me for the rest of my life.

I waited until just before noon. Hope had all but vanished and I was about to face the horror of eating human flesh when a crow landed on a branch just a few feet above my head. My gun was at my side, but, as much as I tried, I had no strength to load the bullet. It was then I saw a soldier rise slowly from the ground. I thought he was dead, but he used his final drops of strength to load his gun. He took aim and shot the bird. And then he died. I ate everything. Feathers, intestines, beak, claws, the lot.

The crow was the first of many miracles, the biggest miracle being my survival to tell this story. By the end of that journey, only sixteen of us remained. The rest either took their own lives, died of starvation or dehydration, were ambushed, became lost in the wild, or fell victim to disease.

When I looked back on that terrible journey, I understood the root of my ability to endure. I recalled the tragedies of my childhood, the burning of my village, the orphaned children burying their dead, the babies dying of starvation. I knew that, despite its vilest attempts, that journey never managed to extinguish the flame of my desire to stay alive and play a part in preventing the suffering of my people. I wanted to be a pilot, a doctor, an engineer. I might not have achieved those dreams—my role in fact lay elsewhere—but one thing remains clear: I am now part of a solution. And I am in a peaceful place where there is milk and honey.

To endure, one must have a dream and the hope to make it happen. Yes, some things we can do by ourselves, but others require faith, backed up by hard work. When that happens, a person can create luck for themselves.

Human beings are like dolphins. In times of hopelessness, depression, and stress they are capable of taking their own lives. Both species must also ride out storms if they are to survive. In my journey I have learned that storms come, and sometimes they are fearful, but they always go. I also understand that purpose and vision allow endurance to shine within us. It is purpose and vision that have given me so many second chances.

No matter what our circumstances, there is always, always hope, and hope has the power to create a way when there seems to be no way.

20

MY LIFE IS ART

PRINCIPLE 7:

Intuition

I AM FASCINATED BY INTUITION—THE INTELLIGENCE, knowledge, and wisdom it holds.

How is that we wake in the morning, think about somebody, and then they text us? Or we ignore a hunch that to become friends with someone will be a bad idea, only to then end up hurt or exploited?

Intuition does not have a voice. It sends its messages via impulse. The heart is the first recipient and then the brain, which is left to interpret these thoughts, feelings, and words. Making an intuitive decision has no logical explanation. We just feel that it's the right course of action.

During my life as a child soldier, I had different voices speak to me. I had conflicting thoughts and emotions. The voices were like a council of advisors, some more dominant than others. Sometimes I would make decisions faster than my logical mind could detect. They would either work or land me in trouble. My greatest challenge was figuring out which was the right route to take. It takes time to develop that muscle in our brain.

KURKI—A MESSAGE THAT SAVED MY LIFE

Kurki is near Juba, the capital city of South Sudan. I experienced many things there during the civil war, some inspiring and thought-provoking, others harder to digest. One experience always delivers thoughts of gratitude whenever it comes to me in a flashback.

One evening I saw animals crossing the nearby river and birds flying away from the direction of the main city. That night, the wild foxes and dogs gave terrifying howls. Owls gathered around our camp, making chilling sounds, but when the morning came, the songbirds, usually so vocal, were quiet. I knew exactly what this was—a clear sign there was going to be heavy shelling. It made sense. Comrades were not doing well on the front line, suffering a heavy defeat as they tried to take Juba from the government forces, and government troops were advancing in our direction.

I hated many things in the battlefield, but shelling was right at the top of the list. It was impossible to counter, a bombardment as damaging psychologically as it was physically. During the day we would be bombed by jet fighters and helicopters and see missiles rain down on us from government bases. At night, the artillery would take over. I would rather be face-to-face with the enemy any day than to have bombs dropped on or fired at me. I thought of it as cowardly. I knew also that when the bombs came nonstop, it was a clear sign that ground forces were set to attack.

As I recognized the clues in the air, the silence of the birds, the unusual behavior of the animals, I knew this was my signal to leave my one-man shelter, little more than a hole in the ground. I leapt to the next, larger shelter instead.

"Why have you come here?" the guys in the hole asked. But I couldn't explain.

One of them started laughing. "Are you scared?"

"I know what that is called," remarked another. "It is called fear." Everyone laughed, including me. But a captain spoke more seriously.

"Why would you leave? And why can't you explain?"

"Something told me to leave, sir," I responded. "I will go back in a few minutes."

As I spoke, something told me to move closer to the exit. *If you don't*, my head told me, *you are going to die.*

I moved nearer to the exit. Two seconds later, a huge shell exploded outside. A piece of shrapnel flew through the entrance of the bunker, passed within a whisker of my throat, and slammed into the exact spot where I had been standing. At the same time, the pressure from the explosion threw me backward, smashing my head against the wall. The other guys thought I had been hit, but I was okay, just a minor headache and flashbacks of my throat almost being slashed.

After the bombing, I thought I would be punished for disobeying orders and moving shelters. But when he saw that first hole, smashed to pieces, the captain approached me.

"Young man," he said, "you have angels with you. We have to look after you."

He told me how he had once survived an ambush by government soldiers. Given an order to use a specific route to reach a destination, he followed his instinct and took a different path. Those who obeyed were ambushed, saved from death only by the captain and his troops, who had gone the other way.

The captain told me there is a feeling that comes, devoid of logic or reason, to great commanders. The feeling gets into spaces where logic cannot work. He told me to ignore those comrades who said I had left my bunker because I was afraid.

"I understand that feeling. It is different from fear," he told me. "It is a message from God, the angels, your ancestors, or whatever you believe in."

Master those messages, he said, and one day I would be as brilliant at reading situations as those great soldiers I so admired; leaders who were my heroes at that time. As we ate our tea of roasted maize, hot pepper, and salt, I felt uplifted by his words.

I still think about that day in the bunker, and still I have no explanation. It was a message I felt in my heart, gut, and mind—and I obeyed it. If not, I would have been dead.

WHAT IS INTUITION?

In the Bible, they call it the spirit of discernment, which helps us make the right judgments. I also see it as a wealth of knowledge that we have collected in our lifetimes, or perhaps that has been passed on to us by our ancestors, that lets us process information and make accurate decisions.

I have gathered three ways in which we receive messages into our hearts and brains for guidance—**spirit, soul, and body.**

Spirit

When we receive a message from an infinite intelligence, ancestors, angels, or evil forces, we are dealing with spirit.

Such a message may be about our lives, our friends, our community, or our country. It may come to us when we feel a connection or a calling, entering first our heart and then our brain, where it can be translated into words, images, or thoughts. The heart and the mind have to be in agreement for the message to perform its work. Division creates conflict and sabotage.

As the message is translated, we can feel it in our gut. If it is a great and amazing message, we will become excited, drunk with joy. If the message is challenging, then fear is triggered. What matters most is how the heart reacts to the message. If the heart has belief in what we are being told, then it will mobilize our internal governing structure to make that message happen.

Spiritual messages come in different forms—visions, dreams, or feelings. I think back again to the time we, as child soldiers, walked in the desert for days. Our commander warned us not to waste our water.

"Only drink when you are about to pass out," he told us.

We walked slowly, conserving our energy and not sweating valuable moisture. "If you do sweat," a fellow soldier told me, "lick it—there will be no water here."

I took his advice seriously. I walked slowly but the sun was so hot I couldn't avoid sweating. As he directed, I licked it up. It was super salty and disgusting, but it meant I could delay drinking my water. Even so, by midafternoon my bottle was empty. I wasn't alone. Everybody had finished their water. We walked exhausted across an arid savanna with tall elephant grass. There was no sign of birds or fresh footsteps of animals to give us a sense of where we might find water. That night, we slept restlessly. In the early morning, we wiped our hands on the dew and licked them desperately. The dew was our only source of life, the only water that passed our lips.

Based on my experiences in South Sudan, if I were given two choices, starving to death or dying of thirst, I would choose the first. Dehydration is different from starvation. When you are starving, the first day is difficult. Headaches come, while on the second day the stomach hurts slightly. On the third day of starvation, the pain becomes sweet. The headaches disappear as the body begins to eat itself. When starvation came my way, I felt like I had been given a massage and just wanted to sleep. I knew I wanted food to stay alive, but at the same time death was calling me and seemed so appealing. When it comes to dehydration, every cell in your body hurts, the throat is dry, the eyes ache, the eardrums ache, the brain hallucinates, the trees start talking, and the wind forever whispers its death song—that water is ahead. You believe you can see it sparkling in the distance and then, just as you get close, it takes huge strides away from you again. People are dragged off track in its pursuit and never come back.

On the night of the third day without water, we knew this was it. Death wasn't far away. Several people shot themselves. My mind gave up debating with life and praying to God, but my heart stayed hopeful.

At three or four in the morning, I received a message in my heart. A map appeared in my head. It showed water. The image was so clear it was as if I were watching TV. A voice in my head told me to head left. *Keep walking*, it said. *There will be a huge tree ahead of you. Keep it on your right and keep walking.*

I acted on the instruction, but then a doubting voice came, discouraging me. *Where are you going? Why do you believe this message? You are going to be eaten by wild animals. You are so stupid.*

I didn't listen. I allowed my head to keep me moving. I walked for fifteen minutes—and fell in a pool of water. "Water! Water! Water!" I screamed so hard.

I rolled around in the pool and drank and drank. Others joined me. They, too, were saved.

I see that message as coming from the heavens or gods. Maybe ancestors or an infinite intelligence. Had I never listened to that message, I am sure I would be dead. Equally, I am sure all my fellow soldiers were sent the same message but never picked it up. The same intelligence that takes care of everything on our planet knows each and every living organism and gives them directions.

The universe, I learned, has a way in which it looks after its own. I have no further explanation. I just trusted the message, and the message saved my life.

Soul

Soul messages are those already embedded in us. Our soul has a great understanding. It knows our purpose. It guides our heart.

I believe every person on this planet chose their parents, where they wanted to be born, and what problems they would like to fix. I also believe that Earth is the training ground for our souls. It is here we must mature and pass the test laid out before us. Only that way can we be assigned another mission in another galaxy.

When our heart and our soul are united, we experience joy and depth of life. We acquire deep knowledge of ourselves. Our soul knows what we are about. It possesses a profound understanding. It is connected to the infinite intelligence and receives messages to further our well-being. Ask a six-year-old what their purpose is and you will be amazed by their understanding of their role as an adult. It follows then that for an adult to know their purpose, they must surrender themselves to a childlike state of openness, for it is only from this angle that they can see their true purpose.

From a young age, I knew I wanted to be a part of solutions. I followed signs that led me in that direction. Those signs become easier to see when we are spiritual; when we meditate, fast, and pray; when we respect nature and perform acts of kindness; when we feed our soul positive contents. I knew also that listening to the stories of others can lift us to greater heights—our soul guides us better when we find and listen to spiritual beings who are walking in their purpose.

There were two sentences I hated saying when I was a kid: "I love you" and "I am sorry." The genesis of that apprehension came from fear. If I told someone I loved them, maybe I would discover they didn't love me back or were faking their love. I also wanted to be sure I could back up the commitment and responsibilities that came with saying "I love you." The word "sorry," meanwhile, had shame attached to it. I could never be sure if the person to whom I apologized could forgive me. It was how I discovered soul-to-soul communication, starting with my mother. In Chapter 7 (on reprogramming), I revealed how I promised her I would never steal sugar and milk powder again. But I'll admit that on occasion I was unable to resist. On such days I would communicate with her soul.

"Mum," I would say, "I broke the promise. I didn't want to break it but something inside me made me do it. I don't understand why I was not able to resist, but my promise to you is still there. From my whole heart I am sorry. I will try my best not to do it. I will find a way to stop the devil inside me breaking this promise again."

It was soul-to-soul communication that helped me overcome my crime. My conscience became clear, and my mum would welcome me with joy—"Where have you been? I missed you."

From that point on, I knew something happens when we are sincere in our intention. I was not expecting Mum to forgive me but just wanted her to understand. I wanted to talk to her physical being. To work, soul-to-soul communication has to be pure. No manipulation, just expression of yourself.

One day my mother shocked me. She suspected I had again been taking sugar and milk powder. "But," she said, "I am not concerned because I have another feeling inside me that tells me you shall overcome such urges and you are working on yourself."

She blew my mind. I wondered why she wasn't angry. The reason was she had chosen not to judge me. She made me believe in the good me I was working on.

Speaking to people's souls was a survival strategy. I believed in it even though I had no firm evidence—only the reaction of others. Take my experience of bullying at schools in Kenya. The first time I encountered a bully I let him pick on me. I took my time to study his environment, where he liked going, who he hung out with, and his weaknesses. I then meditated to connect with the souls of his friends.

"Hey," I told them, "I came here to study. I don't want to cause trouble. Can I be your friend?" Next time I saw those kids they were smiling back at me.

I then did my best to talk to the bully's soul. If he didn't react positively, I would pick a fight in a public place. My plan was to beat the bully and by so doing gain the friendship of others he had picked on. I did this a few times with bullies and one way or another it worked.

However, on one occasion the confrontation went a step further. A bully smashed my head into a wall. I didn't act in the moment. He was very strong. I would have to approach the situation in a different way. A few nights later I armed myself with a knife and went to his room. The door was open—he was asleep. I lifted my knife. I was in turmoil inside. My soul was unhappy. I knew that what I was doing was wrong. And then it happened—Jesus appeared in front of me. "If this guy continues to bully me," I told him, "I will kill him. I do not want to be bullied. Talk to his soul, educate him, and he will stay alive."

That same week, the bully became my friend. He apologized to me. "I don't know why I bullied you," he said. "You are harmless."

Soul-to-soul communication still works for me today. I use it with family and friends, and I urge others to do the same.

A friend of mine was disowned by his wealthy father and cut out of his will. Growing up the father abused the mother, and he was not treated well. He never wanted to speak to his father again. I would ask him if had forgiven him and always he said no. I convinced him that he needed to forgive his father, for his own sake. He agreed, but he lacked the confidence to do so in person. I then told him about soul-to-soul forgiveness, that he could forgive his father in a different way. Whenever his father crossed his mind, he could send him a positive vibe, the best feeling he could ever want him to have.

"Do not," I told him, "expect anything in return."

A few months later, my friend told me his father had called to say he was thinking of him and wanted to meet. The entire family was reunited. Everyone asked my friend what he did to make it happen.

"I don't have words to explain what I did," he told them, "except to speak to his soul."

Soul messaging has its fun side too. Sending dreams to friends was something I loved doing when I was a kid. The next day, we would laugh as we compared our experiences of the same dream in detail.

Some call it telepathy. I think differently. It is souls communicating with each other at long distance. I understood it as a kid, and I still practice it today.

Body

Our bodies collect information to make intuitive decisions. Our senses collect data and send it to our brains for temporary or long-term use. All experiences, whether we are conscious of them or not, are recorded. The subconscious mind has unlimited space. It records 24/7.

The brain recognizes data quickly, be it feelings, images, voices, tastes, colors, or a million and one other elements of everyday life. When our brain encounters something absent from its data bank, it may react with fear or curiosity.

In our use of stored data, we are no different from every other living thing around us.

Horses

Horses are highly intuitive animals. They have had to be in order to survive. They rely on flight, not fight, and can outrun the majority of their predators.

I once saw a mare defend her newborn foal. Another horse approached. It was acting aggressively. As it leapt toward the foal, its mother planted itself in its path to protect her baby, which was doing its best to scramble clear. One kick would have ended its life. The horses pushed and jostled, rearing, kicking. Those who have something to lose will always fight harder and smarter than any assailant. The mare won the battle convincingly.

Afterward I wondered how the mother knew the other horse wanted to kill its baby. Furthermore, why didn't other horses intervene, and how could a newborn foal understand danger?

The answers came when I was part of a project called Unlikely Collaborators, organized by my good friend, the publisher and writer Elizabeth Koch, where people from diverse backgrounds came together to share our experiences to help others gain strength and learning.

On one of our rest days, Caitlin Powell, a leader in wellness and a curator of experiences, my manager Tania Campbell, and branding and marketing director Justine Fink organized an experience with horses. My son Jal and his mum, Atong Arjok, also came along. The guide told us that the horses could read our emotions. If we were scared, they would know. If we were brave, they would know. I had never ridden a horse before, and it was amazing to see how the horses were able to read my mood. We were trekking in line. I felt uncomfortable where I was in the middle, and I wanted to move up the line. My mount started biting the horse in front. I wondered why. The guide told me it was because the horse wanted to lead the pack. The instructor took me to the front. I was happy there, as was my horse.

After a while, I wanted to be back down the line with my son. I just held the thought. Again, the horse started getting jittery. The guide asked me if there was anything wrong. "Can you please take me to where my son is?" I asked. She did so, and again the horse was calm.

From that day, a belief was planted in me that horses can read how we feel at a cellular level. I was further convinced when I met healer and animal anthropologist Shelly Burton. Shelly uses horses to heal trauma and anxiety and emphasizes that they can sense pain and heal with love. They sense our inner disposition, read our movements and tone of voice, and take energy from our cells. Cellular communication—incredible but true.

The Head-Banging Snake

Chickens, dogs, pigs, and snakes can all detect earthquakes faster than humans. In China's Guangxi Province, snakes are used as an early warning system, because it has been proven that they can detect movement deep beneath the surface days before an actual quake occurs and many miles away from the epicenter. For China, an early warning is vital. The country is often hit by earthquakes, which result in the loss of thousands of lives. Scientists experimented with different animals and found snakes to be the most reliable. The normally calm reptiles would behave erratically, even launching themselves headfirst into walls, to escape the approaching event. Snakes are now used by twelve Chinese cities vulnerable to earthquakes.

It amazes me how animals are able to sense volatility before it happens. I believe humans have similar abilities. Our downfall is that we don't use our senses in the best way to serve us. We act on information received, rather than awareness and intuition.

WOMEN

One of the most powerful gifts that women possess is intuition. When women step into a room, they read people quickly. Even though I possess this gift, I am still working on the art of putting it into practice. I have picked people to work with me, only for it to turn out disastrously. They might smile with me, eat with me, but on the side they plan to crucify me.

In interviews, I would pick people based on their capacity to do the job, adding an element of intuition based on what I could see and hear.

I wanted to make my intuition stronger, to learn how to differentiate my subconscious mind, conscious mind, and emotions. I had been great at using intuition when I was in a war zone, but in the concrete jungle it became more complicated.

I conducted an experiment with two friends who had never met before. I will call them Mary and Chi to protect their identities. They came to my house early one evening on the pretext that their meeting could lead to future work collaborations. They appeared to get on well, the conversation flowing as well as the laughter. We had a delicious meal, everyone was happy, and they exchanged phone numbers. The next day, I asked Mary what she thought of Chi.

"She is a troublemaker," she replied. "Be careful what you tell her and who you introduce her to. She will tear you apart." She was really concerned about what Chi might do.

The following day, I met Chi and asked her about Mary. "Be careful," she told me. "Mary is very controlling. She said that in so many words, she will entice you with sweet words and fatten you for the kill. She will sabotage your business."

Chi could not be friends with Mary ("I don't trust her"), and Mary could not be friends with Chi ("she's a drama queen"). I ignored their words of advice.

It wasn't long after that my friend, speaker and entrepreneur

Kalista Zackhariyas, told me of a terrible dream. In it she saw Mary as described by Chi, and vice versa. I ignored all these insights. I just thought Mary and Chi were jealous and making up stories about each other. I was interested only in their value and ability. I was never concerned about any damage they could bring to my life. Yet a few months later, everything the women spoke about had happened. I asked myself how they were able to judge each other's characters with such accuracy. Trust was broken and relationships lost, both business and personal. The psychological and emotional cost could have no price tag.

I asked Kalista, who dreamed about Mary and Chi, how she came to harbor such thoughts about them.

"I felt it in my gut the moment I met each one of them," she said—the exact same answer given by both Mary and Chi when I had asked why they felt so vehemently about their opposite number.

Thankfully, I have improved my intuition. I am now able to read people consciously and subconsciously by listening, observing, and feeling their energy. Most of the time, my interpretation is accurate—intuition happening at a cellular level. When cells talk to each other, they share our current experiences as well as our past and future worries. If there is a disagreement at the cellular level, we do not feel a connection with one another. Look at it as the body's Bluetooth, passing a connection—or not—to those we encounter.

Ever heard the term "presence," as in the impression a person has on others? I believe some people have a huge presence, one that can extend miles from where they are, while others have a presence that extends only a short distance. Look at public speakers. One may be talented but have no presence; another's words may not be amazing but are carried straight into the audience's heart. We all present ourselves in different ways, ranging from the calming to the intense to the aggressive.

When we meet people, our presence can put them in flight, calm, or fight mode. The most highly intuitive people can read if someone is trustworthy, but to some extent we all possess the ability to discern one another's characters. The challenge is evaluating the accuracy of our radar—our intuition—that has gathered the information for interpretation. We must also keep in mind that intuition is neutral. It is merely an advisor and, as such, will respect our decision.

We receive intuitive messages in three ways: spirit, soul, and body. Make decisions guided by spirits, and we are spiritually intuitive. Make decisions guided by our souls, and we are emotionally intuitive. Make decisions guided by our body, and we create intuition from the data collected by our senses and stored in our brain; we are mentally intuitive. Some decisions require a mix of all three. Some need just one. Ever heard somebody say, "My heart says yes, my head says no, and my spirit is disturbed"? When I find myself in a situation like that, I take a deep breath. I connect with my spiritual advice and make a decision accordingly. You may see things differently, but always remember there are three supreme advisors in you.

Use them.

21

MY LIFE IS ART

PRINCIPLE 8:

Sagaciousness (Wisdom)

TO BE SAGACIOUS IS TO BE OPEN, TO BE THOUGHTFUL, AND to show consideration to other people and their needs. It is having the understanding that the world revolves not just around us but around everything. Sagaciousness is a great habit to develop because it can help us in many ways and is needed in all aspects of life.

A sagacious person is one who is able to organize their thoughts to produce the most positive outcome. To be sagacious is to be wise. It is the perfect application of what we know, based on our experiences and knowledge, good or bad, to make life and the world better. Possessing the gift of wisdom allows us to quickly absorb information for current and future use. It allows us to solve both simple and complex problems.

THE SEARCH FOR WISDOM

An ancient African king and queen were looking for an advisor. They gathered the wise men and women of the land and informed them they would be asked three questions.

"Give a wrong answer," they were told, "and you will be hanged in public. Alternatively, admit you don't know the answer and you can go home."

The three questions were:

How can a family use an elephant's body without wasting a single part?

How could they put what is inedible to good use?

Could they teach such wisdom to others?

Some said to use every part of an elephant was impossible. Others gave vague answers. Still more wanted extra time to think. Only a few delivered a viable solution. They stated that to eat an entire elephant would necessitate the meat being dried to stop it rotting and the building of a secure storeroom to protect it from rats, wild dogs, and insects. Internal organs, more prone to decay, would have to be eaten first. Bone marrow would be turned into oil, and any other inedible material would be mixed with elephant dung to make fertilizer. The skeleton, meanwhile, would become a work of art.

While others, as promised, were either hanged or dismissed, those who found such solutions were made advisors.

Wisdom is about asking questions to find answers. Wisdom is about taking time to think. Wisdom is putting guesswork to one side and working only with facts, with what you are certain of and believe can work.

TYPES OF SAGACIOUSNESS

Inherited

A great African king was known for hiring great wise people, warriors, and servants to be part of his inner circle. He believed greatness to be inherited, so to aid his selection he would look at family history. This king also would not let mistakes pass by. He wanted things done perfectly. A mistake would warrant punishment, which few survived.

The king was known for keeping tigers, cheetahs, wild dogs, hyenas, and lions as pets, each trained to listen to his orders. When the king ordered an execution, he would also choose an animal to eat the victim as the public watched.

On one occasion the king ordered the execution of a servant who had made an error. The servant fell to his knees and begged. "Please, your royal highness, you have transformed my life and the life of my family. And I have failed to show you my worth. Give me ten days to prove my worth." The king agreed, but the threat of death hung heavy in the air.

The servant wasted no time. For the next ten days he fed the king's animals. He earned their trust to the extent that they would even lick his hands.

When the ten days were up, the king could see no evidence of the servant proving his worth, and the execution was arranged. But when the servant was thrown into the arena, the hyenas would only lick his feet. The tigers and lions, meanwhile, hugged him, as did the wild dogs. The king became angry and anxious in equal measure. Eventually, the servant dropped to his knees.

"Your royal highness," he shouted, "my grandfather served your father until his old age. My father did the same for you. For ten years I, too, have served you with all my heart, soul, and spirit—and yet you have forgotten me. I have served these animals for just ten days and they remember me."

The king was embarrassed. He began to cry and ordered the servant not only to be released but to be elevated to serve as a wise man. The wisdom inherited from his lineage had saved his life.

Hardship

I often travel to the U.S. from the U.K. Sometimes I meet amazing customs officers, sometimes not. On one particular occasion, the officer I encountered was exceptionally aggressive.

He looked at my passport. "You are from Sudan," he spat. "You fucking refugees are draining our country's resources. You are parasites. You come here and beg and take. When are you guys going to stand on your own feet?"

I couldn't speak. It was as if I had been punched in the stomach. However, past experience with aggressive people told me I should stay calm. Never pick a fight for which you are not prepared. I took a deep breath, controlled my emotions, and showed no sign of shock or fear. I considered the worst possible outcome of confrontation—me being denied entry to the country. Being calm was the only wise option.

"You are coming here to America to blackmail our citizens with your fucking child soldier story," the officer continued.

"I am an activist," I replied calmly.

"Oh, so you are a troublemaker," he replied.

I tried to explain. "Shut your fucking mouth until I ask you a question," he snapped. Another officer gave him a look, signaling for him to take it easy. He took my interrogator to one side.

"This young man," he told him, "is incredible. He is doing his best to leave this world better than he found it."

The first officer took me to another area where I sat for two hours. Every now and then I would be called for more questioning. He asked for my credit card details, checked my address, wondered if I had a girlfriend in the U.S., or a child, and inquired how long I was staying for. So many questions—and every time I tried to answer I was interrupted. The officer was looking for any opportunity to deny me entrance.

Whenever I returned to my seat, I meditated, prayed, and applied gratitude to manage my emotions and ego. I charged myself with positive emotions.

"Relax, Jal," I told myself. "This is not worse than the desert walk you endured. This is like eating a plate of cookies compared to that."

My mind also reminded me that it was being denied entry to a country that led me to the path I am still taking today. As a student, I was denied a U.K. visa five times. Had I been granted that visa, I would not have become the recording artist I am today. I would be an electrical engineer or stressed out by working in a factory. My wisdom told me that every negative brings a positive. I tapped into past experiences that reminded me of who I am, my purpose and vision. Doing so gave me the peace to accept any negative outcomes.

In the end, my case was handed to another officer. He took five minutes to assess the situation.

"You are a great young man doing his best to make our world better," he told me. "Welcome to New York."

The day had been saved by the multiple previous experiences which replayed in my mind, convincing me to be calm. I watched as another Black man, given the same sort of grilling, acted more emotionally and was denied entry. I felt for him, trapped in this one-sided exchange, and sent him a soul message. I had understood from the start that, had I shown any opposition, even the good officers would have sided with their colleague, because that's what comrades do.

Remember, every experience brings wisdom and knowledge that we can apply in the future.

Educational

This is the wisdom we acquire through formal education. Here we are taught what to think, almost like robots. This type of thinking allows us to go by the book and solve problems logically; it allows us to manage complicated systems. People are put under pressure to learn such wisdom and then display it in exams or tests. They then have to learn how to apply it in their daily life.

Growing up, I admired people with this type of wisdom. In my village, anyone with a pen in their pocket was treated with respect. I recall a man once writing my name. I watched in wonder and then copied it again and again on the ground to practice and show off to the other kids. When those kids then asked me to write their name in the earth, of course I couldn't do it. At that point I stopped showing off.

I was so curious growing up, fascinated by planes, tanks, bicycles, cars—even biscuits. I wanted to learn the most difficult of tasks. When I saw somebody with a book, I wanted to know exactly what it was about and plead with them to read it to me. When finally I learned how to read a little and write my name, I felt so much joy and happiness.

The wisdom I acquired from formal education set me apart. When

I was able to read and write properly, I became popular. Once I was in a marketplace in South Sudan with a pen in my hand and one in my pocket. Within a few minutes, there was a line of people paying me to show them how to write their names or help them write a letter to a member of their family. Just like the men I had respected in my village, now others respected me for being able to write names and letters.

Such wisdom has helped me enormously. I can now organize my thoughts and write them down. I can plan and strategize. Educational wisdom introduced me to modern thinking. It set me up for success. But such wisdom can be expensive and lead to disparity. Look at how differently a graduate from a top university such as Harvard is treated compared to someone with a degree from the University of Juba in South Sudan. Educational wisdom causes so much good and so much mess at the same time.

Spiritual

This type of wisdom, acquired through spirituality, is given to us by God or by following religious or ancient Indigenous beliefs.

Jesus applied spiritual wisdom when faced with a difficult situation. A woman accused of adultery was brought to him by religious leaders. They wished to test Jesus's wisdom and lay a trap for him so he would have to approve their plan to stone the woman to death.

Jesus's response was immediate. "Let he who has no sin throw the first stone," he decreed. Each of the leaders left without saying a word. He had saved the woman's life.

ONCE YOU HAVE WISDOM IT CAN BE EITHER CORRUPT OR PURE

Corrupted Wisdom

Sadly, wisdom is used by many to promote evil. There are those who direct their corrupted wisdom to control humans, using fear, worry, torture, death, and poverty to ensure that the masses rely on them.

They use one hand to give and the other to kill. They bring violence, rape, chop people's hands off, and murder children. They loot property and burn down entire villages. The reason for their actions is to install software into the minds of their victims so they can control them and their entire circle of family and friends for the rest of their lives. When the victims meet their loved ones, they, too, become infected by bitterness, hate, anger, and pain. Their minds lose their pure function. Now, if they get an opportunity, they will take revenge, doing the same to the enemy, perhaps even worse. Soon, as poverty begins to fester and worry and fear dominates minds, entire communities are afflicted by this desire to harm others.

Wisdom as a Savior

Wisdom gives us the ability to think fast—sometimes with our lives at stake. I am reminded of the story of an SPLA general, Peter Gatdet, during a conflict in Sudan. After a plane flight over enemy territory, his pilot made a potentially catastrophic navigation error and landed before the plane was back on home ground. Immediately the aircraft was surrounded by opposition troops.

"I come to make peace," General Gatdet told his counterpart as he emerged from the plane. "It is time we put an end to this conflict. I am serious. Let's not kill each other anymore. I will tell our soldiers to stop firing."

The other general wasn't convinced. "Are you really sure?" he asked. "What about the thing that is bothering your arsehole. Is that not going to itch anymore?"

But Peter Gatdet was adamant. "For me there will be no itching. We are going to build on peace."

His rival was delighted. The two celebrated and drank together before General Gatdet reboarded his plane. They waved at one another as the plane left the runway.

Just before he landed at his destination, General Gatdet phoned his counterpart.

"I was lying the whole time," he told him. "I am coming for your head tonight."

Through his corrupt wisdom, his quick thinking, the general had saved himself.

Of course, some people are wise where others only see a fool. I am reminded of a story I once heard about a farmer. For many days he dug a huge hole. All anyone could do was laugh at him.

"What are you doing?" they asked him scornfully. "If you think you will find water, you are wasting your time."

But the farmer carried on digging. Again and again, the doubters mocked him. Until one day he found the water he knew was beneath his feet. Unlike those who had been so keen to judge, he now had an endless supply of water from his well.

No matter what doubts and insults people threw at him, he had carried on. His wisdom made him eliminate any thoughts of failure. What others thought was foolishness was in fact short-term suffering for long-term gain.

SAGACIOUSNESS IS OUR SURVIVAL GUIDE

Modern society can be seen as a huge trap. Sagaciousness is our survival guide. It gives us a 360-degree view and directs us to apply all we know to produce positive outcomes.

Without wisdom we are like a frog that has jumped into a pot of cold water on a fire. As the frog adapts to the changing temperature, it doesn't notice that it is slowly boiling to death. If we become too self-centered, we, too, can all too easily fail to notice the danger around us, the system fattening us up for the kill, and we fail to take the necessary steps to reverse it. Global warming is a case in point. The ice caps are melting, sea levels are rising, desertification is increasing. Our ecosystem is being devastated. Such issues could be prevented by leadership that is accompanied by wisdom. The lack of collective wisdom is failing us all. The pursuit of riches dominates, but as the Book of Proverbs says, wisdom is better than silver, gold, and jewels.

There is imbalance in our world. Some rely on spiritual wisdom, others on educational or inherited wisdom, or sagaciousness learned from hardship. My belief is that to make the truly huge impact we need to transform the planet and our lives, we must achieve the ultimate positivity by utilizing all four elements of sagaciousness. If we don't, how can we ever say to future generations that we gave them the best chance?

22

MY LIFE IS ART

PRINCIPLE 9:

Action

IN TORONTO, I BECAME A LIFE PERFORMANCE COACH, DE-livering retreats, workshops, and one-on-one support for hundreds of people. After each event, we would do a ninety-day challenge. The idea was to correct our behavior by creating new positive habits and beliefs to increase our mental power. We would meet every month and check our progress.

"Did you meditate every day?" I would ask. "Did you infuse yourself daily with positive stories? Did you carry out the daily practice of habits and beliefs?

"What are you grateful about?" I would continue. "Have you had any breakthroughs? What stories would you like to share? What did you learn that you can teach us?"

Two people who attended the meetings stuck out: Chantelle Edwards and Charles Perroud, who ended up becoming teachers themselves, as well as my friends. At every meeting they had stories to share and so much to teach us.

Chantelle had been raised in foster care. Against the odds, she did well in her education and became a zoologist. But life battles kept following her. She married a man who abused her emotionally and left her in financial crisis. At work, she faced a tough job and a tough boss.

Unsurprisingly, she suffered from severe anxiety and felt tormented by her life when she was alone. By following the steps in the course, however, Chantelle began to change. Every time we spoke to her, she seemed renewed. Now Chantelle, too, is a life performance coach, supporting others with her experience and learning.

Charles, meanwhile, had suffered a series of catastrophic events. His son died of an incurable brain disease, he was divorced, and his best friend died of cancer. Charles's life energy had been sucked away by endless worry. Meet Charles now and you will not believe how far he has come. An activist, biochemist, storyteller, and spiritual leader, he does 850 speeches a year. He builds cultures in schools that support learning and coaches teachers and principals for free. I am truly humbled to know him.

The opposite of Chantelle and Charles are those who expect results without doing the work. It's like going to the doctor, not taking the medicine they prescribe, and then expecting to heal. Or signing up for a fitness course, continuing to eat junk food, and then asking the coach at the end of the month why you haven't lost weight or gained muscles. Do half the work and you get half the results.

Whatever we want will not happen. As a Christian might say, "Faith without action is dead."

In my experience, what wins is hard work, which leads me to another thought that resonates with my reality. What wins is not hate or love: what wins is action.

Why is it that hate so easily takes control while love must fight for freedom? What side are you on? The truth is it doesn't matter. What matters is doing something, acting to get what we desire.

If we died today, could we honestly say to ourselves that we did our best—that we read, gathered wisdom, asked questions, developed our skills and talents? Could we say we persisted, trained, prepared for opportunities that came, touched lives, added value, and acted with a burning desire to achieve?

Action wins even if we can't immediately see the impact. Action is problem-solving, making ideas reality, taking courage in the creative process, and getting work done. It is not a competition. Everybody can take the journey at their own pace. But ultimately action is required. If you don't take action, others will take it on your behalf, and you may not like the results.

Successful people are action oriented, hungry for know-how, and they always seek solutions to improve their lives and the lives of others. They don't stand by and hope things will just happen. There are people who believe that if they pray, a big fat check will appear in the mail with their name written on it. The world doesn't work like that. A great idea that you don't act on will never happen, but a worse idea supported by action will see a positive result. To be successful, one must be action and goal oriented. To achieve requires a greater force than to resist. Look at the great battles of history. To win, each soldier had to pick up their weapon and fight harder and smarter than their counterpart. Action is what converts resistance into reward. Action is the force of manifestation.

This quote from the Bible drives the message home for me: "Those who sow sparingly will reap sparingly and those who sow bountifully will reap bountifully" (2 Corinthians 9:6).

THE TRIANGLE

I have been meditating in a triangle for years. It eases my stress, adjusts my focus, and trains my imagination. Yet the tangible meaning of the shape remained a mystery to me for years.

The answer came to me after an out-of-body experience on Richard Branson's Necker Island. I was there at the invitation of Richard and Chris Anderson, the head of TED, the nonprofit organization that delivers inspirational conferences and talks.

I'd spoken and performed on three previous occasions, but this visit was different and set me on a new path of unlimited possibilities that I am still reaping daily.

I was at my lowest point since my desert walk. My country was at war with itself and my activism work was hitting a dead end. One night the devil visited me in my dreams and told me he was watching me. "You are grazing on my green pastures without my permission. My eyes are on you, Jal." That vision set me off—I interpreted every-day occurrences in terrifying ways. I had formidable nightmares every night.

On the island, I was surrounded by people who were the very best in their fields. I was honored to be among them, but mentally, spiritually, and emotionally I was on the floor. The experience was exuberant, spectacular, and mind-blowing—I had never done any-thing like it before—yet my mind and my heart couldn't enjoy it. My head was set on "self-destruct." It felt like having a cold, sore throat, and malaria all in one go. My painkiller was my purpose, which did its best to pump joy from my heart and ignite life in different parts of my body.

High and low moments intermingled, the days better than the nights. In the day, my energy allowed me to at least consider just what I was experiencing. It had never crossed my mind that one day I would be on an island with thirty millionaires and billionaires, talking and dining with them. It was like being part of a secret society where big, audacious ideas were formed to transform evil to good; great plans to make our world better. Few of those billionaires, however, were very friendly. I felt on occasion as if they were scared of me. I was instructed not to bother them. "We want them to relax," I was told. "Everyone is chasing them for their money and ideas."

Others, however, could not have been more generous with their time. One night I stayed on nearby Eustatia Island, talking with Google cofounder Larry Page. I played chess with Richard Branson and chilled out with eBay's first president, Jeff Skoll. Chris Anderson spoke passionately about the idea of collaboration. His wife, Jacque-line Novogratz, founder and CEO of Acumen, a nonprofit organiza-tion using entrepreneurial approaches to address global poverty, was so intuitive, always checking on me to make sure I wouldn't collapse. I don't know if she was able to read my emotions or see beyond my soul, but whatever she did, it was cool, and I needed it. When I get super-triggered, my mind cannot receive advice from others; it makes me isolate to regroup. Only after I have cleared space can it take advice. Trauma, poverty, and stress occupied a lot of room in my mind, so even five minutes alone in a toilet cubicle allowed me some mental freedom.

When the conference was over, I finally got time for myself and went through a super-meditation to face my inner demons. In times of extreme challenges, I feel maybe the creator can upgrade me to the next level. I ate nothing. Instead, I meditated on my bed until I was unaware of my existence. That night, my soul came out of my body. As I hovered above my room, I could see only my TV and bed; everywhere else was dark.

I heard a voice. *Do not be afraid. The darkness in your life gives you the resources to create. It is part of your triangle.*

Leaving my body was terrifying, but when I heard the voice, I relaxed, and in so doing my soul returned to my body. I couldn't understand what was happening. I felt a complete shift in myself, as if I were possessed, and fetched my computer, notebook, and pen. I began collecting thoughts and writing down what I considered might be the meaning of the triangle. It blew my mind when I realized it was the missing link of my meditation.

For months after that experience, as I sank myself more and more into meditation, more revelations illuminated the knowledge and wisdom that was missing in my daily practice. The books I was reading made more sense and my subconscious reorganized my thoughts into a more comprehensible form. My mornings became joyful and happy, and I completely surrendered myself to my purpose. I became even stronger.

Anyone who practices the triangle will see their life change forever. I died and came back to life with my experience. There can be no bigger change than that. It gave me more energy to confront myself and demanded that I work from deep within to create the greatest impact I possibly can.

What Is the Triangle?

The triangle is purpose; genetic wealth enhanced by education, plus acquired skills and talent driven by desire; and problems.

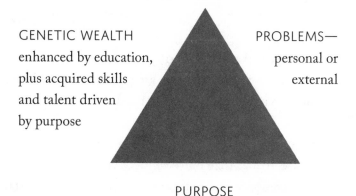

GENETIC WEALTH
enhanced by education,
plus acquired skills
and talent driven
by purpose

PROBLEMS—
personal or
external

PURPOSE

It is made up of three fundamental principles that show us who we are, what we are about, and what we were created for. It gives our lives direction, meaning, and reason, and it adds value to ourselves and others. It allows us to achieve success in the direction we most desire.

Use of the Triangle

For your triangle to provide viable help, your day must revolve around it. To do this:

- Lead by questions, with direction provided by the triangle.
- Debate, plans, and conversation must be directed by the triangle.
- Analysis and deep research should be directed by the triangle.
- Decisions should be directed by the triangle.
- Anything outside of your triangle is a trap, a Trojan horse, a virus that will infect you, corrupt you, and destroy you.

THE SIXTH AND SEVENTH SENSES

Purpose is about spreading love and being kind to all; it is the conscious awakening of self that comes with the opening of the sixth and seventh senses.

The sixth sense is when we come to realize that the world doesn't just revolve around us but around everything. At that point we understand that we can become active without expecting anything in return.

The seventh sense is the highest form of consciousness, awakening when a person comes to understand there are five factors that make everything complete: matter, energy, time, space, and the creator. In this awakening, a person appreciates everything around them and seeks more knowledge of the creator. The seventh sense delivers the highest call to serve a cause greater than ourselves, receiving the universe's joy as our reward. That purpose can be as simple as taking care of our family, volunteering, respecting the natural world, or supporting a cause and devoting time to be grateful and praise the creator for its unending creativity.

DISCOVERING OUR PURPOSE

The six pillars of purpose are passion, belief, love, care, a forgiving heart, and gratitude. Purpose is the creator's will. It allows the creator to work with us so we can become the light, the peace, the joy, the hope, the freedom, the equality, and the dignity.

The benefit of purpose is joy, peace of heart and mind, courage, faith, energy, focus, health, spiritual wealth, perseverance, longevity, endurance, hard work, wellness, and emotional and spiritual intelligence.

Knowing our purpose has value. It can give us clues about our direction and what we are capable of.

Ask yourself the following questions:

- What am I passionate about?
- What are my beliefs?
- What do I love doing?
- What do I care about?
- Do I have a forgiving heart?
- Is gratitude my daily practice?

These questions are relevant to us all. I will answer them myself.

What am I passionate about?

Ever since I was a child, I wanted to be part of a solution, and that passion remains. To do so, I share my experiences for social and emotional learning and create a conscious global awakening through the arts, business, and philanthropy. I like giving without expecting anything in return, which led me to found the Gua Africa charity, which works with families and individuals to help them overcome the effects of war and poverty.

What are my beliefs?

I believe in giving back. I believe in justice, equality, and freedom for all. I believe there is something only I can do or contribute to restore balance in our world. I believe I am not here for competition, but for collaboration and contribution. I believe there is a creator who made all things. I believe purpose generates luck. I believe success is not a competition. Everybody can be successful in their own way. Such beliefs become our built-in motivation circuit, impacting daily decisions.

What do I love doing?

Being part of a solution. I love teaching others what I have learned. I love creating opportunities for others, putting injustice, inequality, and violation of human rights in the spotlight. I love telling stories, psychology, creating experiences that give people joy (in my case, dancing, performing, making music, telling jokes). I love history, community, brotherhood, sisterhood, family, friends, art, science, information, acts of kindness, music, films, food.

What do I care about?

The well-being of people, mentally, spiritually, physically, emotionally, and socially. I care about what I have been trusted to do. I care about the environment and my country.

Do I have a forgiving heart?

Whenever somebody causes me harm, I forgive them without an apology. I constantly forgive myself for the harm I have caused myself. I am constantly waiting for my body to send me memories of those who have caused me harm. When it does so, I forgive them and also forgive myself.

Is gratitude my daily practice?

Yes. When life presents me with challenges, I reflect on the choices I've made that have led me to this moment. Good or bad, my experiences have enriched my life and I am grateful for the opportunity to learn.

Find Your Purpose

What do you do that gives you joy? What are the things that give you joy? For me, sharing my experiences, giving time and energy to support others, gives me joy, as does having no expectations of them doing anything in return. Sharing my blessings gives me joy.

The things that give me joy include people smiling, dancing, being happy, and doing well. I would also put nature, forests, landscapes, ocean, rivers, family, friends, culture, and the human spirit on that list. And especially gratitude. I am always grateful to the force that allows us to exist and notice the gifts it has given us.

My purpose is the creator's will, to be part of a solution, restore balance, give without expecting anything in return, and create experiences that give people joy and balance.

Taking the information in this chapter, can you define your purpose by allowing your heart and mind to write a purpose statement?

What is your purpose?

23

GENETIC WEALTH

GENETIC WEALTH, ENHANCED BY EDUCATION, SKILLS, AND talents and driven by purpose, is a powerful entity. As much as we can inherit material wealth from our parents and grandparents, we can also inherit their survival tactics, hustling skills, talents, traumas, kindnesses, beliefs, and both good and bad habits.

It is important to note that every human being in this world is unique, designed perfectly by nature or the creator to either contribute to or restore balance on the planet. Our health, mental power, heart power, shape, size, and height all have a purpose. These features are genetically encoded.

TALENTS AND SKILLS DRIVEN BY A PURPOSE

When I was in primary and high school I loved science, but science hated me. As mentioned previously, I was always bottom of the class. The thing is, I was not exposed to science as a kid. My parents and grandparents were not disposed to science, so I didn't inherit that genetic wealth and the subject became difficult for me to learn. Easier subjects for me were those my parents and grandparents had access to, but at that point I wasn't interested in teaching, creativity, spoken storytelling, agriculture, or business.

We are not destined always to be interested in what is given to us by genetic wealth. I wanted to be a doctor or electronic engineer, so I was desperate to be good at science. I had persistence on my side. Good thing, because it took years for me to be encoded. Only at university, after more than ten years of science humiliation, was my system able to accept math and science and allow it to become part of me. I apply both now in my daily activities. Purpose and passion allowed me to reach that position.

I dropped out of university because I was refused a visa to study in the U.K. Unable to enroll elsewhere because of the fees, creativity came to my rescue. Still, for a long time I longed to study. Only when I further investigated genetic analysis did I accept what I was encoded to do. I am now using my science knowledge to create superfoods such as Jal Gua, and I have other exciting science projects, which I will introduce to the world in the near future.

IDENTIFYING YOUR GENETIC WEALTH

Genetic wealth can be defined as the skills, talents, and attributes we inherit from our parents and families. We all have these. They are genetically encoded within us. They are ours to embrace and to use for excellence.

If I identify my genetic wealth, I look at the fact that I am Black, tall, and fearfully and wonderfully made. I am thin with defined muscles, healthy, capable of running long distances, and have good eyes, legs, and hands. I am a dancer and storyteller—a purpose-driven, spiritual, open teacher. I have courage and high sexual energy, and am creative and entrepreneurial. I am imaginative, an entertainer.

My genetic wealth has given me the ability to speak and express myself, to be self-motivated and driven to teach and motivate others. I am also a problem-solver, emotionally intelligent, and able to communicate well, mobilizing others toward a cause. I have vision, optimism, curiosity, kindness, and the instincts of a warrior.

From my mum, a teacher, nurse, and community leader, I inherited leadership skills, a likable personality, motivation, endurance, and spirituality. From my dad, a policeman and a commander in the rebel army leadership, I inherited the ability to speak with courage, be a warrior, and build a strategy. They did not teach me those skills; they passed them down to me. From my grandparents, I took generosity, a work ethic, and contentment. My grandmother on my mother's side, for instance, was a philanthropist who opened her doors to many needy children. She was also an entrepreneur. She made the best alcohol in town. Nobody could compete with her until the war disrupted her business. She was a hustler, hardworking, charismatic, humble, and popular.

Identify your genetic wealth in terms of skills and talents passed on to you by your parents and grandparents. If possible, travel further back in time and track the history of your ancestors. What skills and talents did they bestow on you from previous centuries?

Genetic Wealth and Our Environment

Genetic wealth also comes from our environment. Whether it be our immediate vicinity or the world at large, our environment is always taking us in new directions, teaching us new and important lessons. COVID-19 is a case in point. The disease came from our environment; equally our environment influenced how we coped, how we survived, how we got through it. None of us could swim to a submarine in the middle of nowhere and live out the outbreak in isolation. We survived by influencing one another in our behavioral response to the pandemic.

Our environment will also affect our cultural behavior. If a person goes from a polygamous culture to one where they can have just one partner, they may find themselves caught between the law and their genetic wealth. Not easy if that genetic wealth is wired in.

When it comes to my own environment, I saw early on that being focused, audacious, persistent, disciplined, goal driven, and able to plan and organize were great attributes. That knowledge added as much to my self-development as any formal education. Such wealth may have come from my surroundings in my village, but equally it came from the voices of those I respected, including within the sporting environments of the boxing ring, football pitch, and basketball court.

My environment taught me how to hustle, focus, and be audacious and goal driven. It schooled me in planning, organization, strategy, patience, persistence, discipline, awareness, and self-development.

Identify skills and talents brought to you by your environment.

Genetic Wealth Enhanced by Education

My education was sporadic and interrupted. Even so, by enhancing my genetic coding with education, I better equipped myself for life. Science upgraded my genetic wealth. So much of what I now do is attached to science.

My formal education also gave me a better understanding of the Naath language, storytelling, courage, teaching, book and lyric writing, sales and marketing, management, and public speaking.

Being at the bottom of the class at school made me feel stupid, but my experience shows we can help rewire ourselves with purpose.

My skills and talents, enhanced by education, will now be added to the genetic wealth of those who follow me.

Identify skills and talents brought to you through education.

Creator's Gifts

Do you have talents with no apparent source or beginning? These are the creator's gifts. See if you can identify a gift or talent that is not inherited or hasn't come from your environment or education. My creator's gifts include purpose, problem-solving, wisdom, entertainment, and a healthy life.

Identify your creator's gifts.

ACQUIRED SKILLS AND TALENTS DRIVEN BY PURPOSE

Some skills and talents we acquire are driven by our purpose or desire. They have no trace in our DNA or our environment—we acquire them because somebody inspired us or we were advised to better ourselves by taking them on board. With learning and practice, we then become great at them.

In my case, such skills include speaking five languages (English, Kiswahili, Naath, Dinka, and Arabic) and a good understanding of physics, mathematics, chemistry, geography, biology, literature, and poetry. The latter two help me write lyrics and develop my style of rapping. At the same time, I have taken on board much philosophy and history and have a huge interest in using food as medicine. I also know as much about business as I do about modern warfare and weaponry. Again, those skills and talents will now be added to the genetic wealth of those who follow me.

Do you have skills and talents driven by a purpose?

Doing Everything Is Doing Nothing

To shine like a star, a person must organize their dominant skills and talents in order of importance and spend time developing them. They must train every day and enhance those skills further through education.

If I were to identify my top five skills and talents, they would be creativity (storytelling, music, public speaking, dancing, and performing); teaching; writing (lyrics, poetry, and books); entrepreneurship (business, sales, and marketing); and the ability to think big and solve problems.

What makes a person shine like a star are genetic skills and talents, enhanced by the skills and talents acquired through education and driven by purpose.

PROBLEMS

Until I was four, I was shielded from the many problems life threw at me by my parents, grandparents, aunties, and the community at large. My circle of protection got weaker the older I got. By five I was becoming aware of lots of rules, lectures about life and how to become a better child, and disciplinary beatings from strangers. At six and seven, I began to feel the heat. The protective shield had been removed. Laughter and joy were being stolen away from me every day, replaced by psychological and emotional issues and external problems that just got bigger and bigger. What bothered me the most was when we moved from one village to another. My problems didn't disappear; they followed me, added to by even bigger problems when we arrived. One problem always seems to attract more and more.

Even when I made it to Kenya, there was no escape. There were just new and different problems. Each and every headmaster had the same mantra: "Jal is a problematic child." The only shield preventing me from breaking down mentally and emotionally was my purpose. Without it I was suicidal. My purpose was all that prevented me from taking my own life.

It was listening to stories of those who have achieved great things against the odds that made me accept my problems with dignity. I developed a belief that transformed my life—that problems are my mission, and the only way for me to know that the creator, shah, or God loves me and trusts me is by his providing me with more of them.

Have only one problem in life and you are on your deathbed. Have many problems but don't know how to manage them, then you are effectively a dead person who is alive. Have many problems but know how to manage them, then you are blessed. Have no problems at all and you are dead. Problems are the way to life. There is no progress without a problem.

Types of Problems

Internal Problems

Internal problems are those we acquire from our experiences. They include:

- Fear
- Worry
- Anxiety
- Stress
- Unworthiness
- Bitterness
- Hate
- Poverty
- Negative habits and beliefs
- Trauma

Internal problems include genetic curse problems—those we inherit from our parents, grandparents, community, country, and ancestors. Fear, bitterness, worry, anxiety, poverty, hate, and trauma also come into this category.

External Problems

External problems come from a place out of our control. They include problems concerning:

- Family
- Relationships
- Friends
- Community

- ◘ Other countries
- ◘ Organizations
- ◘ Global issues
- ◘ Universal issues

You will see there is an overlap between internal, genetic, and external problems. The only difference is from where they come.

Internal problems must be addressed. Doing so gives us enormous energy to handle those that come from other sources. How do we do so? By working on our core pillars to create a better us. Purpose, gratitude, calm, courage, feeding the soul, peace of mind, patience, love, faith, forgiveness, knowledge, wisdom, and a positive mindset all deliver ultra-strong supports.

Internal and external pressure has to be balanced. It is how our planet operates to achieve success. But internal threats tend to be more threatening than those on the outside. That's why winning an internal battle can never be seen as the end of the war. We must still maintain great habits and beliefs to prevent the rebels from rising up again within us, which is where meditation proves so valuable.

Problems and Purpose

Problems are infinite. They keep coming and keep piling up, whether family problems, relationship problems, issues with friends or community, or global problems. But by knowing our purpose in life, both individually and as a species, we can convert our problems into infinite resources for creation. They ignite our burning desire for change. They challenge our thinking and worth. Without problems, vision wouldn't exist. It is our problems that reveal great and audacious goals. It is also true that managing our personal and internal problems gives us the ultimate force to create and handle everything on the outside.

Even though I found my purpose early in life, I still felt as if there were monsters draining my energy. I set my mind to find them; not to kill them, but to embrace them. I learned to fall in love with my problems and manage them with dignity because solving each one offered a gateway to hope and freedom.

To be effective in our lives, we have to turn our attention to ourselves and fix our internal problems. It's not a single day's work, or that of a week, a month, a year—it's a lifetime commitment, guided by incremental steps and daily practices. When I understood that my external impact became greater as I became stronger internally, I fully committed to applying order and structure to my head and mind.

My Big Battles

The basic steps I took to set myself up for success involved waging several major internal battles, but none were easy. I still have to constantly defend against enemy incursions. The losing sides are rebels. They still seek the occasional skirmish.

Battle 1. Liberating my heart and mind from bitterness

Heavy in the extreme, bitterness weighs you down. I hope never to carry it again. I would rather travel light and allow my heart to forgive people indiscriminately. That way bitterness can never even enter my head.

Battle 2. Uniting my heart and mind so they could work together

A human body is like a kingdom, and any kingdom that is not united shall be destroyed.

Battle 3. Trauma

Trauma is mental genocide, soul murder, an invasion of demons that fills your head and leaves you lonely, exhausted, defeated, and tormented. Winning this battle gave my mind more space to be creative, active, and free. Mental space allowed me to create, think, and plan. Heart space gave me constant motivation and joy, delivering positive emotions to guide me every day. Having heart space means we can be patient and kind, and have more love to give. It allows us to become more human.

Battle 4. Mental poverty/lack of confidence and dignity

Mental poverty is when we are unable to engage our being to do what we want. It can lead to lack of courage, confidence, focus, and clearly defined goals. Being able to engage our mind to do what we want is so important in life. Defeating mental poverty gave me an ability to see life's endless opportunities. It delivered a conscious awakening and discovery of who I am. I saw my purpose—to share my experiences for social and emotional learning, and to create conscious global awakening through the arts, business, and philanthropy. I understood that all human beings are wealthy, but all too often we fall into the trap of believing poverty means a bleak void of emptiness. Actually it is that very space that offers the chance to grow by providing fertile ground, in which lies an untapped gold mine.

Battle 5. Stress

The stress I experienced growing up in difficult times kept me connected to myself and others. It made me productive and active. But stress in the Western world made me disconnect from myself and others and blurred my focus. As a result I became less productive. It also gave me high blood pressure and feebleness. Stress can make us primitive and feeble if we don't find an outlet for it.

Battle 6. Engaging my mind to solve complex problems and implement my clearly defined goals

I am currently fighting this great battle. But that is okay. Suffering is hell; struggle is sweet; success is boring. Creating the life I want is exciting. I know also from past victories that I live on the winning side. Look at my We Want Peace campaign, raising awareness on fundamental principles of justice, equality, and freedom for all through the

power of music worldwide. Look also at my becoming a recording artist, motivational speaker, life coach, entertainer, and storyteller. Each
role came from applying brainpower to a problem, accompanied by a
purpose, to create the life I want. It's exciting knowing I am fashioning
a work of art, a final masterpiece that only those I leave behind will be
able to experience and see. Our chapter isn't closed until we depart this
world.

Take Some Time to Think

Can you name your internal problems? Poverty? Fear? Indiscipline?
Anxiety?

What are your genetic problems? Are they the same?

What about your external problems? Family? Finance? Health?
Friends? Community? Environment?

Write them all down.

What do you think is the way to solve your problems? What steps do
you think are necessary?

What plan are you putting in place? What is your strategy to win?

Ask yourself:

- What problems are you addressing right now?
- What is working in handling these challenges?
- Who is supporting you to handle these problems?
- What is your plan?
- What is your strategy?

Remember:

- Your purpose will fuel you. It will keep shining as you enhance
  your genetic skills and hone your talents through education. You

will become bold, strong, competent, and prepared, and you will
see problems as opportunities.

◘ Your purpose will give your life meaning at every stage,
including when you are suffering.

◘ When those opportunities come, they will spark a conscious
awakening that shifts your paradigms.

◘ If you are unprepared, such opportunities may be seen as sources
of anxiety, producing negativity that damages your mental state.

◘ If you have purpose, you will learn, grow, and prepare for the
next opportunity. It is purpose that gives you the necessary fuel
to keep moving.

◘ Enhance your genetic wealth with education and you will be
stronger in the face of problems and reap the rewards.

24

GUIDING STEPS

WORRY. POVERTY. FEAR OF FAILURE. FEAR OF DEATH. ALL are major weapons used to prevent us from being successful. If we are not careful, these weapons can own our minds and hold us captive.

Worry can create mental clutter. It can weaken our immune system and expose our bodies to deadly diseases that cripple us and make us unproductive. But I prefer to look at it a different way—as something that can prepare us for a challenge. Address its ruthlessness and we can see that worry has the potential to make our lives great. Much better to spend our time acting positively to improve our situation than entertain negative thoughts that can only bring more worry.

Poverty, not nuclear bombs, is the major threat to humankind. People are so crushed by poverty that they spend all their time worrying about it instead of investing time in skills and talents that can get them out of it. Poverty has a way of dominating the human mind and sucking the energy out of a person. It has a way of torturing people, beating them down into the form of a slave, reducing them even to the status of a domestic animal.

Poverty can hide our potential, our talents and skills, and make us feel useless. It acts like trauma, snatching away our worth, confidence, willpower, courage, and dignity. Many people are more afraid of being poor than of death itself.

A lack of basic human needs—food, clean water, shelter, clothing, education, and health care—is the biggest threat to our existence. But the creator didn't make any human being poor. Sadly, poverty is man-made. The creator gave us genetic wealth—a mind with which to gain both spiritual and physical blessings. Acknowledge this fact and poverty can be seen as a mindset. Change that mindset and we can find a solution.

Fear of failure should never be our companion. Failure is an infinite source of intelligence—simple feedback telling us to take a different approach. Those who have become successful have failed many more times than those who haven't. If we fail, we try again. Keep trying until we succeed. It is not failure that is damaging, but the negative thoughts that come with it.

When such a situation arises, it is important to reflect. "Yes, things didn't go as I had wished. But this is not the end. I will continue to learn, and I will find other ways to make this situation work in my favor."

Fear of death is only natural. Everyone will die someday. But being afraid to die doesn't change that fact. Since we will all lose our life, why not make an adventure of it?

In Naath culture, people are encouraged to face death. Death is reunification with ancestors. Also, as in many other cultures, a man or woman is respected when they die fighting for what they believe in.

Ask yourself what you believe in, what you are willing to die for, and death will suddenly have a context that allows you to overcome your fear.

24 ELEMENTS THAT PREVENT US FROM SUCCEEDING

- Failing to identify what we want in life—a lack of vision
- Lack of ambition or drive
- Failure to define clear steps forward
- Fear of what others will think if we start something but don't succeed
- Taking shortcuts
- Giving up before we've started
- Giving up after one or multiple defeats
- Making wrong choices
- Procrastination
- Lacking a mind and heart for contribution and collaboration
- Lack of drive to gain a specific skill
- Refusal to gain knowledge and wisdom
- Inability to prepare, think ahead, and recognize opportunities when they come
- Lack of goal-oriented habits
- Failing to understand health as wealth
- Poor environment
- Lack of faith—believing more in failing than in succeeding
- Lack of self-governing purpose, rituals, and principles
- Failing to love ourselves and others
- Allowing negative cognition to govern our lives
- Worry, anxiety, and lack of courage
- Lack of gratitude
- Not knowing who we are and what we are great at
- Lack of positive beliefs and right habits

It is hugely important to define what success means to us. To me, it means finding enlightenment and in so doing bettering my life. It means showing others how I obtained that enlightenment so they, too, can have a better life. Success is putting all you know into producing positive outcomes.

USING POSITIVE INFLUENCES

How amazing would it be to gather all the forces who have influenced my life in one room? To just hang out with Jesus Christ or the Nuer prophet Ngundeng Bong? What about sitting down to chat with Martin Luther King Jr., Mahatma Gandhi, Nelson and Winnie Mandela, William Wilberforce, the pharaoh King Taharqa, Mother Teresa, the prophet Mohamed, and not forgetting, of course, my mother Nyakong Nguanhok and grandmother Nyapan Deng? How good it would be to see Emma McCune, as well as SPLA commanders Dr. John Garang, William Nyuon Bany, Nyariaka Choul, and Dr. Riek Machar? How useful would it be to converse with the self-help guru Napoleon Hill, Winston Churchill, Angelica Fuentes, Tupac, Bob Marley, Genghis Khan, President John F. Kennedy, African independence hero Julius Nyerere, former Kenyan president Daniel arap Moi and current president William Ruto? Then there's the Ghanaian and Haitian revolutionaries Kwame Nkrumah and Toussaint Louverture, Raila Odinga, Burkina Faso ex-president Thomas Sankara, Congolese independence leader Patrice Lumumba, Scottish independence hero William Wallace, the Dalai Lama, South Sudan president Salva Kiir Mayardit, Mozambican politician and humanitarian Graca Machel, Sudanese defense minister Angelina Thomas Kuma Khan, Fathna Ramthala, who rescued and cared for me at a difficult time, Sudan vice president Taban Deng Gai, Nuer artist Luany, and Mary, mother of Jesus. The list of people who have been a positive influence on my life has no end. There are too many to mention.

All would offer such sage advice—and they do. When it comes to guiding steps, I look upon these people, and others, as my council of elders. Some of these people are dead, but the flame of their desire to pass on wisdom has far from been extinguished.

You, too, should have a list of elders, a combined list of the living and the dead. You should read their books, study their lives, listen to their words, enter into dialogue and organize a meeting with them in your mind. When you face a difficult time, they can be there for you. It is possible for you to ask them for advice and hear their answer.

I am not the only one to go down this route. Napoleon Hill would have imaginary meetings with elders, although I find that getting them all together in an imaginary board meeting can be a challenge. African traditions especially encourage communication with ancestors. However, in most religions it is not encouraged.

Imaginary meetings need not be deadly sincere. I sometimes use them for pleasure. If I like a girl, for instance, I won't tell her. Instead, I will organize meetings with her in my mind. I might crack jokes with her, and if she doesn't laugh, I will take it as a sign she isn't interested in me. If she is more friendly, and finds me funny, then I might actually express my interest in her.

Whatever my situation, I know my imagination is there if I need it. If I am in a mess, I know it will take me to somewhere better, or tell me to think not about problems but about being part of a solution. At such times, I will immerse myself in its vision. I will feel good. The imagination is always a place of revelation.

A Soldier's Story

Before you read the following story, imagine you have been given two options. One is to be killed instantly by a shot from a pistol. The other is to be dropped in the Sahara desert without a map. Which one would you choose?

A soldier was captured and made a prisoner of war. He and his comrades became slaves, forced to do heavy lifting work for their captors. It was mentally, emotionally, and physically draining. They were fed one meal a day. If any of them got sick, there was no treatment. If they couldn't work, they were shot dead. Every day the soldier would hear the flurry of bullets from the firing squad. Every day he would pray to God to keep him alive so he could see his family again.

One day a guard came to his cell. "The prison is full and the numbers have to be reduced," he told him. "You have two options." He pointed at two doors. "Walk out of the door on the right-hand side and you have a chance of freedom. Walk out the door on the left and you will be shot by the firing squad."

The prisoner looked out the window. He saw thick forest beyond the right-hand door. It disturbed him and made him afraid. He decided instead to take the firing squad.

"Are you sure?" the guard asked.

His reply was instant. "Yes."

Lined up in front of the firing squad door, the soldier asked the guard to tell him what was really beyond the door. All the guard could tell him was that 20 percent of those who went through the door found a perfect life, 20 percent became mentally ill, 10 percent suffered serious physical impairment, and the other 50 percent died. He asked the soldier again, "Would you like to walk through the right-hand door?"

"I prefer the firing squad," he replied.

Ask yourself, if you were in the soldier's shoes, which door would you have chosen? I ask because all through life we have similar choices. We have visions, things we yearn for. Yet most of us, perhaps without even realizing, choose the firing squad.

Some people have great ideas, big dreams, but never find the courage to explore them. Because only a minority have stayed upright on that path, they fear they, too, will fall. They turn their back on chasing their dreams, on self-development and taking the initiative to improve their own lives and those of others. The truth is that most humans are afraid to walk into the unknown. They choose to live with the devil they know.

The right-hand door of the soldier's story presents itself to us all the time in the form of an idea. That idea could rescue us from our challenges, but equally there is no guarantee it will be successful. At that point, all too often we choose to stay where we are and suffer or die in pain.

Death and failure are unavoidable. But unless we walk through the door of the unknown with confidence, courage, and faith that everything will turn out well in our favor, then we will never know anything different. Even if the situation doesn't turn out the way we want, we will have learned valuable lessons for ourselves and others. And we can find solutions that will make it easier when we try again in the future. A failure is not a failure when it is corrected.

We will never know the potential of our ideas until we give them a chance.

Success is like a person seeking a partner; a journey that requires a lot of emotion to examine ourselves spiritually and mentally, and to never give up. Similarly, if success feels it cannot trust us, it will run away from us. While poverty is hungry, bold, and ruthless, forever keen to manifest itself in the physical world, success is subtle. We must work smart mentally to make it manifest in our physical world.

MY LIFE IS ART LIFE MAP

Fill in the map to the right according to how My Life Is Art applies to you. The following acronyms will help you split the map into relevant groups.

PVM—Purpose, Vision, Mission

GIWTRIICEEP—Goals, Industry, Well-Being, Time, Resources, Impact, Income, Community, Expenses, Energy, Plan

SOCSS—Strength, Opportunities, Challenges, Solutions, Strategy

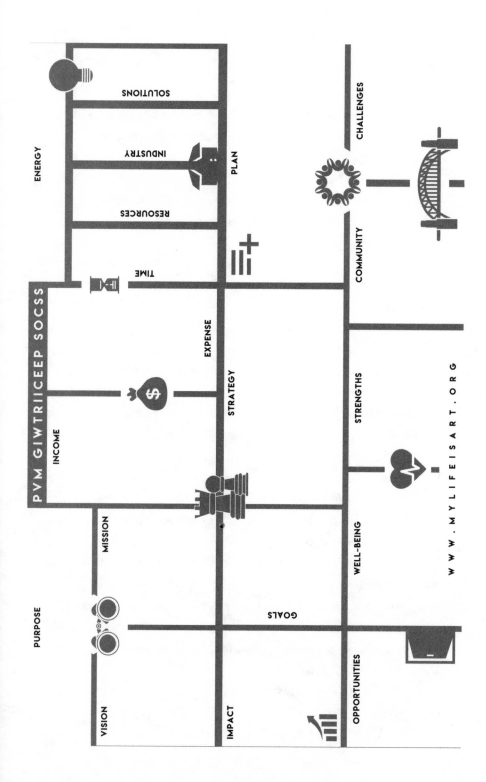

PURPOSE

PVM GIWTRIICEEP SOCSS

ENERGY

VISION

MISSION

INCOME

TIME

RESOURCES

INDUSTRY

SOLUTIONS

IMPACT

STRATEGY

EXPENSE

PLAN

GOALS

WELL-BEING

STRENGTHS

COMMUNITY

CHALLENGES

OPPORTUNITIES

W W W . M Y L I F E I S A R T . O R G

PVM
Create:

1. **A purpose statement**—The impact you wish to create without expecting anything in return. Remember, purpose is the foundation for your vision and your mission. It guides all your actions, behaviors, and goals.

2. **A vision statement**—Your ultimate aim for your life. The endgame, the overarching goal of where you want to be in your life.

3. **A mission statement**—What you do in your daily life to achieve your vision. A guide for your daily behavior and actions.

GIWTRIICEEP

Goals—The targets that guide your plans and life strategy. Break goals down into years, months, weeks, and days.

Industry—The market in which you would like to make an impact. The place where you want to bring value—workplace, home life, community, etc.

Well-Being—The focus here is on your self-development, self-improvement, health (food, exercise, sleep, spirituality), and creating time for meditation, self-reflection, and programming of self. Indicate your focus areas—the elements you wish to concentrate on.

Time—There are twenty-four hours in a day. How are you using your time? Think about your TI^2. What is the impact you are making when using your time, and what benefits are you receiving? For example, sleep, self-development, self-care, learning, projects, work, family, friends, thinking, planning, community, and entertainment.

Resources—What financial resources do you have (e.g., car, house, land, real estate, intellectual property, savings, bonds, profitable businesses, etc.)?

Impact—What impact do you want to create? Consider impact across your entire life. How will your impact affect your family, friends, community, and the industry you are working in?

Income—Consider all streams of your income. Where are you getting your money? Are you able to make your money work for you? Are you able to save and invest?

Community—Your support network: elders, family, friends, colleagues, etc. How are you using them? What support are you providing in return? What value are you giving your community? Are you surrounded by positive individuals who believe and value you?

Expenses—Your outgoing costs. Food, shelter, clothing, transportation, insurance, donations to charity, loan repayments, mortgage, entertainment. The goal here is making sure that your expenses do not exceed your streams of income.

Energy—What is the best use of your health and energy? Are you using your energy reserves to the best of your ability? How can you make better use of your energy?

Plan—This is your action plan. What steps are you going to take to achieve your goals? Write down your plan for the day, week, month, and year. Review your plan regularly and revise as needed. Assess yourself and grade your progress. Your plan is what you want to do, but not wholly thought through.

SOCSS

Strengths—What are you best at? Everyone has strengths, and you know yours better than anyone. What are they? Not sure? Ask your family and friends.

Opportunities—Look across all facets of your life and think about the existing opportunities that can help you achieve your goals.

Challenges—What is preventing you from achieving your goals? Do any opportunities come from these challenges?

Solutions—These are the ideas to overcome and tackle your challenges.

Strategy—This is your plan of action, with clearly defined goals, roles, tactics, and solutions backed up by well-researched data, including challenges experienced in the past, those in the present, and those foreseen. Strategy enables us to concentrate our energy, time, and resources in the place of least resistance with the greatest return. With a great strategy we can avoid failure. Apply strategic thinking, the 360-degree approach to decision-making, to have the best chance of achieving your overall goal. Also use strategic planning to put the plan of action in place, and strategic foresight and data to put resources in place to support future plans. With data, we can change our strategy to fit the situation. Brainstorm, question, and research. It is in the detail of preparation where battles are won. A strategy is a well-thought-through plan of action where failure is not visible.

MY LIFE IS ART BUSINESS MAP

Fill in the map to the right according to how My Life Is Art applies to you and business. The following acronyms will help you split the map into relevant groups.

PVM—Purpose, Vision, Mission

GAC—Goals, Area, Customer Relations

TRIIPEEP—Time, Resources, Impact, Income, Partners, Expenses, Energy, Plan

DOCS—Distribution Channels, Organization Structure, Current State, Strategy

PVM
Purpose—The ethics and values of the company.
Vision—What the company wants to create—its impact.
Mission—The mission statement that describes the focus of your organization, which can guide your daily activities.

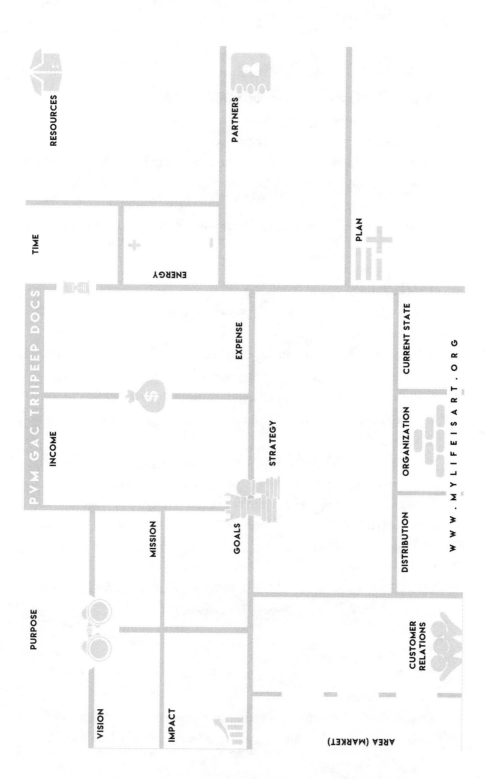

PVM GAC TRIIPEEP DOCS

RESOURCES

PARTNERS

TIME

PLAN

ENERGY

EXPENSE

CURRENT STATE

INCOME

STRATEGY

ORGANIZATION

MISSION

GOALS

DISTRIBUTION

PURPOSE

WWW.MYLIFEISART.ORG

VISION

IMPACT

CUSTOMER RELATIONS

AREA (MARKET)

GAC

Goals—Key activities, major objectives, and tasks.

Area—Your chosen sphere. Your target customers and marketplace. Where can you find them? How can you get them to buy your products?

Customer Relations—Who are your customers? How can you build a stronger bond with them? Are they happy with your goods and services? How can you keep them? And how can you grow them? The all-around customer experience. Your focus on the needs and wants of customers.

TRIIPEEP

Time—Are you releasing your products at the right time? How much time are you allocating for each area of your business?

Resources—Human resources, financial capital, loans, credit, assets.

Impact—The value you give customers, the problems you solve.

Income—Revenue streams. Understanding the most popular products and services and organizing time and energy to maximize the flow of revenue.

Partners—The efficiency of partners—i.e., the suppliers of raw materials, services, and goods to your business and investors.

Expenses—The costs involved in running the operation: wages, phone bills, rent, liabilities, etc.

Energy—Your health, mental agility, and ability to deliver the needs of your business.

Plan—The blueprint on which to build your strategy. What plan do you have? One year? Five years? Thirty years?

DOCS

Distribution—How your products reach your customers. Online? Retail? Wholesale?

Organization Structure—Putting in place a structure that defines clear roles and responsibilities. Who is in charge of what? How can people be held accountable for falling short? Organizational structure is everything.

Current State—Your organization's present state.

Strategy—The concentration and combination of energy, time, and resources with faith, focus, persistence, discipline, and consistency in the place of least resistance that provides the greatest returns. Strategy makes unforeseen failure unimaginable. A strategy is a well-thought-through plan where failure is not visible, where you can do something about it.

25

MY LIFE IS ART

PRINCIPLE 10:

Reading

IN ORDER TO LEAD, YOU MUST READ.

While reading, naturally, still revolves largely around the written word, I prefer to redefine its meaning. For me, reading is based on all our five senses. Reading is listening, touching, smelling, tasting, and seeing. We read to learn, to experience, and to acquire information. We gather this harvest of goodness through our entire sensory network. Those who read have a better chance of surviving and thriving in life than those who don't.

READING WITH THE FIVE SENSES

Hearing

When my son Shang was eight years old, I asked him a few questions.

"Shang, why did God give us two ears?"

"God wanted us to listen more than talk," he answered.

"Shang, why do we listen?"

"We listen to learn."

"If we don't learn, what happens?"

"If we don't learn," he said, "we become stupid."

Shang's answers were simple and straight to the point. The conversation sparked childhood memories as well as my imagination. I was asking Shang these questions only because I was curious to hear his answers. What actually happened was that he reminded me of an intrinsic part of my life, and one with great value.

Growing up, sometimes I would stay awake at night to listen to the incredible array of sounds—hyenas, lions, birds, dogs, rats, cats, goats, sheep, cows, and trees dancing and swaying in the wind. My ears were so good that I could recognize sounds from miles away. I became so adept at listening to the animals that I was able to tell from their reaction if there was danger around. On several occasions my nighttime vigil saved my family from being attacked.

On one occasion I heard the birds making a fearful noise and dogs barking loudly. Then silence—a silence so stark it made my throat tight and my stomach heave with nausea. The hush was broken by footsteps. An animal of some kind searched our hut for a weak point. My mother, brothers and sisters, and Aunt Nyagai were oblivious to the danger, fast asleep. I tried to alert them, but my throat was so constricted, I couldn't say a word. Instead, I hit my aunt on the arm. She woke, her senses immediately attuned to the danger, and roused my mum. As she did so, the animal started to open the door. It was flimsy, made out of wood and grass. Had I been asleep, the beast would have had no trouble getting in undisturbed.

My mum grabbed a huge spear. At the same time, her fear prompted a change in her tone of voice. She now sounded like a man.

"Who is it?" she asked. But her voice didn't scare the animal.

By now, my aunt was wrestling to stop the unwelcome visitor from pulling open the door. But the animal was strong. As it inched its way inside, Mum raised the spear and stabbed it in the neck. At the same time, we shouted our lungs out to scare it away. The animal squealed its displeasure and stormed off. The noise was phenomenal and within a minute there were village warriors outside.

At no point could I see clearly enough to tell what animal it was. But the incident was no great surprise. Wild animals were well-known for breaking into huts. As it was, some villagers stayed with us to act as guards in case the intruder came back. I was so scared, but I realized also that allowing Mother Nature to teach me her nighttime sounds had saved our lives. My ears had read my environment and processed the information.

Can you think of a time where your ears read your environment and gave you important information?

Smelling

As a kid I was fascinated by dogs, particularly their reliance on smell. Our dogs were so embarrassing. They would smell anything—legs, mouths, bottoms, the lot. One evening we were in a circle, dancing and singing with other kids, when, without me knowing, our puppy sneaked behind me. I happened to fart, and the puppy was so excited that it sank its tiny teeth into my backside.

I jumped up screaming. Everyone thought it was funny, except me.

To mimic the dog, we kids started smelling games of our own. We would close our eyes while other children brought different delights— wet cow dung, dry cow dung, goat urine, goat dung, sheep dung, dog poo, flowers, sweet coconut, fruits, leaves, and so on—for us to smell. Whoever identified the most odors was declared the winner.

One day I asked an adult why dogs love smelling things. They explained that dogs build a bank of knowledge through smells. It is their equivalent of reading. The more a dog smells, the better its chances of surviving. I didn't take the adult's words seriously, but at the same time, thanks to our game, I was becoming so good at identifying smells that I could tell the difference between my mum, dad, brothers, and sisters, same as I could cows, goats, donkeys, sheep, and dogs. I knew also the different aromas of numerous plants.

That knowledge would come to be a potential lifesaver. One time we were traveling at night to a nearby village. People were moving along, oblivious to their environment. I was worried.

"Please stop!" I told the soldier with us. "I smell something. It is disturbing. I think it's a lion."

"How do you know'" he asked.

"I don't for sure, but its smell is disturbing and different."

He asked where the smell was coming from. I pointed to a bush beside the path ahead. The soldier told everybody to stop and moved forward with his gun ready. As he neared the bush, the animal emerged—a lion, as my sense had suspected—and charged toward the soldier. Everyone screamed and the soldier fired. The lion stormed off.

It wasn't the last time my sense of smell rescued me. On my childhood trek to Ethiopia, I identified wild plants that I and others could eat.

When we allow all our senses to read our environment, our chances for survival are higher. Sadly, our modern life is making our senses numb to nature.

Touching

There are four senses of touch: warm, cold, pain, and pressure.

Touch is especially important in early childhood. It is how we learn about the world. A baby will grab a toy, rub it on their face, smell it, or even try to eat it. They are learning without even realizing, thanks to the millions of sensors which provide our brains with information for future and current use.

All four senses of touch have been responsible for many life-improving and lifesaving innovations. Whether in heating, architecture, clothing, medicine, travel, or any one of a million other areas, it is our desire to satisfy our sense of touch that has constantly sparked invention. In every way, our senses of touch have allowed us to make sense of our environment.

My own touch senses were vital in helping me avoid mutilation and deadly diseases from rats. As kids, when we slept, rats would come to eat the skin from our feet. A rat would bite my foot, jolting me awake. The rat would then expel air on the bite to take away the pain, a method I recognized only too well. Whenever I fell down and hurt myself, my mum would blow on the graze to make it better.

As soon as I fell back asleep the rat would return. Other nights,

I would sense a rat was about to bite, wake up, and scare it away. It worked, but my disturbed sleep would badly affect my mood.

Catching the rats every time was impossible. One time I was so deeply asleep that I woke in the morning to find my toes covered in blood. The skin had been eaten away. I could barely stand as I tried to run around and play with the other kids.

I wasn't a fan of cats, but at this point an adult suggested I had no option but to love them if I wanted to save my feet from being chewed off. I had many reasons for disliking cats, the biggest being their habit of snoring, which annoyed me at night, but if saving my feet meant having cats in the house then so be it. And it worked. The rats were no more. But it was my collective sense of touch that had saved me. Without it the rats would have torn my skin away. They would have riddled me with disease for which we had no medicine.

Tasting

Our sense of taste is not simply there so we can experience flavor. It is there for our well-being. The taste buds on our tongue can detect five flavors: sweet, bitter, salty, sour, and umami (savory). Each plays an important role in our lives, keeping us in balance and steering us away from illness. Too much salt, for instance, can lead to high blood pressure, kidney disease, osteoporosis, and strokes. Our taste buds act as a warning system so we know we are not ingesting dangerous amounts. In that way, our taste buds can read information hidden to our other senses.

When I was first exposed to a modern lifestyle, I drowned in sugary foods and drinks and salty food. The sweet food made me develop early symptoms of diabetes. The salty food gave me high blood pressure, which almost ended my life twice, saved only by the quick thinking of others.

My behavior around food was so different from when I was a child soldier surviving in the wild. Then, my senses were so good I was able to know whether something was harmful just from tasting it.

After recovering from my high blood pressure, I retrained my sense of taste to aid my health.

Failing to Listen to Our Taste Buds

One time I went to a restaurant where I was served meat stew and injera. When the meat landed in my mouth, I felt a signal warning me that this food was not good and that if I ate it I would get food poisoning. I didn't listen because I was so hungry and continued eating. That night I had food poisoning. The experience was so bad that it made me hate eating meat for six months. Every time I smelled meat, my body recoiled in disgust.

Seeing

A monkey was trying to crack a nut. I watched as it placed the nut on the ground and hit it with a rock several times. The nut didn't crack. The monkey placed it on a log and again struck it with the rock. Still it didn't crack. The monkey became frustrated. It climbed a tree and lay down alongside the nut, looking at it all the time, as if meditating, strategizing, seeking a solution.

After a while, the monkey jumped down. This time it placed the nut on a rock and hit it with a much larger stone. The nut cracked.

I was inspired. So often we look for inspiration from our fellow human beings, but this animal taught me so much about myself. In our lives we are always trying to crack nuts, to find a solution to challenging scenarios. The monkey reminded me to never give up; to take time to rest, think, and try new methods.

Ask yourself, what nut are you trying to crack? Are you taking time to rest? To meditate? To try different solutions?

THE POWER OF READING

In the early days of mankind, we learned by observation, and from that many other forms of learning evolved. Stories were passed on through the generations or through sculpture and art. Eventually, we learned to read and write.

I used to hate reading. In school I hardly did it. I loved listening to stories but was reluctant to read, a fact that was reflected in my grades. I had the desire to learn, but my brain wasn't interested.

My eureka moment came when my thinking was challenged by a Naath elder, a former South Sudanese ambassador to South Africa. He took me out for dinner.

"Jal," he told me, "you have done a great job. You are a very important role model in our community." He paused. "I want to know what books you are reading."

His question took me by surprise. I couldn't remember the last time I completed a book.

"Who inspires you?" he asked.

Instantly I reeled off a list of names: Nelson Mandela, Martin Luther King Jr., Malcolm X, Thomas Sankara, Patrice Lumumba, William Wilberforce, Winston Churchill, Dr. Riek Machar, and Dr. John Garang.

He looked into my eyes. "Those men have one thing in common. They read books. You are now treading on the ground of the smartest, but if you are not reading you will soon be empty. You will not learn to plan, strategize, and think for yourself. Reading is the mental workout for the elite. Don't be just another musician who doesn't know who they are and drowns in their talent."

I understood. I had to read and lead to succeed.

The ambassador continued. "The more you read, the more mental wealth you accumulate. Knowledge is power. Those who shape the world have books in their houses. They trust their books more than any wealth they have accumulated."

Education

As Nelson Mandela once said, "Education is the most powerful weapon which you can use to change the world."

Gaining education for self-enlightenment means we can serve the world better. Acquiring knowledge means we not only acquire new skills but can work toward the aim of specializing in something, then nurturing those skills for the common good.

One time in school, I thought I had done really well. In fact, I had done terribly. It was Year 11 and I had just finished my exams. When the results came out, I was so excited to be given a grade called UN. I associated UN with the United Nations; therefore, it had to be good, right? When I got home, somebody told me what UN really meant—ungraded, unclassified.

"Do you mean I passed so well that I can't be classified?" I asked optimistically.

"No," he said. "UN is even below a fail."

I was upset. That UN weighed down on me, made me feel insignificant. I transformed that energy to convincing myself that I should always be able to be classified. I made it my mission never to be unclassified ever again.

"How can I improve my grades?" I asked at the school.

"Develop a habit of reading, listening, and studying," I was told.

At that time, I just wanted to have fun, write lyrics, and listen to music. But when I made an effort to read, my grades improved massively. If I stopped reading they would again be terrible. But I wanted to improve myself, so when I applied to the University of Westminster in London, I worked hard and read voraciously. I not only made the grades but excelled. In math I received 100 percent and in physics 98 percent.

Later, the reading habit once again deserted me, hence the conversation with the ambassador. Even now, as an activist, storyteller, artist, life coach, and entrepreneur, I know that to achieve my future ambitions, my big audacious goals, I must commit myself to self-development. I now read several books a month and have learned habits to be disciplined. I remind myself that acquiring knowledge is good exercise for the brain. Processing thoughts generates new ways to solve complex problems, and it also provides the brain with more material to use in deep thinking.

Knowledge

Knowledge is not gained to exploit others. It is gained to better serve humanity. We live in a broken world, and knowledge is the solution. It is the only way to fix our problems. Knowledge helps us gain confidence. It helps us learn skills, discover, and polish our talents. Through reading, our perspectives change. We generate different thoughts and emotions that act as the fuel to drive us to solve problems and look at them as opportunities.

If we don't know how to fix our problems, then someone will always be there to exploit them for profit.

The most valuable element on Earth is not gold, it is thought. But many people either don't want to think—maybe they have been conditioned that way—or believe themselves incapable of doing so in a way that will effect change. To be a thinker doesn't necessarily mean going to school. It means graduating to be a person with knowledge and experience. We can all solve problems with what we know.

As human beings, we have lived through natural disasters, devastating diseases, and our many, many wars. We have developed a mechanism for survival. Our brains are built that way. But to function at their optimum requires exposing them to knowledge and information. In order to thrive, each individual must grow emotionally, socially, mentally, spiritually, and physically. So much of that growth is acquired through reading and by allowing all our senses to collect data for us. Whether we have all five senses working efficiently doesn't matter. For those lacking in a certain area, nature has a way of compensating by strengthening elsewhere.

Benefiting from the Senses of Others

Growing up, I would hang around old people and generals and ask them to tell me a story or just listen to them talk. Hearing them shaped my thinking. It added to my success. Before our systems were broken down by war, we had a culture where we had mentors all over. A child raised by a village learns from uncles, aunties, elders, parents, and strangers. Even animals and nature.

When I was exposed to Western culture, I came to learn about coaches and mentors—and how expensive some of them are. With my own community fractured by conflict, and elders not to be found, I asked myself how I could still access great advice. *Books, speeches, and documentaries*, my mind told me. I would go on the internet to see what books those I admired were reading, and then I would spend my money on them. That way I heard about people such as Jim Rohn, a motivational speaker who believed we are the average of the five people with whom we spend the most time. This made me ask, "How can I surround myself with people who are successful and who I like?" The answer was for me to access the books, podcasts, YouTube lectures, and TED Talks of five people who qualify as friends, something which I still do and which has given me knowledge and strength.

Considering the wealth of knowledge now readily available digitally and in books, there is no excuse for anyone to say they don't have a mentor. All kinds of advice are there to read, watch, and rewind. Even so, I still consider books to be my best friends. An author puts their heart and mind into writing a book. When we read it, their heart and mind is implanted in us. We learn how they think and allow their thinking to shape our own. We allow their writing to expand our imagination.

In my case, the knowledge I gathered helped me to form the community that is My Life Is Art. It made me want to create a collective where everyone is a student and a teacher at the same time.

We become wealth, knowledge, wisdom, and understanding when we read our collective senses.

Reading the right books adds value to everybody's lives.

26

MY LIFE IS ART

PRINCIPLE II:

Training

I FIRST CAME ACROSS TRAINING WHEN I WAS BEING DRILLED as a child soldier. I have no idea how I completed that training. It was brutal, far more so than the actual battlefield.

The first principle I was introduced to was discipline. Without it, order could not have been established. We would have been nothing more than a bunch of kids, giggling, laughing, and messing about. Now, if we behaved that way, our trainer would stare into our faces and shout so loudly our entire bodies would shake.

He further cemented his authority by dishing out punishments. Trusted child soldiers or the military police would turn up, order us to lie on our fronts, and deliver thirty lashes—two people delivering lash after lash so fast that counting could never be possible. The thrashing never seemed to end and the other children would watch, overwhelmed by fear. One young boy was so badly beaten he couldn't sit for days. I heard later that he had died.

Establishing order was key. Parade in the morning, parade in the afternoon, and parade in the evening, plus endless other activities requiring us to wake at some ungodly hour. I most dreaded waking up at 4:00 a.m. for the 5:00 a.m. jog, between four and ten kilometers every day, with multiple push-ups along the way. I didn't see the point, but twice a day we would be required to perform this exercise. I hated it so much. To boost morale, we would sing as we went along.

One time, a commander stood up and made a speech. "Young men, your gun is your father and mother. Your brothers are your comrades." His words have forever stuck in my head. "We don't win the battle on the battleground," he continued. "We win the battle here in the training. We have to be smarter, more disciplined, more adaptable than the enemy. Our failure shouldn't be predictable. Any mistake you make here will catch up with you on the battlefield."

He asked for questions. Everybody put a hand up, but I was picked. "Why do we have to jog and do push-ups every day?"

"You will not understand this, soldier," he told me. "But what I can tell you is that jogging and push-ups will save your life and those of your comrades."

When I first experienced a real battle, his words rang out in my head. Running, ducking, dropping to the ground, getting up—over and over again. War has a rhythm, and we had learned it. My hands, lungs, heart, and legs burned with pain until it just became normal. I ran and ran and ran, whole days sometimes, from 4:00 a.m. to 5:00 p.m. If I stopped, the guns would immediately fire in my direction. Just as the commander had promised, jogging saved my life.

Training is preparation for the future, and those who don't bother, like a boxer who has not worked hard to face a challenger, will be taught a merciless lesson. Training is creating routine. It is repeating what you already know to perfect the art. A boxer has to dream boxing, breathe boxing, be boxing, so that when they are in the ring they can fight with their subconscious as well as their conscious mind. Training is how the subconscious learns best. Whenever I research the greatest people in their field—the military, martial arts, whatever—I see it again and again. Their ability always comes from training. Mastering an art takes time. In Naath culture, the title of elder is given only to somebody who has mastered a skill over a long period. By the time they earn the title, they have gray hair. The more gray the hair, the more respect they get.

In ancient Egyptian times, to earn the greatest respect and be considered a god, or close to it, a person had to have practiced their area of expertise for forty years. The author Malcolm Gladwell, meanwhile, talks about the ten thousand–hour rule, stating that a person can become a master in their field if they practice ninety minutes per day for twenty years. In other words, there is no shortcut to greatness.

I once asked SPLA founding father William Nyuon Bany why it is that the top generals are always older.

"They have fought more battles than the young generals," he told me, "and made more mistakes. They may not be as strong physically, but mentally they are a gold mine. It doesn't take a single year to become a great general. It takes years of failure and practice."

If that was the case, I wondered how come our leader Dr. John Garang was younger than our generals. What had he done to deserve such a title?

He told me that Dr. Garang had a wealth of knowledge. He had learned the art of our oppressors and was trusted to outthink the enemy. Wisdom and knowledge plus experience means thoughts can be productive. Such a person can be trusted to lead. Preparing, he reiterated, is how we win.

What I learned as a child soldier was hard, but later in life it gave me the patience to develop my art. In my early days, I invited a group called the Gospel Fathers to appear at Brookhouse School in Nairobi. I performed first and received just one clap. I still remember the name of the child—Iddi Ajawin. He stood up to applaud, for which I was extremely grateful. When the Gospel Fathers took the stage, on the other hand, it was like everyone was hypnotized—cheering, screaming, clapping, and dancing. I had never seen people go so crazy. "Wow!" I said to myself. "These guys are great."

Part of my brain wondered if I could make music as captivating as theirs. Another told me that there was no point trying. *You got burned, bro. You are dead.*

Afterward, I approached the Gospel Fathers. "How come you guys are so amazing?"

"The Lord," one of them told me. "Jesus, and a lot of practice at crafting our art. You have to find out what an audience likes and practice and practice."

Another time I was performing with the Somali Canadian poet, rapper, and singer K'naan in South Africa. It was a time when there was so much hype around me and my story. I did my set and was burned alive, to the extent I said never again.

What actually happened was that both those experiences made me practice. I would perform in my dreams and cowrite with top artists like the Bahamian-born songwriter Clinton Outten. Both experiences set me on a path of no return. Now I never burn. When I perform, people cry, dance, laugh, and experience joy, all of which came with training.

At the same time, rather than rush into any situation, I learned diplomacy, thinking things through to find the best strategy. That way we can win without firing a bullet. Diplomacy buys time and delivers the best results.

RUDY RUETTIGER'S STORY

Rudy Ruettiger is an extraordinary man. He wanted to be somebody but found barriers in the way of his ambitions, especially academically. To find relief from his troubles, he played for American football teams run by the renowned and record-breaking coach Gordie Gillespie. His real dream, however, was to enroll at the University of Notre Dame, in Indiana, and play for the famed Notre Dame Fighting Irish football team. After working hard on his grades, discovering he had dyslexia along the way, he was finally accepted by the university on his fourth attempt.

Rudy was only five foot six, so he was at an immediate disadvantage when it came to making the team. However, he never gave up, always practicing, always learning about the game, imagining himself participating in the play. Rudy made the team at his very last opportunity. He looked like a kid lost in a field of giants, but he put in a tackle on an opponent much bigger than him and won his side a huge advantage. At the end he was carried off the pitch by his teammates, the first player in the history of the team to be so honored. The stadium erupted in celebration. Rudy had come from nowhere to having the ultimate tribute paid to him. All his hard work paid off.

But Rudy's triumph was no accident. When a prepared talent meets an opportunity, it sparks a conscious awakening.

WHAT HAPPENS WHEN WE TRAIN?

Our brain is built to learn and adapt. Learning a skill or developing a talent sparks links between nerve cells—synapses—which allow us to attain knowledge and adapt. But what makes us truly shine is myelin, a substance that surrounds nerve cells and acts as an insulator, increasing the rate at which electrical impulses are transmitted. Myelin is what creates talent, forming our habits, beliefs, and skills. It is what makes us ourselves. The more we practice, the more myelin is formed, the better it insulates, and the faster and more accurate our thoughts and movements become.

It is astonishing to think that we quite literally contain tools to redesign ourselves, do our internal engineering, and create new habits and beliefs. Those tools give us courage, confidence, discipline, meditation, and mental strength. And they all come from training.

Not everything is easy to redesign. My traumatic experiences still exist, but I also have new pathways for communication in my brain, each growing stronger and stronger every day through My Life Is Art meditation.

Whatever pathway you want to create, it can be done through acquiring knowledge, practicing habits, and repeating daily mantras to create the necessary beliefs.

When it comes to training, we can always learn from the greats. Muhammad Ali was once asked at what point he starts counting his push-ups. His answer was simple: "When I start feeling pain." He was right. If we don't push ourselves, then we are not learning. It is determination that creates neuroplasticity, the ability of the brain to form and reorganize synaptic connections. Every time we practice, our entire body learns. As Bruce Lee said, "I fear not the man who has practiced ten thousand kicks once. I fear the man who has practiced one kick ten thousand times."

Training means immersing yourself in a skill so it becomes part of you when you face a challenging situation. Even when you're struggling, your subconscious can continue the fight for you. Training gives us the confidence to walk tall. Train and we give our brain pleasure. We program ourselves to replace bad habits with good habits.

As part of my own training, I have written a short story with which I wish to end this book. I love creating stories in my head. It is writing them that has always been the challenge, but I have trained myself to be better.

A MOTHER AND CHILD

A single mum was raising a son who was being bullied in school and was also struggling in class. She decided to act. She gave her son a challenge. If he completed it, she would give him whatever he asked for, so long as it was in her power to do so. The son accepted the challenge.

To start with, they would both go to bed before 11:00 p.m. and wake at five in the morning. They would then say positive words to themselves—"I am smart. I am great. I am beautiful." "I will do great things. I am special. I fear no one." "I am a giver. My future is beautiful."

Next, they would undertake physical exercise and yoga and listen to motivational speeches before showering, having a cup of tea, and reading or studying for two hours, at which time the mother would help her son with his homework and show him how to improve his reading. They did this for a month—at which point the regime had become not a challenge but a lifestyle. The boy's reading skills improved—he handed his homework in on time and went from bottom of the class to the top. The entire school could not believe his improvement. His confidence was sky-high.

One day a bully approached the boy, punched him on the nose, and pushed him against a wall. Other kids stood around laughing. But the boy had changed. It took him just a single slap to knock the bully down.

Meanwhile, the mum, happier in herself, was promoted at work, going on to become a motivational speaker and a positive force in the community.

Remember, no one is born a genius, but everyone can improve their skills or talents through repetition and practice. We can all reprogram ourselves and boost our confidence through training. That doesn't mean my traumatic experiences or bad habits have gone. But I have rewired my brain to detach my emotions from the pain of the past so that I am able to see the value it brings into my life. I have created new habits and beliefs that allow me to live in the present and create the future I want.

If you are reading this, I would love to find you and tell you how you inspired me. If you are reading this and this is your reality, I would love to find you and say you are my hero too.

AFTERWORD

MY PURPOSE IN WRITING THIS BOOK WAS TO CREATE change: in you, in myself, and in our planet at large. My belief is that words change worlds. They are what make us sit back and consider. Without them, we cannot focus, we cannot meditate, we cannot formulate a way to make things better, to make life work.

It is words that create imagery, that deliver an internal dialogue that makes us understand there are other ways of looking at existence. That our purpose may not be what we assume it to be. That we have the energy, the wherewithal, the spiritual know-how, to change the hand that we have been given.

My life has always been art, but for years I never knew it. In many ways, if it hadn't been for the darkness, the rough seas under a moonless sky, I might never have seen the light. When the waves were at their most turbulent, I managed not to drown. Instead, I sensed the safety of dry land on the horizon. I knew it would draw on every last fiber of my mental and physical energy to reach it.

With that dry land beneath my feet, I realized I was only at the start of my journey. My life as a war child was finished, but my relationship with the world, my understanding of it, had barely begun. People look at me as if I am mad when I say I am lucky to have experienced those seemingly relentless hard times. But I am. It was that life, and its endless succession of challenges, its repeated forays into the fields of tragedy and death, that built a mind able to see an ultimate truth—that we must never stop searching for betterment if we are to achieve true joy, purpose, and satisfaction.

For that reason, this book can never be a full stop; this chapter can never be a conclusion. *My Life Is Art*, like existence itself, is fluid, a meandering stream. One day a flood will come, another the bed will run dry. And at points like those we have to reassess, determine how we are going to negotiate our way forward; how we are going to not just survive, but flourish. At such times, new skills, new outlooks, and new approaches may be found. In the same way, a prolonged period of calm may allow our minds to discover pathways previously blocked by the barricades of turmoil.

I want you, the reader, to carry this book with you, not in your hands but in your head and heart. Those two entities are its natural home. The head and the heart are our internal librarians, our search engine, and if you invest in the guidance in this book, they will lead you to the relevant words to help you take off and fly.

Too often books sit gathering dust on shelves. *My Life Is Art* will never do so because it is part of us. It is a shared spiritual and physical experience, as fresh as the last breath we took. Our inner selves will never need an index to find the best piece of advice, the most relevant story or effective plan. Reaching for that information will be as automatic as the connection of nerves, the interaction of cells. At that point, you can stop, embrace the silence, breathe in, and say to yourself with 100 percent belief and honesty—"My Life Is Art."

ACKNOWLEDGMENTS

I'M GRATEFUL TO THE CREATOR OF ALL THINGS FOR CREAT-
ing me and trusting me with the knowledge that I am sharing with the
world. I'm grateful to my family, my mother, Nyakong Nguanhook, my
father, Simon Jok, my grandmothers, Nyadiangah Pan and Nyaduop
Nyakoang.

My uncle John Biliu, thank you for the constant support. My sis-
ters, Nyaruach and Nyakuoth, and my brothers, Miri and Marnath,
I am thankful to still have you alongside me. I am grateful to Emma
McCune for being a turning point of my life.

Thank you also to uncle Riek Machar for raising me up as one his sons,
and to Taban Deng Gai for providing me with the situations where I
learn practical life lessons. Joseph Mumo, thank you for investing in me.

To my nonbiological mothers who loved me and guided me—
Emma McCune, Mary Nyarieka Chol, Mrs Rhoda Thenya and Angelina Kuma Khan.

Friends: A friend is anyone who comes into your mind and makes
you feel safe, protected, joyful, and empowered. Here are some of
my friends: Nyakor Riam, Connie Abbe, Jeff Gunn, Tanika Charles,
Anika Mattrasingh, Amy Campbell Golding, Sue Mulholland, Davina
Kemble, Julius Owino, Nelly Furtado, Chris Adwar, Davidson Lynch-
Shyllon, Jesse Bukindu, Clinton Outten, Kemi Davies, Ruth Gumm,

Kate Gumm, Johnny McCune, Sally Dudmesh, Paul Lindley, Kalista Zackhariyas, Zane Wilemon, Khan Elijah, Lam Tungwuar, Nyuol Maghook, Andrew Mumo, Lul Ruai, Sarah Ajawin, Gonyi Ajawin, Mimi Teny, Mareika Muller, Michael Fox, John Paul Mallo, Radek Sali, Jane Tewson, Jean Oelwang, Caitlin Powell-Bowman, Heather Dennison, Irene Tunya, John Mark, Atong Arjok, Cari Flammia, Karen Francis, Bigoa Daniel, Angelica Fuentes, and Charles Perroud.

Thanks to Dharmini Dee for the illustrations.

A special thank-you to my manager, Tania Campbell Golding, book agent, James Wills, and cowriter, John Wood, for creating opportunities and working with me to make this book come to life.

Elizabeth Koch, thank you for trusting this book to come to the world. Thank you for creating the platform for it be heard. You are a sister and a friend.

I am grateful to all the angels who came along my path to feed me, clothe me, and offer me shelter, and for the great experiences that have set me up for success.

If I didn't mention your name as a friend or anywhere here, just know you are printed in my heart and DNA forever and I appreciate you walking with me. This book is our collective success, and it would not have been possible without your power and love.

Jal.

© Emmanuel Jambo

EMMANUEL JAL started his life as a child soldier in the war-torn region of South Sudan. He is an activist, author, entrepreneur, and recording artist. He is the subject of the full-length award-winning documentary *War Child* and the author of the book by the same title. He now lives in Toronto, Canada. Find out more at emmanueljal.com.